The Politics of Regime Complexity In International Derivatives Regulation

The Politics of Regime Complexity In International Derivatives Regulation

LUCIA QUAGLIA

OXFORD
UNIVERSITY PRESS

OXFORD
UNIVERSITY PRESS

Great Clarendon Street, Oxford, OX2 6DP,
United Kingdom

Oxford University Press is a department of the University of Oxford. It furthers the University's objective of excellence in research, scholarship, and education by publishing worldwide. Oxford is a registered trade mark of Oxford University Press in the UK and in certain other countries

First Edition published in 2020

Published in the United States of America by Oxford University Press
198 Madison Avenue, New York, NY 10016, United States of America

British Library Cataloguing in Publication Data
Data available

Library of Congress Control Number: 2020946536

ISBN 978–0–19–886607–7

DOI: 10.1093/oso/9780198866077.001.0001

Preface

The international financial crisis that reached its peak in the autumn of 2008 brought the world to the verge of a financial collapse. The financial instruments of derivatives, which constitute one of the world's largest markets, contributed massively to the escalation of the crisis. Although financier Warren Buffett called derivatives, especially over-the-counter derivatives (OTCDs), 'financial weapons of mass destruction', these instruments were for the most part unregulated prior to the crisis, except for some private sector governance. After the crisis, there was an overhaul of financial regulations at domestic, regional, and international levels. At the international level, almost all the standard-setters in finance were involved in the post-crisis reforms concerning derivatives and several standards were jointly issued by two (or more) bodies. These regulatory efforts required considerable *joined-up thinking*: it was like a gigantic jigsaw, whose pieces had to be 'tailored' and put into the right place. This resulted in 'over-crowded' regulatory space and an international 'regime complex'.

This book examines the international regulation of derivatives after the crisis, by explaining what factors drove international standard setting for various aspects of derivatives markets, why international regime complexity emerged, how it was managed, with what effects. Specifically, this research investigates the panoply of international standards that were issued by a 'potpourri' of organizations and committees that set out to regulate derivatives trading, clearing, and reporting; the resilience, recovery, and resolution of central counterparties (CCPs); the capital for bank exposures to CCPs and derivatives; and the margins for uncleared derivatives. The aim is to provide a theoretically informed and empirically grounded account of the post-crisis reform of international derivatives regulation.

While writing this book, several challenges arose. First, international financial regulation on derivatives is a moving target, therefore, the content of the book had to be updated over time. Some assessments are provisional because international financial regulation remains a work in progress. Yet, most of the post-crisis regulatory reforms concerning derivatives markets are in place by now. Second, there is a trade-off between the scope of the research and the depth of analysis, including its level of detail. I opted for broad coverage and, therefore, it was necessary to be selective about the material included (or not) in each chapter. Since this book is about international regulation, the domestic level is examined only in so far as it is useful for shedding light on the international standard-setting process. Third, I wanted to write a book that could be of interest and accessible to political scientists, political economists, and public policy scholars. Thus, a similar structure was adopted for each of the empirical chapters. In each chapter, the main issues at stake are discussed regarding a specific aspect (or elemental regime) of derivatives markets and the international standard-setting process. Then, the explanatory power of the analytical framework put forward in Chapter 2 is assessed against the empirical record. The concluding chapter carries out a comparative assessment across elemental regimes for derivatives.

I am especially grateful to Aneta Spendzharova, Scott James, and David Howarth with whom I have had several intellectual exchanges and very productive collaboration over the years. Some of the material on derivatives trade reporting in Chapter 5 and CCPs in Chapter 6 is based on collaborative research with Aneta. Elliot Posner provided insightful comments on several chapters of the book. Since I started my research, many academics have generously given me their advice and commented on parts of the book, conference papers, and other academic publications in which some of the findings of my research were presented. In particular, I would like to thank Michele Chang, Pepper Culpepper, Shawn Donnelly, Scott James, Philippe Genschel, Dermot Hodson, David Howarth, Peter Knaack, Mark Thatcher, Manuela Moschella, Stefano Pagliari, Elliot Posner, Aneta Spendzharova, and Eleni Tsingou. I further benefited from a range of comments offered by participants at various conferences, in particular, the European Union Studies Association and the European Consortium for Political Research as well as a research workshop held at the Bank of England. I also wish to thank the anonymous reviewers of my book proposal and part of the manuscript for their constructive comments. Research funding from the Department of Political Science at the University of Bologna is gratefully acknowledged.

The primary research for this book could not have been completed without the help of many practitioners and experts in international financial institutions, regulatory agencies, and interest organizations. I was able to benefit from a range of forthcoming and helpful interlocutors, who generously gave me their time, despite their busy schedules. I am very grateful to all of them. With all the interviewees, it was agreed that, although I would use the information they provided, they would not be identified. Several interviewees were willing to provide information for background purposes only. All errors, omissions, and interpretations in this book are mine.

Last but surely not least, at Oxford University Press, I wish to thank the commissioning editor, Dominic Byatt, for his prompt interest in and unfaltering commitment to this project. I also wish to thank Oliva Wells, senior assistant commissioning editor, Markcus Sandanraj, the project manager and Martin Noble, the copyeditor.

Lucia Quaglia

Contents

List of Figures and Tables

Figures

Tables

List of Abbreviations

BCBS	Basel Committee on Banking Supervision
BIS	Bank for International Settlements
CCP	Central Counterparty
CDS	Credit Default Swap
CFTC	Commodity Futures Trading Commission
CGFS	Committee on the Global Financial System
CPMI	Committee on Payments and Market Infrastructures
CPSS	Committee on Payment and Settlement Systems
CVA	Credit Valuation Adjustment
ECB	European Central Bank
EMIR	European Market Infrastructure Regulation
ESMA	European Securities and Markets Authority
EU	European Union
FDIC	Federal Deposit Insurance Corporation
FSA	Financial Services Authority
FSB	Financial Stability Board
FSF	Financial Stability Forum
G20	Group of Twenty
IASB	International Accounting Standards Board
IIF	Institute of International Finance
IMF	International Monetary Fund
IOSCO	International Organization of Securities Commissions
ISDA	International Swaps and Derivatives Association
ISO	International Organization for Standardization
LEI	Legal Entity Identifiers
MOU	Memorandum of Understanding
NIMM	Non-internal Model Method
OECD	Organization for Economic Co-operation and Development
OTCD	Over the counter derivatives
QIS	Quantitative Impact Study
SEC	Securities and Exchange Commission
UK	United Kingdom
UPI	Unique Product Identifier
US	United States
UTI	Unique Transaction Identifier
WTO	World Trade Organization

1
Introduction

The international financial crisis of 2008 brought into the spotlight the importance of derivatives markets, which played a significant role in fuelling and amplifying the crisis (Brunnermeier et al. 2009; Group of Thirty 2009; De Larosière et al. 2009; Financial Services Authority 2009). Indeed, derivatives contributed to fragility and volatility in the financial system by facilitating the growth of speculative trading and by enabling banks to become over-leveraged and accumulate counterparty risk. For example, over the counter derivatives (OTCDs) played an important part in the collapse of the investment bank, Lehman Brothers,[1] and the near failure of the insurance giant AIG[2] (*Financial Times*, 6 January 2010). Consequently, after the crisis, several regulatory reforms at international, regional and national levels focused on derivatives, to be precise, over-the-counter derivatives (OTCDs) (for an overview, see Helleiner, Pagliari, and Spagna 2018). Indeed, this was perhaps the main area of post-crisis regulatory reform in finance.

A derivative is a contract between two or more parties (or counterparties), the value of which is derived from an underlying asset, such as stocks, bonds, commodities, currencies, interest rates, and market indexes. Typically, derivatives are used for 'hedging' as they provide a form of insurance against risk generated by fluctuations in the value of the underlying asset. However, they can also be used for speculation in betting on the future price of an asset, or movements in exchange rates or interest rates. The most common types of derivative contracts are futures (an agreement between two parties for the sale of an asset at an agreed-upon price), options (similar to futures, but without the obligation to undertake the transaction), and swaps (an agreement to exchange cash flows or liabilities). Derivative contracts can be traded over an exchange and centrally cleared, which increases transparency and reduces

[1] When Lehman Brothers failed in late 2008, it had a $35 trillion portfolio of both cleared and uncleared derivatives.

[2] The American International Group (AIG)—the world's largest insurance company that had about $1 trillion in assets prior to the crisis—lost $99.2 billion in 2008. The Federal Reserve Bank of New York provided a loan of $85 billion to prevent AIG's failure. The company lost $30 billion on credit default swaps (McDonald and Paulson 2015, 2017).

The Politics of Regime Complexity In International Derivatives Regulation. Lucia Quaglia, Oxford University Press (2020).
 DOI: 10.1093/oso/9780198866077.003.0001

counterparty risk (i.e. the risk of default by one party from the contract). However, in the decade prior to the crisis, there was a massive growth in the use of OTCDs, especially interest rate derivatives and credit default swaps (CDS), which were traded and cleared directly between two parties and accounted for approximately 90% of the market. As Helleiner, Pagliari, and Spagna (2018) point out, it was and is 'the world's biggest market'.

Pre-crisis derivatives markets, in particular, OTCDs, were mostly subject to industry private sector governance, namely, industry self-regulation (Helleiner and Pagliari 2010; Pagliari 2012; Lockwood 2018; Tsingou 2006). After the crisis, there was a concerted effort to regulate various aspects of derivatives. At the national level, the main jurisdictions, notably, the United States (US) and the European Union (EU), carried out significant regulatory reforms (see Helleiner, Pagliari and Spagna 2018; Clapp and Helleiner 2012; Kastner 2014; Knaack 2015; Newman and Posner 2018; Pagliari 2013a,b; Pagliari and Young 2014; Posner 2015, 2018; Young and Pagliari 2015; Ryan and Ziegler 2015).[3] So far, most academic research has focused on domestic regulatory changes, specifically, the post-crisis regulation of derivatives in the US and the EU, and the regulatory disputes that ensued from it, often due to the different content of domestic rules (Knaack 2015), their extra-territorial reach (Coffee 2014; Griffith 2014; Scott 2014; Gravelle and Pagliari 2018; Zaring 2013; Quaglia 2017b) and the sequencing in the adoption of domestic rules in various jurisdictions (Newman and Posner 2018; Pagliari 2013b; Posner 2018).

At the international level, a post-crisis regulatory overhaul was agreed upon by the Group of Twenty (G20) (Cooper and Thakur 2013; Kirton 2016; Helleiner and Pagliari 2011). It was followed by a multitude of 'soft laws' (Brummer 2010a,b, 2015), that is to say, international standards issued by various transgovernmental fora of domestic financial regulators (Bach and Newman 2014, 2010; Gadinis 2015; Jordana 2017; Slaughter 2004; Slaughter and Zaring 2006; Verdier 2009).[4] According to the Financial Stability Board (FSB 2018a), international standards set out 'principles, practices, or guidelines in a given area'.[5] The few academic studies that have examined the

[3] For some legal analyses, see Coffee 2014; Duff and Zaring 2013; Ferran, Moloney, Hill, Coffee 2012; Scott 2014; Zaring 2013.

[4] Keohane and Nye (1974: 43) define transgovernmental relations 'as sets of direct interactions among sub-units of different governments that are not controlled or closely guided by the policies of the cabinets or chief executives of those governments'.

[5] International standards are non-legally binding. They can be sectoral, when they cover a specific financial sector, such as banking, securities, and insurance; or they can be functional, covering areas such as governance, accounting, transparency, capital adequacy, information sharing, risk management, and so on.

international regulation of derivatives have tended to focus on one or two sets of standards, such as the *Principles for Financial Market Infrastructures* (2012a), issued by the Committee on Payment and Settlement Systems (CPSS) and the International Organisation of Securities Commissions (IOSCO) (Posner 2018), or the *Margin Requirements for Non-Centrally-Cleared Derivatives* (2013), issued by the Basel Committee on Banking Supervision (BCBS) and the IOSCO (Spagna 2019).

This rather narrow focus reflects a broader trend in researching international standard setting in finance whereby the attention has generally been on one standard at a time, albeit with notable exceptions (Drezner 2007; Simmons 2001; Singer 2007; Mügge and Perry 2014; Quaglia 2014a). Prominent examples were scholarly works that focused on the Basel accords, issued by the BCBS (Kapstein 1989, 1992; Howarth and Quaglia 2016; Goldbach 2015a,b; Lall 2012; Thiemann 2018, 2014; Young 2012; Wood 2005); the rules and the memoranda of understanding of the IOSCO on insider trading (Bach and Newman 2010); the rules issued by the Financial Stability Board (FSB) on the resolution of financial institutions (Quaglia 2017a) and the repo market (Gabor 2016a); as well as the work of the Bank for International Settlements (BIS) on macro-prudential regulation (Baker 2013a,b).[6] Furthermore, the few scholarly works that examined international standard setting across various financial services (Drezner 2007; Simmons 2001; Singer 2007; Mügge 2014; Quaglia 2014a) mainly did so in a comparative perspective in order to explain similarities and differences across segments of the financial sector, rather than to explain how the various standards interacted with each other (for an exception, see Mügge and Perry 2014).

A vast array of international standard-setting bodies contributed to the post-crisis reform of derivatives regulation (see Table 1.1). Indeed, almost all the main international standard-setters in finance were involved, in addition to private standard-setters such as the International Swaps and Derivatives Association (ISDA). In certain cases, also non-financial standard-setters, such as the International Standardisation Organisation (ISO), became involved (for instance, in setting rules on derivatives trade reporting), and new ad-hoc bodies, such as the Global Legal Entity Identifier (LEI) Foundation, were

[6] There were also international standards issued by private standards setters, notably, international accounting standards (Botzem 2014, 2013; Botzem and Quack 2009; Büthe and Mattli 2011; Perry and Nolke 2006; Cafferman and Zeff 2006).

Table 1.1 Main international standard-setting bodies and standards concerning derivatives

International standard-setting bodies	International standards (principles, guidance, etc)
BCBS	Regulatory Framework for More Resilient Banks and Banking Systems (2010) (Basel III) Interim Capital Requirements for Bank Exposures to CCP (2012)* Basel III Leverage Ratio Framework (2014) Capital Requirements for Bank Exposures to CCPs (2014)* Basel III: Finalizing post-crisis reforms (Basel IV) (2017)
BCBS-IOSCO	Margins Requirements for Uncleared Derivatives (2013) Revised Margins Requirements for Uncleared Derivatives (2015)
IOSCO	Report on Trading of OTC Derivatives (2011, 2012) Requirements for Mandatory Clearing (2012)
CPSS-IOSCO	Principles for Financial Market Infrastructures (2012)Assessment Methodology (2012) Authorities' Access to Trade Repository Data (2013)
CPMI-IOSCO	Report on Recovery for Financial Market Infrastructures (2014) Guidance on UTI (2017) Guidance on Principles for Financial Market Infrastructures (2017) Guidance on UPI (2017) Guidance on other Critical Data (2018) Framework for Supervisory Stress Testing of CCPs (2018)
FSB	Global LEI Governance (2012) Key Attributes of Effective Resolution Regimes for Financial Institutions + Annex 1 Resolution of Financial Market Infrastructures (2014) Governance of UTI (2017) Guidance on Resolution of CCPs (2017) Governance of UPI (2018) Review of OTC Derivatives Market Reforms (2018)
ISO	LEI code (2012)
ISO & GLEI	Technical work (2017)

* Issued by the BCBS in collaboration with the CPSS-IOSCO.

set up. Moreover, several standards were jointly issued by two (or more) international standard-setters. For example, *OTCDs Data Reporting and Aggregation Requirements* (CPSS-IOSCO 2012b) were jointly issued by the CPSS—which, later, was renamed as the Committee on Payments and Market Infrastructures (CPMI)—and the IOSCO. *Capital Requirements for Bank Exposures to Central Counterparties* (BCBS 2012, 2014d) were issued by the BCBS, in collaboration with the CPSS/CPMI and the IOSCO.

These regulatory efforts required considerable *joined-up thinking*: it was like a gigantic puzzle, whose pieces had to be 'tailored' and put into the right place. The result was an over-crowded regulatory space and an international 'regime complex', characterized by the presence of multiple institutions and elemental regimes governing a set of related issues (Alter and Meunier 2009; Alter and Raustiala 2018; Keohane and Victor 2011; Johnson and Urpelainen 2012; Orsini, Morin, and Young 2013; Pratt 2018; Raustiala and Victor 2004). The post-crisis regulation of derivatives by several international standard-setting bodies is a notable case of international regime complexity, which has become a prominent phenomenon in world politics and the global economy. Scholars have identified regime complexes in a variety of policy areas, ranging from plant genetic resources (Raustiala and Victor 2004), climate change (Keohane and Victor 2011), intellectual property rights (Urpelainen and van de Graaf 2015), trade (Alter and Meunier 2006) and the Troika in the EU (Henning 2017).

However, financial regulation has largely been overlooked by the literature on regime complexity so far (with the recent exception of Heldt and Schmidtke 2019; Breen, Hodson, and Moschella 2020). Yet, regime complexity considerably increased in finance after the crisis of 2008, particularly in areas that previously were not subject to regulation and dealt with several cross-cutting issues. In the case of derivatives, international standards were issued concerning the trading, clearing, and reporting of derivatives; the resilience, recovery, and resolution of central counterparties (CCPs); the capital for bank exposures to CCPs and derivatives trading and clearing; and the margins for derivatives non-centrally cleared via CCPs. These standards represent 'elemental regimes', partly 'nested', partially 'overlapping', partly 'parallel', which are not hierarchically ordered. As explained in Chapter 2, the concept of regime complexity needs some reformulation in order to make it more amenable to financial regulation. Of particular interest is the fact that elemental regimes in finance are often 'interlinked', meaning that rules set in a given elemental regime have direct implications for other regimes.

Puzzles, Research Questions, and Research Design

Post-crisis international standard setting concerning derivatives markets is puzzling for three main reasons. First, whereas derivatives were not subject to much public regulation pre-crisis (Helleiner and Pagliari 2010; Pagliari 2012; Lockwood 2018; Tsingou 2006), despite dire warnings about their potential to be 'financial weapons of mass destruction',[7] a vast array of international standards for derivatives were issued after the crisis of 2008. Second, whereas pre-crisis international financial regulation mainly occurred in a silos-like structure, this was not the case for derivatives after the crisis. Third, whereas pre-crisis international efforts failed to overcome sectoral fragmentation in finance (see Newman and Posner 2018, Chapter 3), post-crisis cooperation was relatively successful in doing so with reference to derivatives.

Derivatives were a particularly 'hard case' for international regulatory cooperation because public regulation was new, without a focal standard-setter. Furthermore, as the Chair of the European Securities and Markets Authority (ESMA), Steven Maijoor (2013b), noted, 'the OTCDs markets are undergoing a massive change from being unregulated to being fully regulated. These changes are not about tinkering around the edges, but rather about a momentous regulatory change. Coordinating a massive regulatory change is obviously more difficult than coordinating a marginal adjustment to an existing regulatory framework.' Yet, as explained in this book, post-crisis international cooperation in regulating derivatives developed over time, and despite the complexity of the regime, overall, the standards issued on derivatives were relatively precise, stringent, and consistent, albeit with considerable variation across standards.

This book sets out to address three interconnected questions regarding the international regulation of derivatives. What factors drove international standard setting concerning derivatives markets post-crisis? Why did international regime complexity emerge? How was it managed and with what outcomes? The focus of this volume is on international standards, not on the domestic implementation of these standards, or other post-crisis domestic regulatory reforms concerning derivatives.

Theoretically, this book brings together the literature on regime complexity in international relations and international standard setting in international political economy. From the literature on regime complexity, this research takes the perspective of analysing the setting of several international standards at the same time, examining how they interact with one another, rather than looking at each of them in isolation. Of particular importance are regulatory interlinkages among various international standards (elemental regimes) that are part of a regime complex. From the literature on international standard

[7] In 2002, financier Warren Buffet noted that 'In my view, derivatives are financial weapons of mass destruction, carrying dangers that, while now latent, are potentially lethal', available at http://www.berkshirehathaway.com/letters/2002pdf.pdf

setting, this research teases out three well-established theoretical approaches that are combined to shed light on regime complexity.

To begin with, the *state-centric* explanation, which emphasizes the preferences and power of the main jurisdictions, accounts for the setting (or not) of international rules and their broad content (Donnelly 2014; Drezner 2007; Fioretos 2011, 2010; Goldbach 2015a,b; Helleiner 2014; Henning 2017; Knaack 2015; Posner 2010; Rixen 2013, 2010; Simmons 2001; Singer 2004, 2007; Thiemann 2014, 2018). It is, however, mediated by the *transgovernmental* explanation, which draws attention to domestic regulators that are gathered in international standard-setting bodies (Bach and Newman 2010, 2014; Newman and Posner 2018; Tsingou 2010a, 2015a; see also legal scholars, such as Brummer 2015; Gadinis 2015; Slaughter and Zaring 2006; Verdier 2009). Finally, the *business-led* explanation stresses the preferences and power of the financial industry, whereby private actors influenced the specific content of the new rules (Baker 2010; Lall 2012; Pagliari and Young 2014; Tsingou 2008; Underhill and Zhang 2008; Young 2012; Young and Pagliari 2015).

Methodologically, this research is operationalized, first, by distinguishing various elemental regimes (or sets of standards) concerning different aspects of derivatives markets, namely: the trading, clearing, and reporting of derivatives; the resilience, recovery, and resolution of CCPs; the capital for bank exposures to CCPs and derivatives; and the margins for derivatives non-centrally cleared via CCPs. For each elemental regime (or set of standards), the book investigates the international standard-setting processes, teasing out the key issues at stake, the preferences and influence of the main jurisdictions and different parts of the financial industry as well as the role of networks of regulators gathered in international standard-setting bodies. Specifically, the theoretical expectations teased out from the literature are assessed against the empirical record in order to gauge the analytical leverage of various explanations within and across case studies.

This material is then used to examine regime complexity, investigating the international cooperation efforts within and across elemental regimes and evaluating the precision, stringency, and consistency of their regulatory outputs. Empirically, the book discusses the making of more than twenty standards (principles, guidelines, etc.) from the peak of the international financial crisis in late 2008 to the present. In order to do so, it relies on a variety of sources, including a systematic survey of press coverage, policy documents, responses to consultations and a set of semi-structured confidential elite interviews with policymakers and stakeholders.

Overall Argument

This book puts forward three main statements about the politics of regime complexity, and specifically, its *causes*, *management*, and *effects*. First, regime complexity can ensue from the multi-dimensionality and the interlinkages of the problem to tackle, especially if it is a new policy area without an existing, focal, international standard-setter. Thus, regime complexity is not always the result of strategic choices by states and interest groups to engage in forum shopping or regime shifting (Bush 2007; Colgan et al. 2012; Helfer 2009; Henning 2017; Morse and Keohane 2014).

Second, the great powers play an important role in managing regime complexity if they value the 'collective goods' produced by elemental regimes within a complex and have, therefore, an incentive to avoid inconsistencies across regimes (Gehring and Faude 2014; Johnson and Urperlainen 2012). It is especially so if inconsistencies can undermine the overall objectives of the regime complex. Transgovernmental networks are instrumental in promoting consistency across and within regimes through formal and informal tools, making up for the limited domestic coordination among regulatory agencies in various jurisdictions. Finally, the financial industry, especially transnational interest groups, contribute to the management of regime complexity if they are negatively affected by inconsistent rules.

Third, the effects of regime complexity can be positive (Keohane and Victor 2011). In fact, regime complexity can trigger an efficient division of work, whereby different international standard-setting bodies tackle specific aspects of the problem on the basis of their respective expertise (Gehring and Faude 2014; Pratt 2018). In the case of derivatives, considering the high level of uncertainty (this was a new and complex area of financial regulation), the large number of policy actors involved (states, private actors, regulators), the presence of nested, parallel, overlapping, and interlinked elemental regimes, and the international cooperation that took place in order to promote regulatory precision, stringency, and consistency in the derivatives regime complex was remarkable.

In order to make sense of regime complexity concerning post-crisis derivatives regulation, this research combines three theoretical accounts put forward by the international political economy literature on standard setting in finance as well as in other policy areas. To begin with, a *state-centric* account, which highlights the preferences and power of the main jurisdictions, notably, the US and, to a lesser extent, the EU, explains why international standards concerning various aspects of derivatives markets were set (or not) as well as most of their content. In a nutshell, international standards were issued if the 'great (financial) powers' (Drezner 2007) had incentives to do so and their preferences were broadly aligned, prompting them to act as 'pace-setters' at the international level. Whenever the great powers, first and foremost, the US, did not sponsor new international standards, these were not set. For example, more wide-ranging reforms of the OTCDs markets were not discussed either domestically in the US, or internationally (Helleiner 2014).

The preferences of the main jurisdictions on each set of standards depended on the domestic regulatory templates (Farrell and Newman 2010; Helleiner 2014; Posner 2010; Quaglia 2014a); the domestic concerns about financial stability and competitiveness (Kapstein 1989, 1992; Singer 2004, 2007), that is to say, negative externalities and adjustment costs (Drezner 2007; Quaglia and Spendzharova 2017; Simmons 2001); and the distributional implications of international rules within and across jurisdictions (Oatley and Nabors 1998; Brummer 2015; Turk 2014; Verdier 2009). The regulatory power of the main jurisdictions depended on their market size (Drezner 2007; Simmons 2001) and regulatory capacity (Bach and Newman 2007; Posner 2009, 2010; Quaglia 2014a), including subject-specific expertise.

With specific reference to regime complexity on derivatives, the great powers had a 'general interest' in avoiding inconsistency across international standards dealing with different aspects of derivatives markets. The US and the EU valued the 'collective goods'—i.e. financial stability and a level playing field—produced by various elemental regimes and were keen to avoid negative spill-overs across them. Yet, the ability of the US and the EU to manage regime complexity was often weakened by the fact that several domestic regulatory agencies were involved in a variety of international bodies, sometimes with limited domestic coordination. These domestic agencies had different compositions, competences, and regulatory outlooks. Furthermore, they sometimes engaged in 'turf fighting' and 'bureaucratic politics' (Adolph 2013; Bach et al. 2016b; Trondal et al. 2013).

Networks of regulators and the financial industry mediated the effects of the state-centric explanation. *Transgovernmental networks of domestic regulators* (Ahdieh 2015; Bach and Newman 2010, 2014; Brummer 2015; Slaughter 2004; Slaughter and Zaring 2006; Turk 2014; Verdier 2009), such as central bankers, banking regulators, and securities markets regulators, contributed to ironing out disagreements among and within jurisdictions. By and large, financial regulators have similar educational training (Chwieroth 2015, 2009), professional backgrounds (Seabrooke and Henriksen 2017; Seabrooke and Wigan 2016), and share the same body of technical knowledge (Seabrooke and

Tsingou 2014; Tsingou 2015a). They are also somewhat insulated from political pressure (Kapstein 1992), albeit less so in the wake of the crisis (Helleiner and Pagliari 2011; Pagliari 2013a). Furthermore, financial regulators have an incentive to sponsor precise, stringent, and consistent rules because of their mandate to protect financial stability. There are, however, important differences across networks in that banking regulators tend to be more 'internationalized' and tightly-knit than regulators dealing with securities markets, including derivatives.

The role of networks of regulators gathered in international standard-setting bodies is often downplayed in the literature because these bodies are considered—generally, by the state-centric explanation—as venues (or 'empty vessels'), where national interests play out and negotiations among various jurisdictions take place. Alternatively, these fora are considered—mainly, by the business-led explanation—as targets for the lobbying activity of the financial industry, which might result in regulatory capture (e.g. Lall 2012; Mattli and Woods 2009). Yet, standard-setting bodies have agency of their own, they are more than the sum of their members (Newman and Posner 2018). In particular, they put in place several formal and informal coordination tools with a view to managing regime complexity (Quaglia and Spendzharova 2020a). Thus, transgovernmental networks make up for limited domestic coordination among regulatory agencies in various jurisdictions. At times, however, there are 'political' and 'bureaucratic' limitations to the activity of regulators.

Finally, the preferences and the structural and instrumental power of the *financial industry* contributed to shaping the content of various international standards, often reducing their precision and stringency (Lall 2012; Mattli and Woods 2009; Pagliari and Young 2014; Young and Pagliari 2015; Underhill and Zhang 2008; Young 2012), although without preventing the adoption of new rules. For instance, margin requirements for non-centrally cleared derivatives (Spagna 2019) and higher bank capital requirements for derivatives trading and clearing were strongly opposed by the industry. Yet, these international standards were adopted. The preferences of private actors derived from the distributional effects of the new rules, that is to say, the expected costs and benefits.

However, the preferences of the financial industry were not homogenous across and within jurisdictions (see, for example, Helleiner 2011; Pagliari and Young 2014; Pagliari 2018), which lessened, partly 'canceling out', the influence of private actors on regulatory outputs. Here, we are mainly interested in business associations and private actors that mobilized at the international level or cross-border (Cerny 2010; McKeen-Edwards and Porter 2013), rather than those that mainly lobbied domestically and which feed into a state-centric explanation. At times, financial associations and firms engaged in international 'venue shopping' (Beyers and Kerremans 2012; Eckhardt and De Bievre 2015), augmenting regime complexity. Other times, whenever imprecise or inconsistent rules across elemental regimes were deemed to be costly for private actors, especially for large associations and firms engaged in cross-border business, these transnational forces contributed to the pursuit of regulatory cooperation, for example, by mobilizing in several venues.

Contributions to the Literature

This book makes three main contributions to the literature. Theoretically, it extends the international relations literature on regime complexity (Alter and Meunier 2009; Keohane and Victor 2011; Johnson and Urpelainen 2012; Orsini, Morin, and Young 2013; Pratt 2018; Raustiala and Victor 2004) to finance. Specifically, it draws attention to the under-explored issues of the intersections between elemental regimes dealing with different aspects of derivatives markets, and the need to coordinate the activities of international standard-setters so as to promote regulatory precision, stringency, and consistency. This topic has become increasingly important, given the augmented complexity of finance and the large number of cross-sectoral issues to tackle. This research maps the over-crowded regulatory space in derivatives by identifying the elemental regimes that regulate it and by highlighting gaps, overlaps, and interlinkages. It also slightly amends the concept of regime complexity in order to make it more amenable to financial regulation by drawing attention to the fact that elemental regimes in finance are often interlinked. By examining the causes, management, and effects of regime complexity on derivatives, this book provides some generalizable explanations that can travel to other areas of financial regulation as well as other policy areas.

This research also contributes to the political economy literature on international standard setting in finance (Botzem 2014; Büthe and Mattli 2011; Drezner 2007; Fioretos 2010; Gabor 2016a; Goldbach 2015a,b; Helleiner 2014; Knaack 2015; Lall 2012, 2014; Mügge and Stellinga 2015; Mügge and Perry 2014; Newman and Posner 2018; Porter 2014a,b; Posner 2010; Rixen 2013; Seabrooke and Wigan 2016, 2017; Sharman 2011, 2006; Simmons 2001; Singer 2004, 2007; Tsingou 2015a,b; Thiemann 2014, 2018; Young 2012, 2014) by innovatively combining mainstream explanations concerning the making of international rules and their consistency. It considers the preferences and power of the main jurisdictions as the independent variables that affect the setting (or not) of international rules as well as most of their content. However, the state-centric explanation is mediated by networks of regulators and the financial industry.

With reference to transgovernmental networks, this research investigates why and how they are instrumental in international standard setting by ironing out disagreements among and within jurisdictions. It highlights their role in managing regime complexity, and it identifies a variety of formal and informal coordination tools used for this purpose. It also points out the limits of cooperation among regulators, whenever the issues dealt with are politically salient, or elicit bureaucratic turf fighting. With reference to the financial industry, the research draws attention to market competition not only across jurisdictions, but also within jurisdictions. In other words, international standards have different distributional implications for various parts of the financial industry. On certain issues, such as the allocation of costs for the recovery and resolution of CCPs, the preferences of different parts of the financial industry (e.g. CCPs, direct users, indirect users) are aligned across jurisdictions. This trend contrasts, for example, with the Basel accords, in which the preferences of the financial industry tend to be homogeneous within national banking systems (Goldbach 2015a, b; Howarth and Quaglia 2016; Thiemann 2018, 2014).

Empirically, this book provides the first comprehensive account of the international regime complex concerning derivatives; whereas the existing literature has primarily focused on national regulations, transatlantic disputes, or one or two international standards for specific aspects of derivatives (Helleiner et al. 2018; Helleiner 2014; Knaack 2015; Newman and Posner 2018; Pagliari 2013b, 2012; Spagna 2019). It is argued that, overall, post-crisis international cooperation was relatively successful in promoting regulatory precision, stringency, and consistency for derivatives. It is true that the international regulation of derivatives trading on exchanges or platforms remained very 'thin'. Other standards, at least initially, lacked precision, for example, concerning the resilience of CCPs (Posner 2018), or data formatting for the reporting of derivatives trades to repositories (Knaack 2018). Or the standards, at first, had limited stringency because they deliberately avoided contentious issues, such as recovery and resolution of CCPs, or the conditions concerning the authorities' access to data held by trade repositories.

The limited granularity of some standards and their gaps were sometimes the price to be paid in order to reach compromises that would be acceptable to various jurisdictions, private actors, and regulators. This partly explains the transatlantic disputes that emerged concerning the regulation of multilateral trading facilities, CCPs, and trade repositories (Knaack 2015; Newman and Posner 2018; Pagliari 2013b). Furthermore, the US and the EU did not always wait for international standards to be set and, instead, acted unilaterally with extraterritorial reach. That said, over time, several standards for derivatives became more precise (notably, those on trade reporting), stringent (notably, those on CCPs), and consistent (notably, capital and margin requirements), dealing with some controversial issues that previously had been side-stepped (for instance, the recovery and resolution of CCPs).

The findings of this research, which highlight the remarkable level of post-crisis international cooperation in regulating derivatives, are at odds with those of previous studies, which have underplayed the extent of international cooperation and have stressed, instead, the regulatory disputes that emerged among jurisdictions (Knaack 2018, 2015; Gravelle and Pagliari 2018; Posner 2018). Furthermore, most academic literature has criticized the limited stringency of post-crisis regulatory reforms in finance, arguing that the pre-crisis status quo continued (Baker and Underhill 2015; Helleiner 2014; Moschella and Tsingou 2013a,b; Maynz 2012, 2015; Tsingou 2015b; Underhill 2015), whereas this book underscores the overhaul that took place in the regulation of derivatives.

Several reasons account for the 'revisionist' view taken in this book. First, previous works tended to consider only one or two derivatives standards at the same time, without looking at the full picture. Second, previous works suffered from case-selection biases in that they selected on the dependent variable by focusing primarily on transatlantic regulatory disputes. Third, while previous studies were accurate at the time they were written, they are now dated because standard-setting for derivatives has substantially expanded over time. The conclusions of existing research were made too soon after the crisis, whereas this book benefits from extra years of observation and can, therefore, give proper weight to a much wider set of derivatives standards.

Structure and Content of the Book

The structure of the book is as follows. Chapter 2 discusses the state of the art, the research design, and the sources used. It outlines the scope of the research, the timeframe, and the empirical coverage. Chapter 3 sets the context in which the international regulation of derivatives markets took place post-crisis.

Chapter 4 examines the international standards for centralized trading and clearing of derivatives. Chapter 5 deals with the international standards for the reporting of derivatives trades to repositories. Chapter 6 discusses the international standards for the resilience, recovery, and resolution of CCPs. Chapter 7 examines the international standards for capital for bank exposures to CCPs and derivative trading and clearing. Chapter 8 deals with the international standards for margins for derivatives non-centrally cleared via CCPs. The concluding chapter engages in a comparative, cross-cutting assessment of various elemental regimes on derivatives. It summarizes the main theoretical and empirical findings, discusses the contributions to the literature, and puts forward proposals for further research.

The empirical chapters offer a complete picture of the post-crisis regime complex on derivatives, rather than examining only certain parts, which provide a piecemeal view of the regulatory reforms undertaken. However, there is a trade-off between the broad scope of the research and the limited amount of detail that can be examined on specific issues. For this reason, although international standards produce domestic changes and feedback effects (Newman and Posner 2018, 2016a,b) as well as compliance problems (Mosley 2003, 2010; Quaglia 2019; Walter 2008), these are beyond the scope of this research, as are also the transatlantic regulatory disputes resulting from domestic rules on derivatives (Knaack 2015; Pagliari 2013b; Quaglia 2017b).

2
State of the Art and Research Design

This chapter begins by reviewing several bodies of scholarly works that are relevant to this research. Then, it outlines the research design, the analytical framework, the methodology, and the sources used. Finally, it clarifies the scope of the research, the empirical coverage, and the timeframe.

State of the Art and Theoretical Framework

There are several conceptual building blocks of this research, which are discussed in turn. We first review the literature on international regime complexity and regulatory consistency. We then discuss mainstream theoretically informed explanations of international standard setting—notably, the state-centric, the transgovernmental, and the business-led accounts—which can be useful to explain how regime complexity in derivatives has been dealt with.

International Regime Complexity

In the international relations literature, the presence of multiple institutions governing a single issue or a set of related issues is referred to as an 'international regime complex' (Alter and Meunier 2009; Alter and Raustiala 2018; Drezner 2009; Keohane and Victor 2011; Johnson and Urpelainen 2012; Orsini, Morin, and Young 2013; Pratt 2018; Raustiala and Victor 2004). Regime complexes are marked by the existence of several sets of rules—also referred to as 'elemental regimes'—that are created and maintained in distinct fora with the participation of different sets of actors (Orsini, Morin, and Young 2013). The increasing number and size of regime complexes reflect the influence of legalization on world politics (Abbott et al. 2000). International regime complexity refers to the presence of nested, partially overlapping, and parallel elemental regimes. Thus, there can be 'nested regimes', where institutions are embedded within each other in concentric

The Politics of Regime Complexity In International Derivatives Regulation. Lucia Quaglia, Oxford University Press (2020).
 DOI: 10.1093/oso/9780198866077.003.0001

circles, like Russian dolls; 'overlapping regimes', where multiple institutions have authority over an issue, but agreements are not mutually exclusive or subsidiary to another; and 'parallel regimes', where there is no formal or direct substantive overlap (Alter and Meunier 2009; Orsini, Morin, and Young 2013). In addition, elemental regimes can be 'interlinked', whereby the rules in a given elemental regime have direct implications for other regimes—this is often the case in finance.

With reference to derivatives, capital requirements for bank exposures to CCPs and for derivatives trading and clearing are nested into the broader set of standards for bank capital. Rules on the centralized trading of derivatives via exchanges or platforms partly overlap with those on the central clearing of derivatives via CCPs because all centrally traded derivatives should also be centrally cleared. Standards for the recovery of CCPs partly overlap with those on the resolution of CCPs because some instruments used in recovery are also used in resolution. These standards are parallel to standards for the reporting of derivatives trades to repositories. Yet, most elemental regimes on derivatives are interlinked. For example, the elemental regime on the centralized clearing of derivatives through CCPs is interlinked with the elemental regime concerning the resilience, recovery, and resolution of CCPs because mandatory clearing means that CCPs need to be made more resilient and resolvable. In turn, standards for the resilience, recovery, and resolution of CCPs are interlinked with the elemental regime on capital requirements for bank exposures to CCPs, so that banks would not become a source of weakness for CCPs and, at the same time, they would be able to withstand the recovery and resolution of CCPs. Margin and bank capital requirements for non-centrally cleared derivatives, which are intended to encourage clearing via CCPs, are interlinked due to their cumulative effects.

The literature on regime complexity identifies several causes for the presence of nested, parallel, and overlapping elemental regimes. Regime complexity is often ascribed to the deliberate attempts by states and, less frequently, interest groups, to pursue their preferences and shift the balance of power by creating new institutions, undermining existing ones, or redesigning them (Colgan et al. 2012; Henning 2017; Urpelainen and de Graaf 2015). Thus, actors can engage in 'strategic inconsistency' (Keohane and Victor 2011), whereby contradictory rules are created in a parallel regime with the intention of undermining a rule in another agreement. Alternatively, actors can pursue 'strategic ambiguity' (Alter and Meunier 2009) by deliberately keeping rules across elemental regimes vague, so that they can be interpreted in different ways. Finally, actors that are unhappy with existing institutions can engage in contested multilateralism by combining 'threats of exit, voice, and the creation of alternative institutions to pursue policies and practices different from those of existing institutions' (Morse and Keohane 2014: 386). However, regime complexity can also be caused by the multidimensionality of the problems to tackle and the absence of a focal standard-setter, as in the case of derivatives.

Regime complexity is often seen as a 'pathology' that undermines governance effectiveness through 'redundancy, inconsistency, and conflict' (Abbott, Genschel, Zangl, et al. 2015: 7). Three main problems ensuing from regime complexity are highlighted in the literature (see Pratt 2018). First, there is an inefficient duplication of rules and institutions (Pratt 2019), which is costly for states as well as for private actors. Second, there is regulatory arbitrage, whereby interested parties (mainly states, but also interest groups) engage in forum shopping (Busch 2007), regime shifting (Helfer 2009) or competitive multilateralism (Morse and Keohane 2014). Third, there are 'negative spillovers' in a regime complex, if 'cooperation in one area undermines the pursuit of objectives in another area' (Johnson and Urpelainen 2012). More generally, 'regime complexes are laden with legal inconsistencies' because the rules in one regime are rarely coordinated closely with overlapping rules in related regimes (Raustiala and Victor 2004, Breen, Hodson, and Moschella 2020). There is, instead, regulatory consistency if the rules issued by various bodies do not contradict each other and are, instead, compatible (Quaglia and Spendzharova 2019, 2020a), that is to say, they work together towards the same purpose. One can observe consistency when, for example, the regulatory objectives and instruments prescribed by one set of rules underpin (or, at least, do not contradict) other rules, or when concepts defined and measured by one set of rules are used in the same way by other rules. Consistency also encompasses 'compatibility'—in the sense that one set of standards does not interfere with others and they both pursue similar objectives—so as to make sure that market participants cannot use sectoral differences in order to 'game the rules'.

In a regime complex, one of the central problems that emerges is that 'the rules in these elemental regimes functionally overlap, yet there is no agreed-upon hierarchy for resolving conflicts between rules' (Raustiala and Victor 2004: 279). At the domestic level, when there is rule overlap or jurisdictional conflict among different actors, the issue is often 'passed on' to a higher level in the government's organizational hierarchy, eventually to be resolved by the relevant minister, or in a collective cabinet discussion (see Peters 2006). However, such vertical transfer of issues upwards to a higher organizational level, in order to resolve jurisdictional overlaps and avoid regulatory inconsistency, is not feasible at the international level in the absence of an overarching government. It is true that certain international regimes are more integrated than others by centralizing coordination through institutional channels across the regimes (Johnson and Urpelainen 2012). For example, the trade regime tends (or, rather, tended) to be highly integrated, with the World Trade Organization (WTO) playing an important coordinating role. By contrast, arms control regimes are quite fragmented, whereas environmental and financial regimes are between these two ends of the spectrum.

State-Centric Explanation

Although the existing literature on the politics and political economy of international financial regulation has not specifically dealt with regime complexity, it has provided several explanations concerning the dynamics of international standard setting in finance. A first body of literature has taken a *state-centric* approach. The early academic literature stressed the preferences and power of the 'hegemonic' country, the US, for or against international harmonization (Simmons 2001; more recently, Helleiner 2014). The assumption was that international regulatory cooperation benefited some countries more than others, and, therefore, had redistributive implications (Oatley and Nabors 1998). Consequently, international cooperation and regulatory harmonization took place only when they were in line with the preferences of the dominant country, as determined by incentives to emulate its rules and by policy specific externalities (Simmons 2001). This approach highlighted the importance of US preferences and its hegemonic bargaining power in shaping international standards.

More recently, Helleiner (2014) pointed out the 'structural power' and 'active policy choices' of the US in order to explain the limited change in the status quo after the international financial crisis. In turn, the power of the US stemmed from the size of its large domestic market (Drezner 2007) and from the fact that US authorities were often 'first-movers' in initiating domestic regulatory reforms, which, then, informed the setting of international standards (Posner 2010). Frequently, the US authorities acted as 'pace-setters' internationally, following the adoption of domestic reforms as first-movers (Ryan and Ziegler 2015) because international regulatory harmonization would help to minimize the competitive disadvantages ensuing for the US financial industry, and would limit negative cross-border externalities for financial stability (Kapstein 1992; Macey 2003; Singer 2004, 2007; Simmons 2001). However, the scope of US domestic regulatory initiatives sets the limits of what the US was willing to endorse at an international level (Helleiner 2014).

Reflecting on the changing global context during the twenty-first century, several works questioned the hegemony of the US in regulating global finance by considering other jurisdictions that have large financial markets. Singer (2007, 2004) investigated the domestic politics of preference formation for or against international financial harmonization in the US, the UK, and Japan. He argued that international cooperation was a way for domestic regulators to restore the balance between domestic financial stability and international competitiveness in response to an external shock, so as to appease elected officials and the industry. Drezner (2007: 5) examined the role of the 'great powers', defined as 'governments that oversee large internal markets', namely, the US and the EU, in a variety of regulatory regimes, including finance. The regulatory preferences of the various jurisdictions depended on the domestic adjustment costs to the new international rules (Drezner 2007) and domestic regulatory institutions, which were the sources of preferences and power in international standard setting (Buthe and Mattli 2011; Farrell and Newman 2010; Posner 2010). Other state-centric works drew attention to the configuration of national economic systems, arguing that national policymakers engaged in international standard setting sought to defend the comparative institutional advantages of their domestic financial industry (Fioretos 2010; Goldbach 2015a, b; Howarth and Quaglia 2016; Macartney 2010; Rixen 2013, 2010; Thiemann 2014, 2018).

State-centric studies generally start from the assumption, grounded in the broad tradition of rational choice analysis, that 'states use international institutions to further their own goals, and they design institutions accordingly' (Koremenos et al. 2001: 762). These authors define international institutions as 'explicit arrangements, negotiated among international actors, that prescribe, proscribe, and/or authorize behavior' and argue that 'many institutional arrangements are best understood through "rational design" among multiple participants' (Koremenos et al. 2001: 766; see also Johnson and Urpelainen 2012; Urpelainen and van de Graaf 2015; Turk 2014). Yet, several works on international financial regulation have shown that the rational pursuit of interest-driven goals by state actors may result in a less than rational institutional design. For example, Kalyanpur and Newman (2017) argue that the evolution of the international securities regime was strongly shaped by an experimental bricolage approach of trying out different solutions to the problems at hand, rather than by comprehensive rational institutional design.

This, in turn, feeds into 'experimentalist governance' (De Burca, Keohane, and Sabel 2013, 2014; Posner 2015; Zeitlin 2015).

On the one hand, international regime complexity can be amplified by states seeking regulatory venues, whose mandates and membership favour the pursuit of national interests. For example, the US and the EU shifted negotiations over intellectual property to the WTO in the 1990s, and linked the result of those negotiations (the Agreement on Trade-Related Aspects of Intellectual Property Rights) to the new WTO dispute settlement system. This dramatically expanded intellectual property protection standards to the benefit of producers in the US and the EU (Helfer 2009).[1] In finance, of particular interests is the alignment of preferences of the US and the EU, which have large domestic financial markets. Drezner (2007) notes that when the 'great powers' have heterogeneous preferences on a certain issue, they are likely to engage in various regulatory venues and promote rival international standards, as in the case of accounting (Botzem 2013; Leblond 2011; Perry and Nölke 2006; Posner 2010). Vice versa, when the preferences of the great powers are aligned, they converge on one set of international standards, such as those adopted in the wake of the Asian financial crisis to increase financial resilience outside the 'core' of the international financial system (Drezner 2007; Walter 2008).

On the other hand, countries that are multiple members of various elemental regimes have a 'general interest in some form of institutional complementarity' within the regime complex because they value the 'collective goods' produced by the elemental regimes of which they are members (Gehring and Faude 2014). Hence, multiple members operate in a setting of 'nested games', whereby, when determining their actions in one regime, they take into account the implications that this will have on other elemental regimes within the complex. Countries that are members of multiple elemental regimes are likely to promote institutional adaptation via 'complementary processes' and the division of work among institutions (Gehring and Faude 2014). Johnson and Urpeleinen (2012) argue that this is more likely if there are 'negative spillovers' across elemental regimes, whereby 'cooperation in one issue area undermines the pursuit of objectives in another issue area'. Yet, the ability of states to manage regime complexity can be constrained by their domestic institutional framework and their capacity to coordinate internally (see Morin and Orsini

[1] Yet, not only the main jurisdictions engage in regime shifting. Indeed, developing countries and civil society groups opposed to strong intellectual property rights under the WTO regime promoted the shift to other international regimes to create counter-regime norms that conflicted with Trade-Related Aspects of Intellectual Property Rights in the WTO (Helfer 2009).

2014). If several domestic regulatory agencies are involved—each with its own composition, competences, and regulatory outlook—and domestic coordination is weak, it is more difficult for states to manage regime complexity.

In the case of derivatives, the great powers were keen to secure financial stability and a level playing field that several elemental regimes set out to protect, and therefore, sought to promote regulatory precision, stringency, and consistency. However, the ability of the US and the EU to manage regime complexity was often constrained by the fragmentation of domestic regulatory institutions (Bach and Newman 2007; Lavelle 2019; Posner 2009; Quaglia 2014b) and their limited capacity to coordinate internally and externally (Moschella and Quaglia 2016; Mügge 2011a; Quaglia 2014c). Domestic coordination is more difficult if domestic regulatory competences are not clearly allocated, or if they are shared by a multitude of regulatory agencies, which, in turn, are active in different international fora. This is notably the case in federal states, such as the US, whose regulatory institutions in finance were deliberately set up and kept fragmented (see Lavelle 2019), and in multi-level jurisdictions, such as the EU (Mügge 2011a, 2014; Moschella and Quaglia 2016, 2013; Quaglia 2014a), where the EU and national authorities are both present in international financial fora. For all these reasons, the main jurisdictions are likely to encounter difficulties in managing regime complexity, even when it is in their interest to do so. From the discussion above, the following hypothesis can be derived.

The main jurisdictions play a prominent role in setting international standards and managing regime complexity, subject to domestic coordination problems.

Transgovernmental Explanation

A second body of literature on international standard setting in finance has highlighted the role of transgovernmental networks of domestic regulators (Ahdieh 2015; Bach and Newman 2010, 2014; Bach et al. 2016a; Coen and Thatcher 2008; Djelic and Quack 2010; Thatcher and Coen 2008; Jordana 2017; Slaughter 2004; Slaughter and Zaring 2006; Tsingou 2010a; Turk 2014; Verdier 2009). International standard setting no longer belongs to the realm of intergovernmental negotiations, but falls within the responsibility of a 'transnational policy community of experts actors' (Tsingou 2008) that have common professional and educational backgrounds (Chwieroth 2015, 2009) and share similar epistemological views (Kapstein 1992). Of particular interest are transgovernmental networks of regulators that have the following core features: they meet in multilateral bodies that are not established pursuant to treaties; their membership consists of domestic regulatory agencies; they work by consensus; and they issue (non-legally binding) soft law (Brummer 2015, 2010b; Verdier 2009). The autonomous role of transgovernmental networks that are gathered in international standard-setting bodies is often downplayed by state-centric accounts because these bodies are considered as 'empty vessels', where national interests play out and negotiations among different jurisdictions take place. Alternatively, these fora are considered by business power accounts as targets for the lobbying activity of the financial industry, which might result in regulatory capture (Lall 2012). Yet, transgovernmental networks of regulators are more than the sum of their members.

On one hand, domestic regulators are 'reluctant diplomats' (Singer 2007: ix) because they have a prominent role in negotiating international standards with their counterparts, given the level of required technical knowledge, but would prefer to stay out of the political limelight. On the other hand, financial regulators are not purely technocratic actors who are insulated from the economy and politics of the national context in which they are embedded (Brummer 2015; Singer 2007, 2004; Verdier 2012). Hence, regulators have to be mindful of the implications of international rules designed to protect financial stability for the competitiveness of domestic financial firms (Kapstein 1989, 1992). Consequently, the process of setting international standards does not simply revolve around establishing consensus on the technical details; it also involves striking a balance between the domestic political economy concerns of various jurisdictions (Quaglia and Spendzharova 2017).[2]

For this reason, some law scholars (Brummer 2015; Verdier 2009) argue that transgovernmental networks can be effective in dealing with information asymmetries in international negotiations, or in reducing the lack of trust among jurisdictions, but are less effective if the domestic preferences of jurisdictions are not aligned (for example, in the case of hedge funds regulation, see Fioretos 2010), or if the international problem to be addressed has major distributional implications (e.g. the regulation of offshore financial centres, Rixen 2013; tax havens, Sharman 2006; and money laundering, Sharman 2011; Tsingou 2010b). Similarly, if an issue has high political

[2] Furthermore, international standard-setting bodies suffer from limited direct democratic accountability to voters (see Black 2008; Mügge 2011b), which is particularly problematic when international standards have potential fiscal implications domestically.

salience—it is no longer 'quiet politics' (Culpepper 2011; Pagliari 2013a; Woll 2013)—elected officials are likely to follow it closely and might seek to intervene directly in the regulatory process. Furthermore, in the wake of the crisis, the transnational policy community in finance was 'under stress' (Tsingou 2010a) because there was 'much less consensus on optimal regulatory models' (Helleiner and Pagliari 2011). For example, in the case of accounting standards, regulators were unable to agree on how and when to apply core principles, such as fair value accounting (Mügge and Stellinga 2015).

Yet, transgovernmental networks of regulators are often engaged in a high degree of horizontal cooperation and act as crucial intermediaries in designing and reforming the international rules governing a given policy area (Jordana 2017). Abbott et al. (2015, see also Abbott, Genschel, Snidal, and Zangl 2016) develop the concept of 'orchestration', which occurs when an international organization 'enlists and supports intermediary actors to address target actors' in the pursuit of the governance goals of the international organization. Hence, orchestration is 'indirect' because the orchestrator works through intermediaries to influence targets, and it is 'soft' because the orchestrator often lacks authoritative control over intermediaries and targets. Indirect governance is especially important at the international level because international organizations often lack direct access to the targets of regulation. Nevertheless, orchestration is less useful in order to explain the management of regime complexity if there is not a lead orchestrator, as in the case of derivatives (as explained in Chapter 3).

The literature on the role of transgovernmental networks in international standard setting in finance speaks to the literature on regime complexity. Indeed, it is the presence of several different transgovernmental networks, each primarily responsible for a given set of standards (or elemental regime), which increases regime complexity. At the same time, these networks can also play an important role in managing regime complexity (Quaglia and Spendzharova 2020a). To begin with, regulators tend to share similar academic and professional experiences, and develop 'deep relationships' and a 'sense of community' that help to foster problem solving (Slaughter 2004), even though these patterns are more common among banking regulators than those of derivatives (Posner 2018). 'Regulators must not only keep abreast of domestic special interests and the expectations of their home governments, but also cultivate allegiances and respond to the concerns of their international homologues' (Brummer 2015: 69). Financial regulators have an incentive to sponsor rule precision, stringency, and consistency because of their mandate to protect financial stability, which would be jeopardized by imprecise, lenient, or inconsistent rules (Quaglia and Spendzharova 2020a). Yet, there are political and bureaucratic limitations to transgovernmental cooperation. In fact, elected officials might decide to intervene in the regulatory process. Or bureaucratic politics might come into play (Peters 2002), whereby regulators seek to protect or expand their particular bureaucratic 'turf' (e.g. James and Quaglia 2020b). On the basis of the discussion above, the following hypothesis can be derived.

Transgovernmental networks facilitate international standard setting and are instrumental in managing regime complexity, subject to political and bureaucratic constraints.

A variety of formal and informal tools can be used by international standard-setting bodies in order to manage regime complexity and coordinate the regulatory activities of transgovernmental networks (see Table 2.1). One important dimension of variation concerns informal vs. formally institutionalized tools. The first formal tool for coordination is the *cross-referencing* of standards, meaning that there is an understanding between two or more standards-setting bodies, whereby each body recognizes the adequacy of the standards issued by other standards-setters. Thus, on a certain issue, one standard-setting body refers to how the matter is regulated by another standard-setter, rather than issuing its own rules. A concept similar to cross-referencing is *institutional deference*, whereby one organization 'formally adopts a set of rules established by a different institution' (Pratt 2018: 562). A third formal mechanism of coordination is the use of *memoranda of understanding* (MoU) among different international standard-setters to set out their tasks and responsibilities. MoUs are statements of intent that do not impose legally binding obligations on signatories. Nevertheless, MoUs introduce more structured formal procedures through which different regulatory bodies may interact. In addition, international

Table 2.1 Informal and formal coordination tools among international bodies

Informal	Formal
Adopting good practices from another body	Cross-referencing of standards
Regulatory dialogue with other bodies, e.g. phone calls, meetings, exchange of information	Joint working groups and joint studies
	Memoranda of Understanding

* Adapted from Quaglia and Spendzharova 2020a

standard-setters may engage in *joint standard setting*, whereby they co-produce standards together as well as carrying out *joint studies*. They generally do so by setting up joint working groups with joint membership and joint chairmanship (Quaglia and Spendzharova 2020a).

Informal coordination tools draw on learning from other international standard-setters or international organizations that have more expertise and may have developed relevant good practices or codes of conduct. In this case, an international standard-setter may choose to replicate the existing *good practices* developed by another body, which, in turn, facilitates coordination. Furthermore, international standard-setters may carry out *regulatory dialogues* with other counterparts regarding their ongoing work of mutual interest and future activities, as well as *exchange information*, for example, through emails, informal meetings, phone calls, cross-membership of the same individuals in working groups of different bodies (Quaglia and Spendzharova 2020a).

Business-Led Explanation

A third body of literature on international standard setting in finance has focused on the role of the business community, arguing that international standards tend to reflect the interests of private actors (Baker 2010; Bell and Hindmoor 2015, 2016, 2018; Graz and Noelke 2008; Mügge 2010; Tsingou 2006; Underhill and Zhang 2008), that is to say, the rules that the financial industry finds more advantageous (or less burdensome), on the basis of the distributional implications of the new rules. In general, the financial industry tends to prefer rules that are less precise and less stringent and, thus, less costly for financial actors. For example, some authors argue that the lowering of bank capital requirements in Basel II was a clear example of a race to the bottom and industry's capture of regulators (Lall 2012; Tsingou 2008; cf. Young 2012). This approach gives attention to the activity of transnational associations (McKeen-Edwards and Porter 2013), such as the Institute of International Finance (IIF) (Newman and Posner 2016b), or the International Swaps and Derivatives Association (ISDA) (Newman and Bach 2014), and the formation of cross-border coalitions in the creation of rules for international finance. Thus, according to Cerny's 'transnational neopluralism' (2010: 4–6), the most important 'movers and shakers' are no longer domestic forces, but rather 'actors that can coordinate their activities across borders'. For instance, Farrell and Newman (2014b, see also 2014a, 2016) and Newman and Posner

(2018) show that cross-border coalitions were instrumental in settling transatlantic regulatory disputes in finance.[3]

Several works on business power and interest groups mobilization maintain that private actors engage in venue shopping by strategically lobbying regulatory venues that are likely to be more conducive to their preferences (Alter and Meunier 2006; Chalmers 2015; De Bièvre, Poletti, Thomann 2014; Eckhardt and De Bièvre 2015). For example, Newman and Posner (2016a) argued that interest groups and other actors that succeeded in embedding themselves within the relevant institutional framework, used their advantageous position through 'policy feedback loops' to pursue regulatory policies that favoured them (and, potentially, disfavoured other groups). With specific reference to regime complexity, research on trade policy shows that venue shopping by private actors can increase regime complexity (Alter and Meunier 2006; De Bièvre, Poletti, Thomann 2014; Eckhardt and De Bièvre 2015).[4]

Yet, the financial industry has an interest in lowering regulatory costs, which can be negatively affected by the imprecision and inconsistency of rules (for instance, concerning the reporting of derivatives trades, or the tools for recovery and resolution of CCPs). Thus, private actors can help to manage regime complexity on derivatives. Indeed, the simultaneous mobilization of (mainly, transnational) private financial actors in several international venues, as well as cross-borders, can facilitate the process of coordination among standard-setters (Cerny 2010; Newman and Posner 2018). The most powerful parts of the financial industry are well-positioned to promote consistency across elemental regimes, depending on the homogeneity of their preferences and the alignment of their economic interests. It should, however, be kept in mind that the quest for consistency is not the main purpose of interest groups and private actors, which are not benevolent welfare maximizers, but rather they are self-interested actors, keen on maximizing their own utility. Therefore, the following hypothesis can be derived.

[3] Other works argue that the structure of the national financial system (or the variety of national financial capitalism) affects national preferences on international standard setting, for example, on hedge funds (Fioretos 2010), shadow banking (Thiemann 2014, 2018), capital requirements for banks (Howarth and Quaglia 2016), tax havens (Hakelberg 2016; Hakelberg and Rixen 2020; Palan, Murphy, and Chavagneux 2013; Rixen 2013; Sharman 2006), money laundering (Sharman 2011) and off-shore centres (Palan 2003), although this strand of the literature is part of the state-centric explanation discussed above.

[4] Moreover, industry lobbying, especially at the national level, can hamper vertical regulatory consistency between international, regional (EU) and national rules (Quaglia and Spendzharova 2019; Young 2014). It can also result in domestic non-compliance (or mock compliance) with international financial standards (Chey 2014, 2007, 2006; Mosley 2003, 2010; Quaglia 2019; Walter 2008).

The financial industry, especially transnational private actors, partly shape the content of international standards and contribute to managing regime complexity, if it is in their interest to do so.

Research Design, Methodology, and Sources

The empirical outcome to be explained by this research concerns international cooperation in regulating post-crisis derivatives markets and specifically: the international institutional architecture for the regulation of derivatives and the degrees of precision, stringency, and consistency of the standards issued. As elaborated in Chapter 3, there are three possible architectures for international regulation: the silos model, hierarchy, and the regime complex. International banking regulation remained quite siloed after the crisis; however, international derivatives regulation fits the regime complexity model. Why? Regarding the second dimension of the empirical outcome to be explained, one would not expect regime complexity to yield rule precision, stringency, and consistency because a variety of institutions and regulatory processes are involved without a clear hierarchy. Yet, post-crisis international standards on derivatives had a considerable degree of precision, stringency, and consistency. Why?

Bringing together the literature on regime complexity in international relations, and the literature on international standard setting in international political economy, the research design innovatively combines three theoretically informed accounts: a state-centric explanation; a transgovernmental explanation; and a business-led explanation. Each of these explanations draws attention to one set of agents—the main jurisdictions (notably, the 'great powers' see Drezner 2007); technical networks of regulators; and powerful private actors (notably, transnational forces)—in international standard setting and in managing regime complexity. Thus, the hypotheses outlined in the previous section can be seen as complementary because they identify several sets of actors that can contribute to regulatory precision, stringency, and consistency. Rather than engaging in competitive theory testing, the research design combines these explanations, following a specific order.

To begin with, the *state-centric* explanation identifies the preferences and power of the main jurisdictions as the principal independent variable that affects the standard setting and the management of regime complexity. Therefore, this research investigates the preferences of the main jurisdictions by considering the trade-off between financial stability and competitiveness in the US, the EU, and the UK,[5] as well as their domestic regulatory templates, which, at times, jurisdictions seek to 'upload' to the international level (Posner 2010; Quaglia 2014a). This research also discusses the distributional implications of international standards across jurisdictions.

Transgovernmental networks act as an intervening variable that affects international standard setting and the management of regime complexity. Networks of domestic financial regulators in international fora can help to iron out disagreement among and within jurisdictions, albeit there are political and bureaucratic limits to what regulators can achieve in promoting rule precision, stringency, and consistency. Therefore, this research outlines the main transgovernmental networks and their interactions in international standard-setting bodies, paying particular attention to the formal and informal tools used to improve coordination.

The *financial industry* acts as a second intervening variable that affects the specific content of standards and their consistency by mobilizing in a variety of regulatory venues. Accordingly, this research investigates the preferences of various parts of the financial industry, mainly based on the distributional implications (i.e. the expected costs and benefits) of international standards and the lobbying activities of the business community, with a view towards influencing regulatory outcomes. The mobilization of private actors in several venues can foster venue shopping, thus increasing regime complexity, but it can also facilitate consistency across elemental regimes.

This research is operationalized, first, by distinguishing various elemental regimes (or sets of standards) concerning different aspects of derivatives markets, namely: the trading, clearing, and reporting of derivatives; the resilience, recovery, and resolution of CCPs; the capital requirements for bank exposures to CCPs and derivatives trading and clearing; and the margin requirements for derivatives non-centrally cleared via CCPs. For each elemental regime (or set of standards), we investigate the international standard-setting processes, teasing out the main issues at stake, the preferences, and influence of the main jurisdictions, the activities of networks of regulators, and the mobilization of different parts of the financial industry. Specifically, the theoretical expectations teased out of the literature, as reviewed above, are applied to the empirical record in order to gauge the analytical leverage of

[5] Although during the time-frame considered by this research, the UK was part of the EU, this country is examined separately because it has a very large financial sector and London is a leading international financial centre. Furthermore, the UK has been very active in international standard setting and has often had preferences that are different from those of the rest of the EU, and similar to those of the US (see James and Quaglia 2020a).

various explanations within and across case studies. We, then, use this material to explain regime complexity, identifying the international cooperation efforts within and across elemental regimes and evaluating the precision, stringency, and consistency of their regulatory outputs.

The empirical research for this book covers all the main international standards concerning various aspects of post-crisis derivatives regulation, whereby the new sets of rules (such as margin requirements for non-centrally cleared derivatives, or capital requirements for bank exposures to CCPs, etc.) are the units of analysis. In line with the FSB, we adopt a broad definition of international standards, which include 'principles', which are usually set out in a general way (for example, the *Principles for Financial Market Infrastructures*); 'guidelines', which provide detailed guidance on the requirements to be met (for example, the *Assessment Methodology* provides guidance for assessing the observance of *Principles for Financial Market Infrastructures*); and reports, whenever they outline various regulatory options for jurisdictions to follow. As far as the time frame is concerned, the research analyses the regulatory activities that have taken place after the international financial crisis of 2008, although a short reference is made to the (few) pre-crisis international standards concerning derivatives as well as to the private sector governance that prevailed in this sector before the crisis.

Data-gathering was carried out by making use of a wealth of primary sources. To begin with, there are documents issued by international standard-setting bodies, such as the BCBS, the IOSCO, the CPSS/CPMI, the FSB, as well as by the national and regional (EU) authorities. Second, there are policy papers, press statements, and responses to consultations issued by international, regional, and national financial associations, large individual companies as well as think tanks. This material is complemented by semi-structured elite interviews comprising a cross-section of policymakers and stakeholders engaged in international standard setting. The interviewees were regulators and representatives of financial industry associations and individual companies. Interviews were also conducted with the secretariats of the main international standard-setting bodies. The main purpose of the interviews was to get a better understanding of the main issues at stake, the preferences of policymakers and stakeholders, the policy-making process, the interactions between various types of policymakers and stakeholders, their influence and so on. All the interviews were confidential, triangulated, and checked against publicly available primary documents and a systematic survey of press coverage. In the following chapters, reference has been made to the interviews conducted, indicating only the dates of interviews, but not the names, locations, and institutional affiliations of the interviewee because the interviews were conducted on a non-attributable basis. Whenever data gathered through the interviews confirmed the information provided in policy documents and newspaper articles, the sources that are publicly available are quoted. In several instances, the material gathered through the interviews could be used for background purposes only.

Conclusion

This chapter has taken stock of the existing literature, outlining the theoretical framework and the research design of the book. The next chapter will provide an overview of the international institutional architecture for derivatives regulation and the vast array of post-crisis international standards issued. The subsequent empirical chapters deal with the main elemental regimes concerning various aspects of derivatives markets. These chapters follow a similar structure, which facilitates the sequential application of the selected theoretical accounts to the empirics. Each chapter begins by discussing the key issues at stake in the regulation of a given aspect of derivatives markets (e.g. trading, clearing, and reporting) and then outlines the international standard-setting process and outcome. Subsequently, the analytical leverage of the state-centric, the transgovernmental, and the industry-led explanations is assessed against the empirical record, paying particular attention to the preferences and power of the main jurisdictions, the coordination tools deployed by networks of regulators in international standard-setting bodies and the mobilization of the financial industry. Finally, each chapter discusses how this feeds into regime complexity.

3

Context and Empirical Patterns

This chapter establishes the outcomes to be explained and provides the context for the rest of the book. To begin with, it argues that the international regulation of derivatives can be considered as a regime complex, that is not a silo-like nor a hierarchal regime, by showing that a variety of international standard-setting bodies were involved, jointly or separately, with no clear hierarchical structure. These bodies issued a panoply of international standards—or elemental regimes—which were often nested, parallel, overlapping, or interlinked. The chapter also assesses the extent of post-crisis regulatory reforms concerning derivatives, as compared to the pre-2008 period, and examines the precision, stringency, and consistency of the main sets of international standards adopted. The chapter is organized as follows. The first section outlines the pre-crisis regulation of derivatives markets, which were largely subject to private sector governance. The second section discusses the post-crisis international institutional architecture for the regulation of derivatives and identifies the main international standard-setting bodies that issued non-legally binding soft law on derivatives. The third section provides an overview of the vast array of post-crisis international standards concerning derivatives and examines their precision, stringency, and consistency.

Pre-crisis Self-regulation of Derivatives Markets

Prior to the crisis, there was limited international regulation concerning derivatives, in particular, OTCDs, and it was primarily issued by the private sector (Lockwood 2018; Pagliari 2012). The ISDA, which was set up in 1985, was de facto the trade association of the global OTCD industry, representing approximately 800 member dealers. Over time, the ISDA produced a standardized Master Agreement concerning legal and operational issues for OTCD transactions, contributing to the development of these markets (Newman and Bach 2014). In 1993, the Group of Thirty, which is a private body composed of senior representatives of the private and public sectors dealing with international economic and financial issues (Tsingou 2015a), issued a series

The Politics of Regime Complexity In International Derivatives Regulation. Lucia Quaglia, Oxford University Press (2020).
 DOI: 10.1093/oso/9780198866077.003.0001

of recommendations, *Derivatives: Practices and Principles*, which became international de facto standards (Tsingou 2006). The twenty-four recommendations of the Group of Thirty mainly targeted derivatives dealers and end-users, highlighting the main types of risk and suggesting risk management procedures. As Pagliari (2013a: 132) notes, these self-regulatory measures fostered the growth of OTCD markets in the years before the crisis and were instrumental in 'preserving the status of these markets outside of the public regulatory umbrella. ISDA and other industry-driven bodies increasingly sought to convey the message that the industry was sufficiently capable of taking care of the regulation of the sector and no additional public regulation was required'.

There were no specific public international standard-setting bodies dealing with derivatives (Posner 2018). It was a bit of a 'no man's land' (interview, June 2018). In the mid-1990s, the BCBS and the IOSCO discussed the matter, but they did not recommend the direct regulation of derivatives markets. Instead, they called for better self-regulation, endorsing the recommendations issued by the Group of Thirty and emphasizing the need for disclosure and risk management (see, for example, the BCBS–IOSCO 1995). CCPs existed, but were not systemically important players. In 2004, the CPSS and the IOSCO published the *Recommendations for Central Counterparties* (CPSS-IOSCO 2004), which were, however, rather generic and mainly relied on voluntary compliance. The CPSS and the IOSCO encouraged CCPs to conduct a self-assessment of their observance of the recommendations.

Helleiner (2014) ascribed the pre-crisis self-regulation of OTCDs to their 'complex' and 'technical' nature; the prevailing 'neo-liberal ideas', especially in the transnational policy community active in this field (see also Tsingou 2006); and the influence of private financial actors, especially the dealer banks, which were the main buyers and sellers of derivatives and which opposed public regulation. Large volumes, opaque markets, and the absence of public regulation made this business very profitable for banks, accounting for about 40% of their profits (Spagna 2019: 8). Dealer banks (Litan 2010 refers to them as the 'derivatives dealers' club') lobbied against regulation at the international and national levels and sought to promote private sector governance, primarily through a transnational industry association, the ISDA, where the dealers carried much weight (Biggins and Scott 2013; Newman and Bach 2014).

Although some observers, for example, financier Warren Buffet, warned that derivatives were 'financial weapons of mass destruction', the US and UK authorities were reluctant to discuss the regulation of OTCDs prior to the crisis (Helleiner 2014; Helleiner and Pagliari 2010). In 2000, the US Congress passed a bill that prevented the domestic regulation of OTCDs. Lockwood (2018) argues that the Federal Reserve, the Bank of England, and the BCBS saw an unregulated OTCD market as serving the public good, and, hence, they ruled out more intrusive regulation. Ex post, the British FSA acknowledged in the Turner Review (FSA 2009: 1) that a proliferation of wholesale financial products, particularly derivatives, had taken place prior to the crisis and that 'the past philosophy of the FSA, shared with market and bank regulators across most of the developed world, has been to assume that wholesale market customers are by definition sophisticated and do not need protection'.

Post-crisis International Institutional Architecture for Derivatives Regulation

After the international financial crisis of 2008, all the main international standard-setting bodies – namely, the BCBS, the IOSCO, the CPSS/CPMI, and the FSB - were involved in the regulation of various aspects of derivatives markets (see Table 1.1 and Figure 3.1). These bodies, which bring together

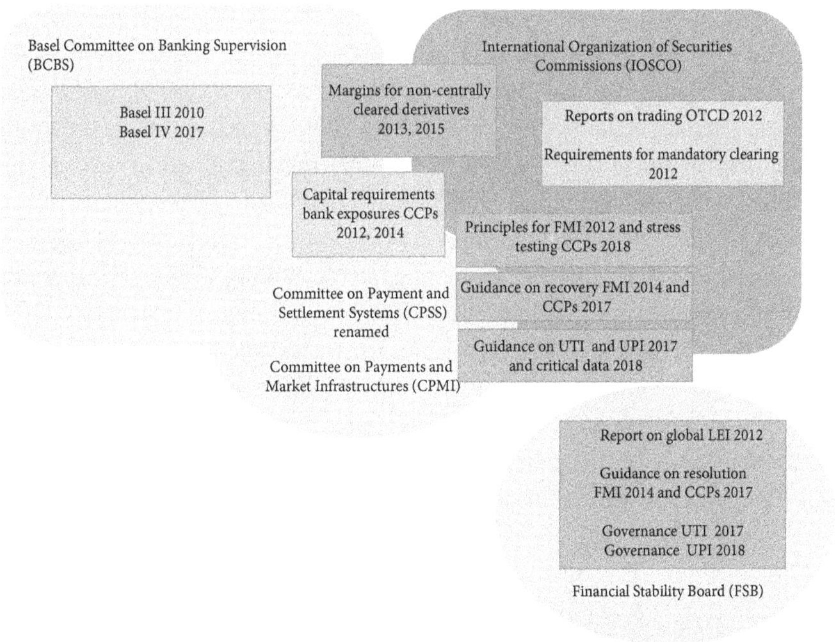

Figure 3.1 Post-crisis international standard setting for derivatives (adapted from Quaglia and Spendzharova 2020a)

transgovernmental networks of domestic regulators, have some core features: they are multilateral bodies that are not established pursuant to treaties; their membership consists of domestic regulatory agencies; they work by consensus; and they issue (not legally binding) soft law (Ahdieh 2015; Barr and Miller 2006; Brummer 2015, 2010a; Bach and Newman 2010, 2014; Gadinis 2015; Slaughter 2004; Slaughter and Zaring 2006; Verdier 2009). The soft law issued by international standard-setters becomes legally binding only when it is incorporated into the domestic legal framework of member jurisdictions. The expectation is that jurisdictions that signed up to the standards will do so. In fact, several authors pointed out the 'hardening of international soft law' in finance when it is incorporated into domestic regulatory frameworks (Arner and Taylor 2009; Karmel and Kelly 2009; Newman and Bach 2014).[1]

The BCBS was established by the Group of Ten countries in 1974 (Goodhart 2011; Wood 2005). Prior to the reform introduced in 2009, the committee's members were from Belgium, Canada, France, Germany, Italy, Japan, Luxembourg, the Netherlands, Spain, Sweden, Switzerland, the UK, and the US. After the financial crisis, the membership of the committee was extended to all countries of the G20, given the fact that financial activity in emerging economies had become more important. Countries are represented in the committee by their central bank and by the authority with formal responsibility for the prudential supervision of banking activities, whenever this is not the central bank. Despite its small staff, the BCBS has recognized expertise in banking regulation (Goodhart 2011; Wood 2005), largely through the work carried out by its working groups of national regulators, which discuss the technical details of regulation and meet regularly. The final versions of the accords are negotiated and agreed upon at the level of governors and chairmen of the supervisory authorities (or their deputies). Although the BCBS does not have enforcement powers, it has implementation working groups that monitor how its capital rules are put into practice across jurisdictions. With reference to derivatives, central bankers and banking regulators mainly deal with bank capital requirements related to derivatives trading and clearing; capital for bank exposures to CCPs; margins on uncleared derivatives; and the oversight of CCPs, together with securities market supervisors.

[1] For example, the EU decided to incorporate the Basel I, II, and III accords into EU legislation (Underhill 1997; Howarth and Quaglia 2013), the Capital Requirements directives, which were revised over time. The EU also decided to incorporate the International Financial Reporting Standards issued by the International Accounting Standards Board (IASB) into EU legislation (Kudrna and Müller 2017; Newman and Bach 2014).

The US is represented in the BCBS by multiple prudential regulators, which reflects the variety of regulatory agencies involved in banking regulation at federal and state levels. Thus, the Board of Governors of the Federal Reserve, the Federal Reserve of New York, the Office of the Comptroller of the Currency, and the FDIC sit in the BCBS. In the US, inter-agency competition in banking has been frequent (see, for example, Lavelle 2013, 2019) and also played out in the negotiations of the Basel accords (Wood 2005), which set capital requirements for internationally active banks. As for the EU, prior to the establishment of the Banking Union, the European Commission and the European Central Bank (ECB) used to participate in the BCBS as observers. After the establishment of the Banking Union, the ECB became a full member of the BCBS. Moreover, several EU countries are directly represented in the Committee by their national central bank and the banking supervisory authority (if separated from the central bank). These are Belgium, France, Germany, Italy, Luxembourg, the Netherlands, Spain, Sweden, and the UK. Previous research regarding the EU and the Basel accords suggests that the EU and its member states have often taken disjointed positions in international negotiations (Goldbach 2015a, b; Wood 2005), not least because of the diversity of national banking systems and regulatory outlooks (e.g. Howarth and Quaglia 2016; Quaglia 2014a, b).

The main international standard-setting body in securities markets is the International Organization of Securities Commissions (IOSCO), whose membership includes more than one hundred jurisdictions. The IOSCO never developed the international status and expertise of its counterpart in banking (Kempthorne 2013; Marcacci 2012, 2014), and, in fact, it did not manage to issue capital requirements for investment firms (Singer 2004, 2007). Instead, the IOSCO focused on the development of bilateral and multilateral memoranda of understanding designed to facilitate information sharing and enforcement across jurisdictions (Bach and Newman 2010). It also developed standardized templates for securities trading (Kempthorne 2013; Underhill and Zhang 2008). After the global financial crisis, the IOSCO revised the code of conduct for rating agencies (Pagliari 2012), issued general principles concerning hedge funds regulation (Fioretos 2010) and did some work on shadow banking (notably, on money market funds and securitization, Gabor 2016a). With reference to derivatives, securities market regulators mainly deal with rules on trading, clearing, and reporting (together with central banks); margins for uncleared derivatives (together with banking regulators); and the regulation of CCPs (together with central banks).

The US is represented in the IOSCO by the Securities and Exchange Commission (SEC) and the Commodity Futures Trading Commission (CFTC). Prior to the crisis of 2008, the SEC used to have a predominant role within the IOSCO (Bach and Newman 2010; Newman and Posner 2018). For example, most of the pre-crisis regulatory output of the IOSCO had been informed by US Securities Law, contributing to the 'spreading of a US-like regulatory philosophy around the world' (Marcacci 2014: 759). After the crisis, with reference to the work of the IOSCO on derivatives, the CFTC became a more influential player, given that domestically it was the primary regulator for OTCDs (Knaack 2015). Several authors (Ryan and Ziegler 2015; Newman and Posner 2018) note that the CFTC was less internationalized than the SEC (i.e. less used to dealing with foreign counterparts) and was understaffed, which contributed to explaining some 'teething problems' that the CFTC encountered in international regulatory cooperation. As for the EU, prior to the crisis, there was no EU representative in the IOSCO. Afterward, the European Commission and the ESMA became associate members. The securities market regulators of most EU member states are ordinary members of the IOSCO.

The CPSS, established in 1990 and renamed as the CPMI in 2014, brings together the central banks of the G20 countries, whereas prior to the international financial crisis it included only the central banks of the Group of Ten. With reference to derivatives, central bankers generally oversee CCPs: oversight, unlike supervision, is system-wide, informal, and based on 'moral suasion'. Therefore, central bankers have an interest in regulating derivatives clearing and reporting, as well as CCPs. The US is represented in the CPSS/CPMI by the Federal Reserve. The EU is represented by the ECB and the national central banks of the member states that are part of the G20. Linked to the CPMI, the Committee on the Global Financial System is a central bank forum that monitors developments in global financial markets and promotes the functioning of these markets.

The FSB brings together central bankers, financial regulators, and treasury ministry officials of the G20 jurisdictions (Arner and Taylor 2009; Donnelly 2012; Gadinis 2014; Helleiner 2010, 2013; Pagliari 2013c). In the case of smaller G20 jurisdictions, only the national central bank is a member of the FSB. The FSB also includes representatives from all other international standard-setting bodies (the CPSS/CPMI, the IOSCO, the BCBS, the IAIS, the IASB), as well as the BIS, the World Bank, the IMF, and the OECD. Given that the FSB includes treasury ministry officials, it is somewhat more intergovernmental and less 'technocratic' than other international standard-setting bodies, such as the BCBS or the CPMI. However, out of about seventy participants in the FSB, only twenty are finance ministry officials, all the others are technical regulators.

The FSB was established by the G20 in the wake of the international financial crisis in 2009, building on its predecessor, the Financial Stability Forum, to promote international financial stability by coordinating the actions of national financial authorities and international standard-setting bodies. The FSB was to act as a transmission mechanism between the G20 (the political level) and international standard-setters composed of domestic regulators (the technical level) (Pagliari 2013c). Its establishment was primarily sponsored by the US, with the support of the EU. With a hyperbole, it was described by US Treasury Minister Geithner as a novel 'fourth pillar' of the global economic architecture, alongside the IMF, the World Bank, and the WTO (Helleiner 2014). Daniel Tarullo (2011b), a member of the Board of Governors of the Federal Reserve, stressed the 'coordinating and gap-filling strengths of the FSB... which can parcel out appropriate components of larger projects to standard-setting committees'. The Charter of the FSB gave this body a specific mandate to 'promote and help coordinate the alignment of the activities' of international standard setters and to 'undertake joint strategic reviews' of their work to ensure it was 'timely, coordinated, focused on priorities and addressing gaps'. However, the FSB charter also stated that the reporting of international standard-setters to the FSB would be 'without prejudice to their existing reporting arrangements or their independence' (Helleiner 2010, 2013).

Given the scope of the post-crisis regulatory efforts and various aspects of derivatives markets to consider, a multitude of international standard-setting bodies were involved (see Table 3.1) and several standards were jointly issued by two or more bodies. By contrast, prior to the crisis, there had been very few standards jointly issued by two or three bodies, specifically: (i) the *Principles for the Supervision of Financial Conglomerates* (1999) and the *Compendium of Standards* (2001), issued by the Joint Forum (1999, 2001), which was established by the BCBS, the IOSCO, and the IAIS, to deal with issues common to the banking, securities, and insurance sectors, most notably, the regulation of financial conglomerates; (ii) the *Recommendations for Securities Settlement Systems* (CPSS-IOSCO 2001) and the *Recommendations for Central Counterparties* (CPSS-IOSCO 2004); (iii) the *Amendment on Application of Basel II to Trading Activities* (BCBS-IOSCO 2005).

At the outset, the division of work on derivatives among various international standard-setting bodies was unclear for several reasons. To begin

Table 3.1 International institutional architecture for derivatives regulation

International standard-setting body	Date of establishment	Membership/ composition	Functions concerning financial services regulation
Basel Committee on Banking Supervision (BCBS)	1974	Central bankers and banking supervisors of 28 jurisdictions (formerly, central bankers and banking supervisors of G10 jurisdictions)	To set international standards in banking To promote cooperation in banking supervision To monitor domestic compliance
International Organization of Securities Commissions (IOSCO)	1983	Securities markets regulators worldwide (more than 100 jurisdictions)	To set international standards in securities markets To promote the exchange of information and supervisory cooperation
Committee on Payments and Market Infrastructures (CPMI) (formerly, Committee on Payment and Settlement Systems (CPSS)	2015 1990	Central bankers of 28 jurisdictions (formerly, central bankers of G10 jurisdictions)	To set international standards and monitor payment, clearing and settlement systems
Financial Stability Board (FSB) (formerly Financial Stability Forum (FSF)	2009 1999	Central bankers, financial supervisors and treasury officials of G20 jurisdictions, plus officials from BCBS, IOSCO, CPSS, IAIS, IMF, BIS, OECD, World Bank (formerly, officials of G10 jurisdictions)	To assess and address the vulnerabilities of the financial system To coordinate the work of international standard-setters To issue standards on specific matters To monitor domestic compliance

with, this was a new area that previously had not been subject to international regulation, so there were no pre-defined standard-setting bodies. Some of the issues discussed were cross-sectoral—thus, it was unclear which specific regulatory body should take the lead—and they cropped up in the regulatory agenda in a non-linear way, and not necessarily in the most logical order (interview, October 2018). Policymakers, especially those of the main jurisdictions that were actively involved in all regulatory workstreams, were aware of this problem. As Daniel Tarullo (2011b: 6), member of the Board of Governors of the Federal Reserve, noted:

> the overlapping, sometimes competing, activities of all the international committees and arrangements are completely understandable in light of the number of new and urgent issues to be tackled. Similarly, the involvement of political officials through the G-20 was imperative to galvanize the legislative and regulatory processes of participating countries to undertake the breadth of needed reforms.... But we must rationalize the often confusing and duplicative process whereby the Basel Committee, the FSB, and some other BIS committees are all involved in the same subjects.

Several actions were taken in order to rationalize standard setting in this area so as to promote regulatory consistency. First, the FSB was given the informal role of coordinating among standard-setters and their regulatory activities, and of imparting some (political) momentum, whenever regulatory discussions in other fora reached an impasse, for instance, in the case of data reporting and aggregation, examined in Chapter 4. The FSB had five workstreams on derivatives dealing with: standardization; exchange and platform trading; central clearing; reporting to trade repositories; capital and margin. Second, a variety of formal and informal coordination tools were used by international standard-setting bodies, as discussed in Chapter 2. The coordination taking place among international standard-setting bodies was crucial because at the domestic level a multitude of agencies was involved in the governance of derivatives. These agencies had different compositions, competences, and regulatory outlooks, and inter-agency coordination was often limited.

In the US, the SEC supervises CCPs clearing non-OTCDs; the CFTC supervises CCPs clearing OTCDs; the Federal Reserve is responsible for the oversight of CCPs; and the FDIC is in charge of the resolution of CCPs. The Dodd-Frank Act also expanded the Federal Reserve's role in the supervision of all systemically important financial market infrastructures, including large CCPs. Trade repositories are supervised by the CFTC. In the EU, the supervision and resolution of CCPs are mainly the competences of the national authorities. The new legislation adopted in mid-2019 only marginally increased the supervisory competences of the ESMA and the oversight powers of the ECB for CCPs (James and Quaglia 2020b). In contrast, trade repositories are supervised at the EU level by the ESMA. Within the EU, the member states allocate competences on CCPs in a variety of ways. In Germany, the unified financial services authority, the Bafin, is the supervisor of CCPs, in close cooperation with the Bundesbank. In France, the supervision of CCPs is shared between the banking supervisory authority, the financial markets authority, and the Bank of France, but the first authority is in the lead. In Italy, CCP supervision is shared between the Bank of Italy and the securities market authority. In the UK, the Bank of England supervises CCPs.

Post-crisis International Regulation of Derivatives

The international financial crisis of 2008 brought into the spotlight the importance of derivatives (Brunnermeier et al. 2009; Group of Thirty 2009; De Larosière et al. 2009; Financial Services Authority 2009), which facilitated the growth of speculative trading and enabled banks to become over-leveraged. After the crisis, it became clear that the perimeter of regulation had to be extended to derivatives, in particular, OTCDs with a view to mitigating systemic risk, improving transparency and protecting against market abuse (G20 2009b). Trading derivatives on stock exchanges or multilateral trading facilities, rather than bilaterally, was intended to protect against market abuse and improve transparency. The central clearing of OTCDs through CCPs was to mitigate systemic risk by reducing counterparty risk (i.e. the risk of default by one party from the contract) because CCPs bear most of the risk between buyers and sellers when they clear transactions. Indeed, clearing is the process by which a third-party acts as the middleman for both the buyer and the seller of a financial instrument. Buyers and sellers deal with the CCP, rather than bilaterally. Reporting derivatives transactions to trade repositories was designed to improve transparency and enable the public authorities to monitor the build-up of potential risks for financial stability. A trade repository centrally collects and maintains the records of derivatives trades.

After the crisis, the private sector moved in earnest in an attempt to prevent the imposition of public regulation (Helleiner and Pagliari 2010; Helleiner 2011; Pagliari 2013a, 2012). In April 2009, the ISDA revised its Master Agreement and introduced the so-called 'Big Bang Protocol' with the objective of improving contractual standardization in CDS markets. Furthermore, in the wake of the crisis, a group of dealer banks issued several commitment letters about OTCD reforms to the authorities in the US and the EU (these letters are discussed in Chapter 4). Yet, these initiatives did not halt the momentum in favour of more stringent rules because the jurisdictions with the largest derivatives markets, namely, the US and UK, reversed their pre-crisis support for self-regulation, and were joined by the EU. In March 2009, Treasury Minister Geithner (2009) in his testimony before Congress stated the need to subject all dealers in OTCDs markets to a strong regulatory and supervisory regime; to force all standardized OTCDs contracts to be cleared through CCPs, subject to comprehensive regulation and oversight; to encourage greater use of exchange-traded instruments; and to require that all non-standardized derivatives contracts be reported to trade repositories. Likewise, the British Treasury (Her Majesty's Treasury 2009) believed that derivatives needed to be standardized and cleared through CCPs. The European Council (2009: 16) pointed out the need to 'enhance the transparency and resilience of credit derivatives markets, especially by promoting the standardization of contracts and the use of CCPs, subject to effective regulation and supervision'.

Recognizing the unique risk that OTCDs posed to their economies, the US, the UK, and the EU began to advocate new international standards (Helleiner and Pagliari 2010; Pagliari 2012; Quaglia 2014a; James and Quaglia 2020a). However, more radical options, such as a ban on CDS, or position limits on derivatives, were not adopted. A ban on short-selling was introduced in the EU to deal with the sovereign debt crisis in the euro area, but this type of a ban was not adopted in the US. Furthermore, the UK opposed the short-selling ban in the EU, and unsuccessfully mounted a legal challenge before the European Court of Justice (*Financial Times,* 22 January 2014). In the US, position limits on commodity derivatives were introduced by the Dodd-Frank Act in 2010, but the EU did not adopt similar rules. These initiatives were primarily the result of crisis management in the EU (Gabor 2016b) and bottom-up political pressure in the US (Clapp and Helleiner 2012). However, they did not feed into international standards.

At an international level, the political drive for the post-crisis regulation of derivatives markets came from the G20, under the impulse of the US, the UK, and the EU. The G20 Leaders (2009b) at the summit in Pittsburgh in September 2009, under the US presidency, agreed to the following objectives for the post-crisis regulation of derivatives markets: all standardized OTCDs contracts should be traded on exchanges or electronic trading platforms, where appropriate, and should be cleared through CCPs; OTCDs contracts should be reported to trade repositories; and non-centrally cleared contracts should be subject to higher capital requirements. Margin requirements on non-centrally cleared derivatives were added to the reform programme by the G20 Leaders (2011) at the summit in Cannes, under the French presidency. Afterward, international standard-setters began to work on all these issues (see

Table 1.1). This resulted in a multiplicity of partly overlapping, partly parallel, partly nested and partly interlinked elemental regimes, which generated a regime complex on derivatives (see Figure 3.1).

To begin with, there were *elemental regimes* on *derivatives trading* and *clearing*, which partly overlapped because all centrally traded derivatives had to be centrally cleared. The international regulatory discussions concerning the trading of OTCDs on exchanges or trading platforms were very limited because jurisdictions had heterogenous preferences and preferred to issue granular rules at the domestic level. The IOSCO prepared the *Report on Trading of OTC Derivatives* in 2011 and a *Follow-on Analysis* in 2012 (IOSCO 2011, 2012b), but these were mainly stock-taking exercises that lacked precision and stringency (see Chapter 4). They were followed by international standards to promote central clearing, that is to say, the clearing of OTCDs via CCPs. The IOSCO issued *Requirements for Mandatory Clearing of OTC Derivatives via CCPs* in 2012 (IOSCO 2012a). The 17 recommendations issued had limited precision and stringency (see Chapter 4). This was partly because jurisdictions preferred to adopt granular rules at the domestic level, partly because other international standards—on capital and margin—were used in order to promote central clearing. Hence, the elemental regime on mandatory clearing was interlinked with elemental regimes on bank capital and margin requirements for uncleared derivatives, as discussed below. Furthermore, central clearing meant that new international standards for CCPs were necessary to improve their resilience and resolvability, given their systemic role post-crisis.

The *elemental regime* on the *reporting of derivatives trades* encompassed a variety of interlinked standards for data format—including legal entity, transaction, and product identifiers—and data access (see Chapter 5). These standards were created from scratch after the crisis. The CPSS-IOSCO issued *Data Reporting and Aggregation* in 2012 (CPSS-IOSCO 2012b), followed by *Authorities' Access to Trade Repository Data* in 2013 (CPSS-IOSCO 2013). These were rather general documents. They were, however, followed by granular standards for LEI (*Governance of the LEI System* issued by the FSB, in 2012), UTI and UPI (*Harmonisation of UTI and UPI*, issued by the CPMI-IOSCO in 2017a,b, and *Governance Arrangements for the UTI and UPI* issued by the FSB in 2017b). Eventually, international rules on LEI, UPI and UTI became very precise and a new governance system was established by the FSB. This system comprised the Global LEI Foundation, which is the only global source of LEI data, the Derivatives Service Bureau, which is the only issuer of UPI codes and the ISO, which was designated as the responsible body for maintaining the UTI data standards. *The CPMI-IOSCO Harmonisation of Critical OTC Derivatives Data Elements (other than UTI and UPI)* was also detailed (it was indeed hundreds of pages long) (CPMI-IOSCO 2018a). Although authorities' access to data and cross-border data sharing remained problematic, the FSB periodically monitored the removal of barriers to data access.

The regime on trade reporting was parallel to other elemental regimes on derivatives and can be regarded as a regime complex in its own right. Hence, various standards for trade reporting needed to be consistent with one another and, to a large extent, they were. In fact, the standards issued by the CPMI-IOSCO on the harmonization of LEI, UPI, UTI and other critical data, the standards issued by the FSB for the governance of LEI, UPI and UPI and the standards issued by ISO and GLEI had the same objectives—to enable cross-border data collection and aggregation. The instruments to be used were also the same, including 'unique' codes on entities, products, and transactions and the harmonization of other critical data. Otherwise, the data reported could not be compared across jurisdictions, nor could it be aggregated to monitor the building up of systemic risk.

The *elemental regime* on *CCPs* included standards for the resilience, recovery, and resolution of CCPs. Initially, the rules on the resilience of CCPs—the *Principles for Financial Market Infrastructures* issued by the CPSS-IOSCO in 2012 (CPSS-IOSCO 2012a)—were rather general and avoided the contentious topics of recovery and resolution. They were followed by more precise and stringent rules on the resilience, recovery, and resolution of CCPs (see Chapter 6). Thus, the CPMI-IOSCO issued *Guidance on the Resilience and Recovery of CCPs* in 2017 (CPMI-IOSCO 2017c), the FSB issued *Guidance on the Resolution of CCPs* in the same year (FSB 2017a) and the CPMI-IOSCO agreed on a framework for supervisory stress testing of CCPs in 2018 (CPMI-IOSCO 2018b). Although international rules on CCPs did not have the level of precision and stringency of international bank capital and margin requirements for uncleared derivatives, they improved over time.

Furthermore, the rules regarding the 3 Rs (resilience, recovery and resolution) of CCPs were interlinked with one another because the *Principles for Financial Market Infrastructures* (CPSS-IOSCO 2012a) set the prudential rules designed to strengthen the resilience of financial market infrastructures, including CCPs, so as to prevent them from getting into trouble, which would then trigger recovery, regulated by the CPMI-IOSCO (2014, 2017c) and resolution, regulated by the FSB (2014b, 2017a). Consequently, the stricter the prudential rules for CCPs, the less likely it was that CCPs would need to undergo recovery and resolution. However, the less profitable CCPs became, the more expensive their use was for dealer banks and end-users. The CPMI-IOSCO (2014, 2017c) rules on the recovery of CCPs had implications for the FSB (2014b, 2017a) rules on the resolution of CCPs and vice versa, given that many instruments used in the recovery of CCPs are also used in their resolution.

Thus, the regime on the 3 Rs of CCPs could be regarded as a regime complex in its own right, and, therefore, standards for the resilience, recovery and resolution needed to be consistent with one another, in particular, recovery and resolution. To a large extent, they were. In fact, the standards issued by the CPMI-IOSCO on recovery, and by the FSB on resolution, had the same objectives: to preserve the critical functions of CCPs, while maintaining financial stability and avoiding bailout through taxpayer money. They also partly prescribed the use of the same instruments, in that several instruments used in recovery were also to be used in resolution (e.g. margin haircutting, cash calls, tearing up of contracts). Furthermore, rules for CCPs were interlinked with other elemental regimes on derivatives, notably, bank capital for exposures to CCPs, hence they needed to be consistent. In fact, the CPSS-IOSCO (2012a) *Principles* set the prudential rules with which CCPs had to comply to be considered as 'qualified CCPs' for the purpose of the *Capital Requirements for Bank Exposures to CCPs* set by the BCBS (2012, 2014d).

The *elemental regime* on *bank capital* for derivatives trading and clearing and for bank exposures to CCPs (see Chapter 7) was nested into the broader regime of capital requirements for banks. The *Basel III Accord*, which was issued by the BCBS in 2010 (BCBS 2010a, revised in 2017) was relatively precise and stringent. It was hundreds of pages long, it included numerical parameters and mathematical formulas and it more than doubled the minimum capital requirements for banks. The leverage ratio (which had a derivative component) had been increased so much in the wake of the crisis that it then had to be recalibrated downward in order to avoid unintended effects deriving from its interlinkages with other elemental regimes on derivatives (BCBS 2013c, 2014b, 2019). In fact, bank capital requirements, together with margins for uncleared derivatives, were a way to encourage central clearing via CCPs, but they had joint cumulative effects. The BCBS (2014d), in cooperation with the CPMI-IOSCO, issued *Capital Requirements for Bank Exposures to CCPs* in 2014, which were relatively precise and stringent standards devised from scratch. They included numerical parameters and mathematical formulas. Furthermore, these standards were interlinked with those on CCPs because the stricter the rules were for the resilience of CCPs, the lower the capital was that banks needed to cope with in their exposures to CCPs and vice versa. And, in fact, capital requirements for bank exposure to CCPs were lower for 'qualifying' CCPs that met the CPSS-IOSCO standards for resilience.

Finally, there was the *elemental regime* on *margins* for OTCDs not cleared through CCPs. The *Margin Requirements for Non-Centrally Cleared Derivatives* issued by the BCBS-IOSCO in 2013 (BCBS-IOSCO 2013, BCBS-IOSCO 2015) had to be devised from scratch (see Chapter 8). These standards were relatively precise (for instance, they included numerical parameters) and were quite stringent. Indeed, their actual implementation had to be delayed to avoid too drastic cumulative effects, partly due to the interlinkages of margin and capital requirements, given that banks trading and clearing derivatives were subject to both. The margins for uncleared derivatives were interlinked to capital for bank exposures to CCPs because the higher the margins, the greater the incentives were to clear via CCPs; whereas, the higher the capital requirements were for bank exposures to CCPs, the greater were the incentives not to clear via CCPs. Margin requirements were also interlinked with the CPSS-IOSCO (2012a) *Principles*, which set margins for derivatives cleared via CCPs because the higher the margins, the safer the CCPs, but it was also more costly to clear via CCPs. Thus, high margins for cleared derivatives as compared with margins for uncleared derivatives would discourage central clearing via CCPs. At the same time, the level of margins for cleared derivatives had implications for the resilience of CCPs, improving their ability to withstand financial stress without resorting to recovery and resolution.

To sum up, the elemental regimes on derivatives had different degrees of precision and stringency. The least precise and stringent were the standards for centralized derivatives trading, followed by those on centralized clearing, followed by rules on CCPs, which, however, became more granular over time. International standards for derivatives trade reporting became considerably more precise over time. The more precise and stringent were the capital requirements for banks and margin requirements for uncleared derivatives. In order to evaluate regulatory consistency across the elemental regimes on derivatives (rule consistency within regimes was discussed above), it is necessary to consider the objectives that they set out to achieve and the instruments to do so.

To begin with, the elemental regimes discussed above pursued the objectives outlined by the G20 (2009a) in the wake of the crisis (with the exception of centralized trading): central clearing through CCPs; reporting of derivative trades to repositories; and higher bank capital requirements and margin requirements for uncleared derivatives. As for instruments, given that precise and stringent international requirements for mandatory clearing via CCPs were not feasible due to the diversity of national markets and the variety of derivatives contracts worldwide, other instruments—notably, bank capital and margin requirements—were used in order to encourage centralized clearing. Thus, higher capital requirements were set by the BCBS for banks trading non-centrally cleared derivatives, and margin requirements—similar to those used by CCPs—were set by the BCBS-IOSCO for banks and other investment firms trading non-centrally cleared derivatives. All these measures increased the costs related to derivatives not cleared via CCPs in order to incentivize central clearing. Yet, these two sets of standards had cumulative effects for banks dealing with derivatives and their calibration was adjusted over time. Furthermore, international standards to improve the resilience, recovery, and resolution of CCPs were issued following mandatory clearing, which made CCPs de facto 'system risk managers' (Tucker 2011).

Bank capital and margin requirements also aimed to increase the resilience of banks to financial shocks so that banks would not become a source of weakness for CCPs and, at the same time, they would be able to withstand the recovery and resolution of CCPs. To this end, capital requirements for bank exposures to CCPs (a potential source of financial stress for banks), were set by the BCBS, in collaboration with CPSS/CPMI-IOSCO, considering the potential losses to which CCPs were exposed. However, in order to encourage the use of soundly managed CCPs, capital requirements were set lower for bank exposures to CCPs that complied with international standards resilience, set by the CPSS-IOSCO. Capital for bank exposures to CCPs set by the BCBS and margins for derivatives cleared via CCPs set by the CPSS-IOSCO, taken together, increased the cost of central clearing, reducing the incentive to clear via CCPs. Yet, they also increased the ability of banks to withstand problems with the CCPs as well as the resilience of CCPs, so that they would not become a source of instability for banks. Given their cumulative effects, these sets of rules had to be calibrated. With reference to bank capital requirements, including client margins in the leverage ratio made the banks safer but it also increased their costs in the provision of clearing services. The BCBS subsequently decided to change the treatment of client margins in the leverage ratio in order to eliminate the disincentive to provide clearing services to clients.

The evaluation of the incentives to centrally clear OTCDs, which was jointly conducted by the FSB, the BCBS, the CPMI and the IOSCO (2018a) to take stock of the effects of post-crisis regulatory reforms, suggested that international standards promoting central clearing worked rather well and with the same purpose. The report found that the reforms—particularly, clearing mandates, capital, and margin requirements—had achieved the goal of promoting central clearing, especially for systemic market participants. However, beyond the systemic core of the derivatives network of CCPs, dealers, and larger clients, the incentives to clear were weaker. In 2009, the clearing levels were around 24% for interest rate derivatives and 5% for credit derivatives. By 2018, these levels were 62% for interest rate derivatives and 37% for credit derivatives. In addition, more collateral (an additional $1 trillion) was held to reduce counterparty credit risks in the financial system. Overall, the consistency achieved within and across elemental regimes on derivatives was remarkable, especially considering the large number of standards-setting bodies and jurisdictions involved. Furthermore, confronted with the extraordinary economic and financial shocks ensuing from the covid pandemic in 2020, global derivatives markets have been rather resilient (FSB 2020).

Conclusion

This chapter has set the context for the rest of the book. It has clarified the empirical patterns to be explained by providing an overview of the post-crisis international financial architecture for derivatives regulation and the main sets of standards—parallel, nested, overlapping, and interlinked elemental regimes—in the regime complex on derivatives. The following chapters examine international standard setting in each elemental regime, systematically assessing the explanatory power of the theoretical accounts put forward by the literature reviewed in the previous chapter. Specifically, the empirical chapters combine the state-centric, the transgovernmental and the business-led explanations.

4

International Standards for Derivatives Trading and Clearing

At the Pittsburgh summit in 2009, the G20 Leaders (2009b) agreed that 'All standardized OTCDs contracts should be traded on exchanges or electronic trading platforms, where appropriate, and cleared through central counterparties by end-2012 at the latest.' Despite the quick agreement reached at the peak of the crisis, subsequent international standards for derivatives trading and clearing remained rather 'thin' for several reasons: the absence of pace-setting jurisdictions and the foot-dragging of some jurisdictions; disagreements among regulators; and the pushback from the financial industry. Furthermore, exchange and platform trading was not crucial to mitigate systemic risk, rather it was instrumental to promote transparency and protect against market abuse. Clearing via CCPs was crucial to mitigate systemic risk. However, other interlinked standards, notably, bank capital and margin requirements, were used to promote clearing via CCPs.

Precise, stringent, and consistent international standards regarding what should be centrally traded and cleared, by whom, and how were not sponsored by the 'great powers', albeit the US and the EU supported centralized trading and clearing after the crisis. Instead, the US and the EU adopted domestic regulatory reforms that had considerable extra-territorial reach in an attempt to deal with the negative externalities deriving from unilateral action. Jurisdictions on the fringe, especially in Asia, resisted centralized trading and delayed the domestic implementation of this commitment. More generally, these jurisdictions waited for the sorting out of transatlantic regulatory disputes before adopting domestic regulation on trading and clearing derivatives. These regulatory reforms, first and foremost, centralized trading, were contested by parts of the financial industry because of their distributional implications (i.e. the expected costs and benefits for private actors). As for transgovernmental networks, these were new issues for securities market regulators gathered in the IOSCO, which found it difficult to reconcile different views among more than one hundred member jurisdictions. This chapter examines, first, the international regulatory discussions concerning the trading

The Politics of Regime Complexity In International Derivatives Regulation. Lucia Quaglia, Oxford University Press (2020).
 DOI: 10.1093/oso/9780198866077.003.0001

of standardized derivatives on exchanges or electronic platforms; then, the discussions concerning the clearing of derivatives via CCPs. For each of these elemental regimes, we examine the key regulatory issues at stake, the international standard-setting process and the explanatory power of the state-centric, industry-led and transgovernmental explanations discussed in Chapter 2.

Key Issues in Regulating Derivatives Trading

In order to trade, traders, first, need to communicate the quantity, the type of contract and the price at which they are willing to trade. This is, then, followed by the recording of the details of the trade. These two steps are often referred to as 'trade execution' (Ruffini and Steigerwald 2014). Derivatives contracts may be traded (or 'executed') on exchanges, over-the-counter (OTC), or through multilateral trading facilities. An exchange is a regulated market for trading listed securities, derivatives or other financial products.[1] Not every financial contract can be traded on an exchange because certain levels of demand and standardization are necessary to ensure liquidity. The price at which the transaction is executed is communicated throughout the market, resulting in a level playing field, which allows market participants to buy/sell at the same price. Moreover, some exchanges designate certain participants as 'market makers' and require them to maintain quotes at which they stand ready to sell or buy throughout the trading day (Dodd 2018).

OTC markets are less formal than exchanges, although they are often well-organized networks of trading relationships centered around one or more dealers (large banks, called 'dealer banks'). Dealers act as market makers by quoting prices at which they stand ready to sell to or buy from other dealers and their clients. That does not mean that they quote the same prices to other dealers and customers, and they do not necessarily quote the same prices to all customers. Moreover, dealers can withdraw from market-making at any time. There are basically two dimensions in OTC markets. In the customer market, bilateral trading occurs between the dealers and their customers, such as individuals, or hedge funds. In the interdealer market, dealers quote prices to each other and there are often interdealer brokers who provide electronic

[1] Examples of stock exchanges include the New York Stock Exchange (NYSE) and the London Stock Exchange (LSE). Derivatives exchanges include Intercontinental Exchange Clear (ICE) Futures and the Chicago Mercantile Exchange (CME).

bulletin boards to give their clients (the dealers) the ability to send quotes to every other dealer in the broker's network. The broker screens are normally not available to end-customers (Dodd 2018). Advances in electronic trading platforms have changed the trading process in many OTC markets, blurring the distinction between traditional OTC markets and exchanges (Ruffini and Steigerwald 2014). In some cases, an electronic brokering platform allows dealers and some non-dealers to trade directly, replicating the multilateral trading that is the hallmark of an exchange—but only for direct participants and, in fact, the dealers resist the participation of non-dealers (Dodd 2018). Moreover, the clearing and settlement of trades are left to the buyer and seller, unlike in exchange transactions.[2]

The main rationales for post-crisis regulatory reforms to encourage the trading of derivatives on exchanges or platforms were to protect against market abuse and to promote transparency. The assumption was that centralized trading was equally beneficial to all market participants. Yet, it had some potential drawbacks, such as reduced liquidity and impaired price formation (Ruffini and Steigerwald 2014). It also has different distributional implications across jurisdictions and within the financial industry, as illustrated below. In the regulation of mandatory trading via exchanges or platforms, the key issues were as follows: which derivatives contracts among which counterparties should be centrally traded (or, to put it another way, which exemptions should be allowed for certain instruments and entities); the characteristics and level of standardization[3] that OTCDs should have in order to be considered eligible for trading on exchanges or platforms; which financial operators would qualify as trading platforms; and the scope of application and the extra-territorial reach of trading rules.

International Standards for Derivatives Trading

Prior to the crisis, the vast majority of derivatives were traded OTC. The G20 Leaders (2009b) at the Pittsburgh summit agreed that 'all standardized OTC derivative contracts should be traded on exchanges or electronic trading platforms, *where appropriate*' (*emphasis* added), hence, recognizing that the

[2] Several electronic platforms for trading OTCDs were developed, for instance, by Bloomberg, Tradeweb, and Tullett Prebon, in response to national legislation implementing the G20 trade execution mandate (Ruffini and Steigerwald 2014).

[3] The standardization of derivatives contracts concerns the legal aspects, the processes of trading, and the characteristics of products. It is a pre-condition for centralized trading and clearing.

benefits of the trade execution mandate would depend on the circumstances. The G20, however, did not provide any guidance about how to determine the suitability for trading on exchanges or platforms. Subsequently, the FSB (2010: 5) stated that it was appropriate to mandate centralized trading 'where the market is sufficiently developed to make such trading practicable and where such trading furthers the objectives set forth by the G20 leaders and provides benefits incremental to those provided by standardization, central clearing, and reporting of transactions to trade repositories'.

In 2011, the IOSCO (2011) Task Force on Derivatives issued a *Report on Trading of OTC Derivatives* that analysed the characteristics of exchanges and electronic platforms; the costs and benefits associated with exchange or platform trading; and the methods to increase the use of exchanges or platforms for trading derivatives. The Task Force recommended a 'flexible approach' to defining exchanges or trading platforms, highlighting seven key characteristics that they should have. An additional characteristic concerned 'the opportunity for platform participants to seek liquidity and trade with multiple liquidity providers within a centralised system' (p. 49). This additional characteristic is generally associated with 'multi-dealer', as opposed to 'single-dealer', platforms. The members of the Task Force could not agree as to whether this characteristic should be considered as a necessary requirement for platforms. US regulators believed that a centralized system, offering access to multiple liquidity providers, was needed. Other members believed that the benefits of centralization would differ according to market structures (this was the view of regulators in Asia), and that the exclusion of single dealers would involve costs, along with benefits (this was the view of regulators in the EU). The Task Force recognized that 'if some jurisdictions choose to establish requirements that give effect to all eight characteristics, while other jurisdictions do not, the resulting regulatory disparities have the potential to influence market participants' choice of venues in which to conduct business' (IOSCO 2011: 50). In other words, there was a risk of regulatory arbitrage.

The FSB requested the IOSCO to undertake further work on the controversial issue of multi-dealer and single-dealer platforms. Thus, the IOSCO (2012b) produced a *Follow-On Analysis to the Report on Trading of OTC Derivatives* that described the different types of trading platforms in various jurisdictions, noting differences concerning participants and products traded. In particular, US regulators (the CFTC and the SEC) adopted the 'multiple to multiple' requirement for swap execution facilities, that is to say, multiple participants had the ability to accept bids and offers made by multiple participants. Although this requirement was subsequently watered down during the domestic rule-making process in the US (Pagliari 2018), it was not met by single-dealer platforms, but was met by most multi-dealer platforms (IOSCO 2012b: 21). In contrast, the EU allowed single-dealer platforms—to be more precise, organized trading facilities operated by an investment firm or a market operator.[4]

Overall, the IOSCO's work on derivatives trading was primarily a stock-taking exercise. Ultimately, the key issues concerning mandatory centralized trading of derivatives were left to be tackled at the domestic level. The very limited precision, stringency, and consistency of international rules on this matter did little to prevent the emergence of transatlantic regulatory disputes ensuing from dissimilar domestic regulation, which often had extra-territorial provisions in an attempt to regulate cross-border business (Posner 2018; Gravelle and Pagliari 2018). The 'thinness' of international standards concerning the centralized trading of derivatives had several explanations, examined in the following sections: the absence of pace-setting jurisdictions and the foot-dragging of some jurisdictions; disagreements among regulators; and the pushback from the financial industry.

State-Centric Explanation of Standard-setting for Derivatives Trading

After the crisis, the US and the EU advocated mandatory centralized trading, but did not sponsor precise, stringent, and consistent international standards for this matter. To begin with, this reform was not essential in order to safeguard financial stability and the negative cross-border externalities deriving from less stringent regulation in other jurisdictions were limited. Second, granular 'one size fits all' rules on this matter were not feasible, due to the diversity of domestic financial systems and regulatory frameworks worldwide. Third, the main jurisdictions preferred to regulate this matter at the domestic level, so as to move faster, side-step potential foot-dragging from other jurisdictions and customize the rules to their domestic market. They used the extra-territoriality of domestic rules in order to limit regulatory arbitrage deriving from unilateral actions.

[4] The IOSCO (2012c) also issued *International Standards for Derivatives Markets Intermediary Regulation*, providing a definition of market participants that should be considered as 'derivatives markets intermediaries', given their level of involvement in the OTCDs markets, and putting forward 15 recommendations concerning their licensing, capital, business conduct, supervision, and recordkeeping.

As early as March 2009, the US Treasury Minister in his testimony before Congress argued that 'We will encourage greater use of exchange-traded instruments' (Geithner 2009). The Dodd-Frank Act (2010) and the enacting regulation issued by the CFTC and the SEC introduced mandatory trading requirements for certain derivatives contracts, which had to be traded on a regulated market (exchange), or a swap execution facility (Pagliari 2018; Ryan and Ziegler 2015). A 'swap execution facility' was a trading platform in which multiple participants could trade swaps by accepting bids and offers made by other participants. These facilities were regulated by the SEC and the CFTC, depending on the types of swaps traded. If no system was available for specific swaps, then the previous OTC method was acceptable. All US persons were required to trade certain instruments on registered swap execution facilities. Exemptions were made for commercial end-users. The CFTC rules, which covered most of the derivatives markets, included a rather broad definition of a US person and, in only a few cases, they permitted 'substituted compliance' with home country rules in lieu of compliance with US rules (Coffee 2014).

In the EU, the Markets in Financial Instruments Directive II (2014), the Markets in Financial Instruments Regulation (2014) and the regulatory technical standards issued by the ESMA introduced a requirement for certain derivatives contracts to be traded on a regulated market, a multilateral trading facility or an organized trading facility (Moloney 2014). A 'multilateral trading facility' was a trading platform that facilitated the exchange of financial instruments, especially, instruments that did not have an official market among multiple parties. These electronic platforms were often controlled by large investment banks. 'Organised trading facilities' were a new category of trading venues operated by an investment firm. The trading requirement was applicable only if the derivatives asset class had been declared to be subject to mandatory clearing under the European Markets Infrastructure Regulation (EMIR); it was traded or admitted to trading on, at least, one relevant trading venue; and it was considered to be sufficiently liquid to trade 'on venue'. The trading requirement applied if both counterparties to the derivatives contract were 'qualifying counterparties' (i.e. financial and non-financial counterparties above a certain threshold). The trading requirement also applied to derivatives contracts between two non-EU counterparties, if those trades had a 'direct, substantial and foreseeable effect' in the EU, or to prevent the evasion of EU trading rules. This wording was a reaction to similar wording in the Dodd-Frank Act, and, like the US rules, it had extraterritorial effects (Quaglia 2015).

Several jurisdictions did not agree on the need for mandatory centralized trading of derivatives. To begin with, the UK authorities were sceptical. In

2009, the FSA and Her Majesty's Treasury (2009) issued a document on the post-crisis reform of derivatives markets, noting that mandating trading on organized markets would be 'harmful' because OTCDs markets allowed for a variety of contracts to be traded. This enabled the management of risk in a way that would not be possible through standardized exchange-traded contracts. Furthermore, mandatory centralized trading would 'severely impact' some OTCDs markets because in certain cases there was 'insufficient liquidity' to sustain trading on organized markets. The document concluded that 'mandating the trading of standardized OTCDs on organized platforms is unlikely to deliver benefits which would warrant the costs of introducing such a policy proposal' (FSA and Her Majesty's Treasury 2009: 29).

Jurisdictions in Asia, where OTCDs thrived in the run-up to and after the crisis, did not support centralized trading. Given the fact that the biggest exchanges and trading platforms were in the US and the EU, the trading mandate was seen to benefit exchanges and platforms in these jurisdictions by providing them with economies of scale (Chen 2017). For instance, a senior official of the Monetary Policy Authority of Singapore (Chuan Teck 2012) pointed out that 'the first challenge is to ensure that the regulatory changes themselves do not overwhelm the market so that it ceases to function effectively.... For example, if we move all trading onto platforms before there is sufficient depth, liquidity could be seriously impaired.... Regulators in less developed markets have to be especially careful in how they implement the reforms. In Singapore, we have been fairly deliberate in the pace of our implementation.... The viability of a trading mandate remains unclear.'

In 2016, policymakers in Singapore reiterated (Chow, Tan, and Won 2016: 8–9) the risk of 'liquidity fragmentation' and 'regulatory arbitrage', which could be particularly acute for 'smaller markets, especially for markets with large international participation', such as Singapore. Another consideration was the market structure, such as the availability of trading infrastructures, the liquidity, and sophistication of market participants. 'Larger markets, typically with a more diverse group of participants, provide a stronger business case for platforms to invest and set up the relevant infrastructure in those jurisdictions, given a higher demand for OTCD platform trading associated with a trading mandate. In smaller markets, by contrast, there could be a lower possibility of the emergence of domestic platforms.' The centralized trading of derivatives was challenging also for China, given the fact that most OTCDs trading in China was on the inter-bank market, among the large commercial banks (Zhou 2016).

Jurisdictions on the fringe were timid foot-draggers at the international level, and were recalcitrant followers in the domestic implementation of mandatory centralized trading. Indeed, outside the core jurisdictions, national regulation on this matter remained feeble and patchy. Only in 2017, the authorities in Singapore published criteria for determining if products should be traded on organized trading platforms and, in 2018, they proposed changes to OTCDs trading, with a view to migrating activity onto electronic venues. This move was part of a broader plan to seek equivalence determinations from the US and the EU for exchanges and other trading platforms in Singapore, so that the OTCDs market in Singapore would be accessible to both regions under the new regime (*The Trade News*, 23 February 2018). As late as 2018, the Hong Kong authorities consulted about whether it would be appropriate to implement the platform trading obligation and, if appropriate, how best to do so. In 2018, legal frameworks and comprehensive criteria for centralized trading were in force in only 12 jurisdictions of the G20 (FSB 2018c)—this was one of the worst implementation records in the post-crisis reform of derivatives markets.

Transgovernmental Explanation of Standard-setting for Derivatives Trading

The transgovernamental explanation of international standard setting does not have much traction in the case of derivatives trading. International regulatory discussions concerning the centralised trading of derivatives fell within the remit of the IOSCO, which brings together securities market regulators, and which had not previously worked on this matter. The IOSCO, unlike the BCBS, the CPSS/CPMI, and the FSB, has universal membership. Thus, it encompasses more than one hundred jurisdictions with very different national financial markets and distinctive domestic regulatory frameworks. Compared to other standard-setters in finance, notably, the BCBS, the IOSCO is a less well-established body and securities market regulators are a less tightly knit network compared to banking regulators (see Chapter 3).

The IOSCO moved in earnest after the crisis by establishing, in 2010, a Task Force on OTCDs regulation with the aim of developing international standards for the trading, clearing, and reporting of derivatives, as well as the oversight of CCPs (IOSCO 2010). The Task Force was led by the SEC (US), the CFTC (US), the FSA (UK), and the Securities and Exchange Board of India. The ESMA, the European Commission, and the CPSS had observer status. However, it soon became clear that several issues concerning derivatives regulation, such as trade reporting and CCPs, were the competence of, or interest to, other international standard-setting bodies and regulators that were not dealing with securities markets. Only derivatives trading, and, to a lesser extent, clearing, were of almost exclusive competence of the IOSCO.

The international discussions on the centralized trading of derivatives via exchanges or platforms started basically from scratch because there were no pre-existing international rules, even though domestic rules were in the process of being discussed in the US. Among regulators in the IOSCO, there was not a consensus on mandatory centralized trading (interview, June 2019). To begin with, regulators recognized that it was not essential to mitigate systemic risk and protect financial stability. At the same time, regulators in the periphery were concerned about the impact of this reform on their markets. Even regulators in the core jurisdictions were not on the same page on this matter, for example, those in the UK remained sceptical. Finally, there was a strong pushback from the financial industry and, indeed, the reform was partly watered down (for example, through exemptions) at the national level, even in the 'core' jurisdictions that advocated centralized trading (Pagliari 2018). Thus, potentially controversial issues concerning specific aspects of trading—notably, which instruments and entities should be subject to centralized trading obligations, which trading platforms qualified to that end, how they should be regulated, and the extraterritoriality of domestic rules—were not tackled by international standards. Yet, this strategy moved the problem down the line because various jurisdictions adopted different, at times incompatible, rules.

Industry-Led Explanation of Standard Setting for Derivatives Trading

The centralized trading of derivatives was controversial for large parts of the financial industry, notably, the dealer banks and some buy-siders. This helps to explain why precise, stringent and consistent international standards were not set, even though, as explained in the previous and following sections, other factors also accounted for this outcome, namely, the absence of pace-setting jurisdictions and disagreements among regulators. This section examines the arguments articulated by stock exchanges, trading platforms, dealer banks, and buy-siders. Their preferences primarily reflected a cost-benefits analysis of mandatory centralized trading. In fact, the centralized trading of derivatives had major distributional implications for private actors—it was expected to benefit some, at the expense of others. Private actors mobilized in order to shape the content of the reforms at the domestic level, given the 'thinness' of international rules.

In a nutshell, the dealer banks opposed centralized trading, which would reduce their profits by moving their (previously bilateral) trades onto exchanges or platforms, and by increasing price transparency. This reform was, instead, supported by stock exchanges and electronic platforms because it would increase their share of the business. It was also supported by platforms that were used for dealer-to-client trades, such as Tradeweb and Bloomberg, as well as by brokers of swaps between dealers, which were eager to qualify as swap execution facilities or trading platforms. Yet, these players were reluctant to support rules mandating centralized trading of derivatives because they feared that they could be required to trade instruments that were not suitable for trading on exchanges or platforms. Buy-siders (e.g. fund managers and insurers, but also corporates) and end-users, which were generally price-takers in OTCD markets, were expected to benefit from centralized trading. However, they were heterogeneous groups, with limited interest in derivatives, which were not their main business. Moreover, some of them worried about increased costs and the inability to trade highly customized derivatives contracts via exchanges or platforms. Let us examine some of these arguments in detail.

Not surprisingly, the New York Stock Exchange—Euronext (2011) pointed out the benefits of exchange trading. 'In contrast with OTC markets, price discovery and transparency will be available to a broader range of market users, and there will be no need to access it via a closed group of specialist intermediaries.... All sectors of the market would benefit from increased liquidity resulting from the increased transparency associated with exchange trading.' These exchanges supported mandatory rules on centralized trading, although they worried that market participants could avoid the rules by deliberate minimal non-standardization of OTCDs contracts. Similarly, the Chicago Mercantile Exchange (CME) (2011a) praised the benefits of trading derivatives on exchanges. Yet, it also cautioned that given the multitude of specialized contracts traded in the OTCDs market, 'mandatory exchange trading of standardized contracts as a replacement for this bespoke market would be ineffective'. The London Stock Exchange (LSE) (2010), which provided a range of different execution venues, including interdealer brokers, electronic trading platforms, and exchanges, argued that there were many efficiencies to be gained from exchange trading (in the strictest sense) as well as from the use of alternative execution venues. However, the LSE warned that the benefits of centralized trading did not apply to all instruments, market segments, or participants.

The Federation of European Stock Exchanges (FESE) (2011) noted that most products with a high degree of standardization as well as those products that were eligible for clearing through CCPs would benefit from exchange trading, which would 'improve liquidity, price formation, transparency, and risk management'. This association supported regulatory efforts to establish a mandatory regime as well as incentives to promote trading on exchanges. According to the FESE, multilateral trading should be clearly defined and should not include OTC trading because regulated markets were subject to very different (stricter) rules as compared to OTC markets. In contrast, Tradeweb (2010), which operated a multilateral trading platform, praised the use of platforms for derivatives trading. Eager to attract business, it argued that multilateral trading platforms offered the benefits of exchanges, while maintaining much of the advantages of the OTC market, and noted that there was scope for greater use of trading platforms, especially for equity derivatives.

The main associations representing the dealer banks, notably, the ISDA, the Association for Financial Markets in Europe (AFME), the Associazione Italiana Intermediari dei Mercati Finanziari, the British Bankers Association (BBA), and the Nordic Securities Association (2010) issued a joint response that stressed the difference between 'centralized clearing' and 'centralized trading' (see also AFME 2011). Clearing through CCPs was a means to manage counterparty risk, while trading methods (via exchanges, platforms, and OTC) affected the way the transaction price was determined, rather than how risk was managed (see also JP Morgan 2011). These associations believed that priority should be given to clearing eligible instruments through CCPs and reporting derivatives transactions to trade repositories. In contrast, these associations resisted mandatory trading requirements as well as regulatory incentives (in particular, capital incentives) to promote platform trading, arguing that the market 'would naturally gravitate to the trading model that is best suited to it'. The dealer banks stressed that organized trading platforms included exchanges, inter-dealer brokers, multilateral dealer platforms, and single dealer platforms (which the dealer banks operated).

The Royal Bank of Scotland (RBS) (2010), a major dealer bank, denied that the financial crisis was attributable to market failures arising from a lack of trading on organized platforms and was, therefore, sceptical of mandating or incentivizing the use of trading platforms in order to reduce systemic risk. It supported the use of organized trading venues only 'where warranted by market liquidity and customer requirements', and believed that policymakers should define trading platforms broadly—thus, including single dealer platforms managed by banks. JP Morgan (2010:7), one of the main dealer banks, spelled out the pros and cons of derivatives trading on exchanges.

> The benefits of exchange trading in terms of liquidity, efficiency and risk reduction are only likely to materialize in relation to markets for which exchange trading is the most effective mode of execution, which are likely to be markets that have naturally gravitated towards exchanges (exchange-traded products trade on exchanges because they are liquid, not vice versa: illiquid products remain illiquid even if an exchange lists them). It follows that while requiring certain products to trade on exchanges may achieve a desired regulatory outcome of transparency, this may in some cases be accompanied by negative implications to the market in terms of reduced trading opportunities and the ability to meet demand for customer solutions.

As for the buy-side, the Alternative Investment Management Association (AIMA) (2011) supported exchange trading, but recognized that there were reasons for maintaining an OTC market. It noted that not all contracts were suitable for exchange trading or for increased standardization. Similarly, the Investment Management Association (IMA) (2011) argued in favour of letting the market take its course. The European Fund and Asset Management Association (EFAMA) (2011) expressed concerns about the move towards centralized trading, considering it as 'premature'—'market participants needed more time to prepare'.

In the wake of the crisis, the financial industry, in particular, the dealer banks and large buy-side companies, engaged in private sector governance, in an attempt to steam off public regulation, notably, through 'commitment letters', discussed later in this chapter. However, none of the pledges they made in the commitment letters specifically related to carrying out derivative transactions on exchanges. As time went by, the mobilization of the financial industry, in particular, private actors engaged in cross-border business, focused on ironing out transatlantic regulatory disputes and reducing international market fragmentation. The ISDA (2015c) believed that it was critical that G20 members, under the IOSCO's leadership, start the 'process of translating the G20's general intent to encourage centralized trading into to a set of common principles to avoid regulatory disparity, market fragmentation, low trading liquidity, and duplicative compliance requirements'.

Key Issues in Regulating Derivatives Clearing

The term *clearing* generally refers to a series of operational and risk management processes that occur after a trade is executed and before the contract is settled. Unlike exchange-traded instruments, where clearing and settlement usually take place through CCPs and central securities depositories, prior to the crisis, the vast majority of OTCDs transactions were cleared and settled bilaterally between the two parties. This meant that the counterparties were exposed for all parts of the transaction lifecycle, not just trade execution.[5] Only a small portion of OTCDs was cleared through CCPs. Clearing through CCPs can have several benefits. First, it reduces the counterparty credit risk—the risk that one party in the contract defaults and cannot meet its obligations. CCPs reduce and 'mutualize'—that is to say, share among members—counterparty credit risk in the markets in which they operate (Murphy and Senior 2013). Another benefit of central clearing is the 'multilateral netting' of transactions between market participants, which simplifies outstanding exposures, compared to a complex web of bilateral trades. Furthermore, CCPs have rules and resources in place to deal with the default of a clearing member (Rehlon and Nixon 2015).

During the financial crisis, a lack of transparency over large bilateral OTCDs that were traded between counterparties, combined with insufficient collaterals, exacerbated existing problems. Notable examples are the collapse of Lehman Brothers and the near-collapse of AIG, both of which were major participants in OTCDs markets, including credit default swaps. When Lehman Brothers failed in late 2008, it had a $35 trillion portfolio of both cleared and uncleared derivatives. Following its collapse, Lehman's uncleared derivatives counterparties filed claims totalling $51 billion and the first payments to these uncleared derivative creditors were made four years later.[6] This contrasted with Lehman's cleared derivatives portfolio: the Lehman Brothers UK subsidiary had a $9 trillion cleared interest rate derivatives portfolio at the London Clearing House (LCH), comprising over 65.000 trades (*Wall Street Journal*, 14 October 2008). Despite the extreme market conditions, it took less than three weeks for the LCH to hedge and close out the entire $9 trillion position (Cunliffe 2018).

[5] This problem was heightened by the fact that OTCDs have long maturities: interest-rate swaps and credit default swaps can have durations up to ten years.

[6] In 2018, claims against Lehman were still ongoing.

Yet, not all OTCDs transactions were suitable for centralized clearing through CCPs. On the one hand, some observers felt that all OTCDs contracts—not just the standardized contracts—should be cleared. On the other hand, requiring CCPs to clear non-standard instruments that posed valuation and risk-management challenges would not reduce the risk for the system as a whole. In fact, if CCPs had difficulty in designing margin and default procedures for such products, they would not be able to effectively manage counterparty credit risk (White 2009). Furthermore, even though it was important to prevent the design of derivatives contracts in such a way as to avoid the central clearing obligation, there could be legitimate economic reasons why standardized contracts did not meet the needs of some users. A senior official at the Federal Reserve, Patricia White (2009), recommended a 'flexible approach' that addressed systemic risk with respect to standardized and non-standardized OTCDs, albeit in different ways.

In the regulation of mandatory clearing via CCPs, the key issues were which derivatives contracts, among which counterparties, should be centrally cleared (or, to put it another way, which exemptions should be allowed for certain instruments and entities); whether all centrally traded contracts should be centrally cleared; whether centralized clearing was a pre-condition for centralized trading; whether regulatory action to incentivize the clearing of standardized products through CCPs could represent an indirect incentive to trade these products on platforms; and the scope of application and the extra-territoriality of domestic clearing rules.

International Standards for Derivatives Clearing

At the international level, the US, the UK, and the EU advocated derivatives clearing via CCPs after the crisis. For instance, the reform blueprints issued by the US Treasury (2009), the European Commission (2009), the British FSA and the HM Treasury (2009) mentioned a commitment to promote central clearing internationally as well as domestically. However, these jurisdictions did not promote precise, stringent and consistent international clearing rules—they preferred to regulate this matter at the domestic level, as explained in the following section. No jurisdiction opposed the introduction of clearing requirements because in the aftermath of the crisis there was a broad consensus that mandatory clearing of standardized OTCDs via CCPs was needed in order to safeguard financial stability (Helleiner and Pagliari 2010). Yet, international rules on this matter remained 'thin'—they did not regulate what was to be cleared, by whom, and how.

The discussion on clearing requirements fell within the remit of the IOSCO, which had done no previous work on this issue. In 2012, the IOSCO issued *Requirements for Mandatory Clearing*, outlining a set of 17 recommendations that the domestic authorities were expected to follow in establishing a mandatory clearing regime in their jurisdiction. These recommendations concerned: whether mandatory clearing obligations should apply to a product or set of products, potential exemptions, and cross-border issues. The report outlined two general approaches to determine whether a product should be subject to mandatory clearing: the 'bottom-up approach', which considered the products that a CCP proposed to or was authorized to clear; and the 'top-down approach', which considered products that should be subject to mandatory clearing, but for which there were no suitable CCPs. The report recommended the use of both the bottom-up and top-down approaches.

The recommendations adopted by the IOSCO were rather general, also to make sure that they would be suitable to be applied in more than one hundred member jurisdictions (interview, June 2019). Controversial issues concerning specific aspects of clearing, such as which entities and products should be exempted from clearing obligations, were not dealt with by international standards, which, deliberately, left them to be regulated by individual jurisdictions. This strategy 'kicked the can down the road' because various jurisdictions adopted different and, at times, incompatible domestic rules on clearing, as elaborated in the following section. It is, however, important to note that, besides mandatory requirements, there were other incentives that could be used to promote central clearing, notably, higher bank capital requirements, and margin requirements for non-centrally cleared derivatives. Consequently, precise, stringent and consistent international standards for capital and margin were instrumental in promoting central clearing through CCPs in the absence of granular international standards for mandatory clearing. But this required regulatory cooperation among various international standard-setting bodies, as discussed in subsequent chapters.

State-Centric Explanation of Standard Setting for Derivatives Clearing

The US and the EU advocated mandatory centralized clearing after the crisis, but did not sponsor precise, stringent, and consistent international standards on this matter for several reasons. To begin with, although clearing via CCPs was important in order to safeguard financial stability, precise 'one size fits all' rules on this matter were not feasible due to the diversity of domestic financial systems and regulatory frameworks. Second, other international standards, notably, bank capital requirements and margin requirements, could be used to incentivize centralized clearing—and the US, the UK, and the EU acted as pace-setters on those. Third, the main jurisdictions preferred to regulate this matter at the domestic level, so as to move faster and customize the rules to their domestic market. They used the extra-territorial reach of domestic rules to limit negative externalities and prevent regulatory arbitrage deriving from unilateral actions.

In the US, the Federal Reserve and the CFTC were the main advocates in favour of clearing derivatives through CCPs. A senior official of the Federal Reserve, Patricia White (2009) argued that 'centralized clearing of standardized OTCDs is a key component of efforts to mitigate systemic risk. One method of achieving centralized clearing is to establish central counterparties, or CCPs, for OTCDs. Market participants have already established several CCPs to provide clearing services for some OTC interest rate, energy, and credit derivative contracts. Regulators both in the US and abroad are seeking to speed the development of new CCPs and to broaden the product line of existing CCPs.' Similarly, the CFTC Commissioner, Jill Sommers (2010), noted that by 'mandating the use of central clearinghouses, financial institutions would become much less interconnected, mitigating risk and increasing transparency'.

The US was a first-mover domestically. In October 2008, the Federal Reserve Bank of New York issued a statement mentioning the formation of CCPs for CDS in the US as one of its priorities. This was followed by the Dodd-Frank Act (2010) and the enacting rules adopted by the CFTC and the SEC. Unlike, for example, in the case of capital requirements for banks, the Dodd-Frank Act did not carve out a specific space for international clearing standards, even though the Act mandated the US authorities to consult and cooperate with their foreign counterparts (Pagliari 2018). US rules distinguished between securities and non-securities-based swaps, regulated, respectively, by the SEC and the CFTC. The asset classes of derivatives subject to mandatory clearing were expanded over time, but foreign exchange derivatives were exempted from central clearing and exchange-trading requirements. Other exemptions applied to commercial end-users, which used swaps to mitigate commercial risk.

The EU supported centralized clearing through CCPs. A member of the Executive Board of the ECB, Benoit Cœuré (2014), listed four benefits of central clearing. First, 'CPPs overcome information asymmetries that typically exist in marketplaces'. Second, 'CCPs offer state-of-the-art margining and risk management methods'. Third, 'CCPs are able to mutualize losses in a transparent and predictable way'. Finally, 'central clearing allows for the multilateral netting of exposures so that a given level of risk protection can be achieved with a smaller amount of collateral'. In the UK, the Deputy Governor of the Bank of England, Paul Tucker (2013), argued that central clearing simplified the 'network of counterparty credit exposures' and made the 'transmission of risk in the global financial system more transparent'. For Jean-Pierre Jouyet (2009), Chairman of the French Autorité des Marchés Financiers, CCPs were 'fire-doors' breaking up the high degree of financial interconnectedness among market actors.

The EU was a second-mover domestically. In 2009, the EU authorities put pressure on market participants to clear CDSs through CCPs (*The Guardian*, 19 February 2009). Afterward, the EMIR (2012) and the regulatory standards issued by the ESMA introduced a clearing mandate for certain asset classes (initially, interest rate derivatives, followed by foreign exchange, equity, and commodity derivatives). The clearing obligation applied if it involved a transaction between two financial counterparties, a financial counterparty and a non-financial counterparty that exceeded the clearing thresholds, two non-financial counterparties that exceeded the threshold, a financial counterparty or a non-financial counterparty that exceeded the threshold and a non-EU entity that would be subject to the clearing obligation if it was established in the EU.

The ECB highlighted the euro area dimension of clearing. It argued that given the importance of CCPs for the safe, efficient, and transparent functioning of OTCDs and the systemic relevance of these markets, there was a strong 'Eurosystem interest' in further developing these infrastructures in the euro area (ECB 2009). In 2011, the ECB proposed that CCPs clearing a significant proportion of euro-denominated financial instruments should be located in the euro area (ECB 2011)—it was the so-called 'location policy' (Buckley, Howarth, and Quaglia 2012). The ECB proposal was strongly opposed by UK policymakers, who were keen to retain the profitable euro clearing business in the City of London. Although the UK government successfully challenged the ECB's plans in the European Court of Justice, efforts to revive the location policy for CCPs clearing large amounts of euro-denominated assets gathered pace in the context of Brexit (see James and Quaglia 2020b).

Jurisdictions on the fringe that had thriving derivatives markets supported clearing via CCPs. A senior official at the Monetary Policy Authority of Singapore (2012) pointed out that 'The Lehman episode provides a good illustration of how useful a reporting and clearing regime could be... most of Lehman's contracts that were centrally cleared could be resolved quickly, without large systemic disruptions' (Chuan Teck 2012). However, the main challenge was that CCPs were relatively undeveloped in Asia prior to the crisis. For example, the first CCP to clear OTCDs in China, the Shanghai Clearing House, was established in 2009. This meant that often 'in addition to drawing up new regulations, regulators in Asia have to work with the industry to develop the right architecture to support the regulations.... In Singapore, we realized shortly after the Pittsburgh communiqué that we cannot impose clearing requirements if there are no CCPs dealing with Asian products that most Asian institutions have ready access to' (Chuan Teck 2012).

Afterward, the problem became the excessive proliferation of CCPs and trade repositories in Asia as well as elsewhere. As one Asian policymaker (Chuan Teck 2012) noted, 'instead of there not being enough CCPs and trade repositories, there may be a case where there are too much, and too many' because many markets were developing their own CCPs and trade repositories. Since some of these entities were too small to be commercially viable, regulators could be tempted to impose onshore reporting or clearing requirements to support the viability of these entities. 'This may create substantial inefficiencies as market participants would need to report to multiple trade repositories and place margins in multiple CCPs' (Chuan Teck 2012). As a result of domestic, somewhat uncoordinated, actions, the US and the EU adopted different rules about which products and which entities should be subject to mandatory clearing obligations, which generated transatlantic regulatory disputes (Knaack 2015; Pagliari 2013b; Posner 2018) and resulted in a potential fragmentation of global derivatives markets (see, for example, ISDA 2015c). The other jurisdictions mainly waited for the US and the EU to iron out their disagreements before adopting domestic clearing rules (Knaack 2015; Li 2018), which also gave them time to establish domestic CCPs. As of 2018, 17 jurisdictions of the G20 had issued criteria to determine when OTCDs should be centrally cleared—it was one of the best implementation records among post-crisis derivatives reforms.

Transgovernmental Explanation of Standard Setting for Derivatives Clearing

The transgovernmental explanation of international standard setting does not have much traction in this case. International regulatory discussions concerning derivatives clearing fell primarily within the remit of the IOSCO, which had done no previous work on this matter. As noted above, the IOSCO is a relatively loose network, which brings together securities market regulators from more than one hundred jurisdictions with different domestic markets and regulatory frameworks. Within the IOSCO, the Task Force on Derivatives was set up in 2010 and was co-chaired by the SEC, the CFTC, the British FSA, and the SEC of India. The international discussions on the centralized trading of derivatives via exchanges or platforms started basically from scratch because there were no pre-existing international rules, even though domestic rules were in the process of being discussed in the US and the EU. In the IOSCO, neither the US authorities (the SEC and the CFTC), the UK (the FSA) nor the EU promoted the issuing of precise, stringent, and consistent international rules on centralized clearing.

Several transgovernmental networks, other than securities markets regulators, were involved in the regulatory discussions on derivatives clearing because a variety of post-crisis standards were instrumental to incentivize clearing via CCPs. Specifically, these standards concerned bank capital requirements, set by the BCBS, whereby higher requirements were prescribed for uncleared derivatives (see Chapter 7); and margin requirements for uncleared derivatives, set by the BCBS-IOSCO, which were supposed to make these transactions more costly (see Chapter 8). Regulators in the main jurisdictions were well aware of the interlinkages among these elemental regimes. Benoît Cœuré (2014b), who was a member of the Executive Board of the ECB, noted that a number of reforms needed to be adopted in order to promote central clearing, including: mandatory clearing, margin requirements for non-centrally cleared derivatives, and higher capital requirements for non-centrally cleared derivatives. He highlighted the 'crucial complementarity' between the regulation of CCPs and the regulation of banks to reduce the 'overall level of risk in the financial system', rather than 'shifting it around', concluding that cooperation between the CPSS/CPMI-IOSCO on one hand, and the BCBS on the other hand, was crucial in this respect.

Furthermore, the mandatory clearing of derivatives and the concentration of counterparty risk into CCPs increased the risk of failure of CCPs. CCPs were transformed from 'niche' operators pre-crisis, to crucial nodes of the financial system post-crisis. Consequently, there was a need to reform the regulation of CCPs (Genito 2019). Within transgovernmental networks, the regulators most alert to the interlinkages between the regime on mandatory clearing and the regime on the resilience, recovery, and resolution of CCPs were regulators of the main jurisdictions, which were actively engaged in all international standard-setting processes concerning derivatives. For example, Paul Tucker (2011), Deputy Governor of the Bank of England, argued that as a consequence of the mandatory clearing of derivatives, international standards were needed to prevent and manage the failure of CCPs. Daniel Tarullo (2011a), a member of the Board of Governors of the Federal Reserve, noted that in order to ensure that a global move towards central clearing of derivatives actually reduced systemic risk, it was critical for CCPs to be 'sound and stable'. Therefore, he argued that it was essential that CPSS and the IOSCO completed their work on the regulation of CCPs as soon as possible. However, a variety of domestic agencies regulated derivatives-related matters in the US and the EU, often with limited domestic coordination. This enhanced the need to coordinate the international regulation of derivatives through transgovernmental networks in which national regulators participated. In other words, the fragmentation of domestic regulatory competences on derivatives increased the need for coordination among international standard-setters, which used a variety of tools to promote the consistency of their regulatory outputs (see Chapter 3).

Industry-Led Explanation of Standard Setting for Derivatives Clearing

For the financial industry, the obligation to centrally clear derivatives was less controversial than the obligation to centrally trade derivatives. Thus, the absence of precise and stringent international clearing standards cannot be ascribed to opposition from the financial industry. Central clearing brought new business to CCPs, and, although it could potentially increase costs for dealer banks, buy-siders, and end-users, it was a way for them to reduce credit risk (i.e. the risk of default or non-payment of the counterparty of the bilateral deal) (Norman 2008). Clearing also allowed the multilateral netting of transactions between market participants. That said, most of the industry preferred market-led action, rather than mandatory clearing requirements. Furthermore, several industry players sought to avoid clearing obligations by advocating exemptions for certain entities, products, or below a certain threshold (Pagliari 2018). The preferences of various parts of the financial industry reflected their cost-benefits analysis of the proposed reform. Private actors mobilized in order to shape the content of the new rules, even though this sort of lobbying took place mainly at the domestic level, when detailed rules were issued.

The dealer banks articulated three main arguments: they preferred incentives and market-led action, rather than mandatory requirements, arguing that it was in the interest of market participants to centrally clear most OTCDs. They also maintained that certain contracts were not suitable for clearing. Initially, the ISDA (2010) tried to stave off public regulation by stating that the industry was committed to delivering 'robust, efficient and accessible central clearing to the OTCDs markets', and by noting that significant steps had been taken by the industry to 'increase the range of products eligible for clearing'. Subsequently, this association argued that some derivatives were not eligible for clearing and that non-centrally cleared OTCDs continued to play an important role in many industries and were used extensively by corporations and investment and pension funds to manage risk (ISDA 2013a).

The European Banking Federation (EBF) (2010) questioned whether mandatory central clearing was the best way to reduce counterparty risk. To achieve that objective, the EBF favoured a combination of several measures: market-driven CCPs clearing; capital incentives for centrally cleared derivatives; and margins for uncleared derivatives. The European Fund and Asset Management Association (EFAMA) (2011) noted that although the buy-side supported the move from bilateral to central clearing, this could produce 'perverse results', 'if the costs of central clearing were not proportionate to the risk'. This association feared that the costs of clearing would be borne disproportionately by the buy-side. However, large companies on the buy-side were less concerned because they benefitted more from the multilateral netting of exposures carried out by CCPs. For instance, BlackRock (2018) argued that 'the reduction in bilateral counterparty credit risk, increased market transparency, together with the improved efficiency in trade execution, outweigh the significant operational costs incurred by market participants and end-investors to comply with clearing mandates. In fact, a number of market participants who are not subject to clearing mandates, including end-investors, do decide to clear voluntarily.'

In the wake of the crisis, the financial industry sought to prevent or limit public regulation concerning derivatives clearing by engaging in private-sector governance. In June 2009, a group of major market participants (the G14 dealer banks) issued a commitment letter to the US public authorities, pledging to use CCPs to clear credit derivatives.[7] In September 2009, the same group established targets for clearing interest rate derivatives and credit derivatives.

[7] These commitment letters are available at: https://www.newyorkfed.org/newsevents/news/markets/2010/ma100301.html

Most of these clearing targets were met afterwards. In the EU, the ISDA and the European Banking Federation (EBF) sent a similar commitment letter to Charlie McCreevy, the EU Commissioner for the Internal Market. Barclays Capital, Citigroup, Credit Suisse, Deutsche Bank, Goldman Sachs, HSBC, JP Morgan, Morgan Stanley, and UBS all signed up to the agreement (*The Guardian*, 19 February 2009). In another commitment letter sent to the US and the EU authorities in March 2010, market participants pledged to: increase market transparency (especially, price transparency) in the OTCDs; expand the range of cleared products and broaden market participation in clearing; and improve standardization of derivatives products.

Following the adoption of post-crisis clearing regulation in the main jurisdictions, notably, the US and the EU, the financial industry (in particular, transnational associations and private actors that engaged in cross-border business) raised concerns about the fragmentation of global derivatives markets as well as regulatory inconsistency across standards, as discussed in the concluding chapter. To begin with, there were regulatory inconsistencies between the US and the EU concerning the criteria to mandate central clearing, or to make certain instruments eligible for clearing. The second issue concerned the extraterritoriality of domestic rules (which generated regulatory overlaps). The third concern raised by the financial industry was that, whereas some standards (e.g. mandatory clearing and margins for uncleared derivatives) were designed to encourage centralized clearing, others (e.g. notably, the leverage ratio in capital requirements for banks) made it more expensive. The interlinkages of these issues are discussed further in the following chapters.

Conclusion

This chapter has discussed the elemental regimes on the centralized trading and clearing of derivatives after the crisis. Although the international agreement on these reforms was reached by the G20 at the peak of the crisis, it was not followed by precise, stringent, and consistent international standards. To begin with, although the US authorities advocated the need for central trading and central clearing, they did not sponsor international standards. They preferred to regulate these matters at the domestic level and were first-movers in doing so. The EU was a second-mover, undertaking domestic regulatory reforms on derivatives trading and clearing, which, at times, clashed with US rules. In order to limit negative externalities deriving from less stringent regulation in other jurisdictions, the US and the EU encouraged other jurisdictions to trade up their domestic rules on derivatives trading and clearing. However, the great powers mainly used the extraterritoriality of domestic rules to do so, rather than sponsoring precise and stringent international standards.

There was considerable pushback from industry concerning centralized trading and, to a lesser extent, clearing of derivatives. In the case of trading on exchanges or platforms, the strongest opposition came from the dealer banks. In the case of clearing via CCPs, the pushback from the financial industry was limited because clearing was seen as having considerable benefits, not only costs, for dealer banks, buy-siders, and end-users. Transgovernmental networks of regulators gathered in the IOSCO were aware that the domestic markets of jurisdictions worldwide were too diverse for meaningful international harmonization, also considering the level of rule granularity that would have been necessary. Thus, international standard-setting bodies issued some general recommendations on centralized trading and clearing and monitored the domestic regulation that implemented these international commitments across jurisdictions.

In terms of regime complexity, the rules on mandatory platform trading partly overlapped with those on mandatory CCPs clearing, in that the expectation was that centrally traded derivatives should also be centrally cleared. Furthermore, the rules on clearing through CCPs were interlinked with most of the other elemental regimes concerning different aspects of derivatives markets discussed in this book, notably, bank capital requirements and margin requirements for non-centrally cleared derivatives. Consequently, international standards issued with reference to these matters were instrumental in promoting central clearing through CCPs in the absence of granular international standards for mandatory clearing.

5

International Standards for the Reporting of Derivatives Trades

This chapter examines the elemental regime concerning the reporting of derivatives trades to repositories, including the harmonization of data format and aggregation, the politically charged issue of authorities' access to data, and the technical issues concerning entities, products, and transactions identifiers. Initially, international standards for trade reporting were not considered as a priority and the attention focused on other areas of derivatives regulation. Consequently, different domestic rules on trade reporting proliferated, making cross-border data sharing and aggregation very difficult. However, as time went by, precise, and consistent international standards concerning entity, product, and transaction identifiers (i.e. the LEI, UPI, and UTI) were issued. Yet, the international harmonization of other critical reporting data was limited and cross-border data sharing remained difficult.

The US were first-movers at the domestic level and belated pace-setters at the international level in promoting the post-crisis reform of the reporting of derivatives trades to repositories. The EU supported the delayed international standard-setting efforts, and was a second-mover, in that it adopted domestic regulation after the US did. The ability of these jurisdictions to promote international standards rested on several inter-related factors: market power (i.e. the size of their financial sector), domestic regulatory capacity and subject-specific expertise. Internationally, there were no foot-draggers, even though several jurisdictions on the fringe were slow in implementing the domestic regulatory changes necessary in order to give effect to the trade reporting mandate because they had to build up trade repositories from scratch.

The financial industry accepted the need for trade reporting after the crisis. Hence, trade reporting requirements, as such, were not contested by private actors, also because these requirements did not have major distributional implications within the financial industry and, initially, their costs were deemed to be fairly limited. Trade reporting became contested once different domestic requirements proliferated and diverged, increasing reporting costs for the industry, which would have preferred harmonized rules, but without

The Politics of Regime Complexity In International Derivatives Regulation. Lucia Quaglia, Oxford University Press (2020).
 DOI: 10.1093/oso/9780198866077.003.0001

having to bear switchover costs. The mobilization of certain private actors, first and foremost, cross-border derivatives traders, contributes to explaining the slow but steady progress made concerning the international harmonization of trade reporting. A private standard setter, the ISDA, also played an important role in fostering international regulatory consistency by collaborating with the public authorities. A variety of transgovernmental networks of domestic regulators dealt with trade reporting. In addition to central bankers gathered in the CPSS (later renamed, the CPMI) and securities market regulators gathered in the IOSCO, treasury officials were also involved through the FSB. A non-financial international standard-setter, the International Standardisation Organisation (ISO), issued rules on the Legal Entity Identifier (LEI) code and was designated as the responsible body for maintaining UTI data standards. Finally, a new body, the Global LEI Foundation, was set up and became the only global source of LEI data, whereas the Derivatives Service Bureau was appointed as the only issuer of UPI codes.

First, this chapter discusses some key issues concerning the regulation of the reporting of derivatives trades to repositories. It then examines three components in the international governance of trade reporting: data format and aggregation; data access and cross-border sharing; legal entity, transaction and product identifiers, which are specific elements of data formatting that require full harmonization. Subsequently, the analytical leverage of the state-led explanation, the transgovernmental explanation, and the industry-led explanation is assessed against the empirical record.

Key Issues in Regulating Derivatives Trade Reporting to Repositories

The crisis, notably the failure of Lehman Brothers, underlined the absence of suitable data concerning derivatives trades, especially OTCDs. Due to the lack of data, there was no comprehensive map of the interconnections in the financial system. Even prior to the crisis, the CPSS (1998) had pointed out the 'cumbersome nature of data on derivatives trades, which were mostly paper-based, were held by banks' back offices and needed to be updated every day. It was also problematic for banks to understand, at the group level, which OTCDs they held and their level of risk exposure' (interview, February 2019). Therefore, after the crisis, there was an international consensus on the need to introduce reporting requirements for derivatives trades.

Trade repositories are entities that maintain a centralized electronic record (database) of OTCDs transactions, gathering market data and making them accessible to regulators. The post-crisis reform that introduced the requirement to report derivatives trades to repositories was intended to improve transparency, mitigate systemic risk, and protect against market abuse by enabling regulators to monitor the market (CPSS-IOSCO 2012b). This reform involved two interrelated aspects: the establishment of trade repositories, including the format of data reporting and data access; and the development of global entity, product, and transaction identifiers in order to make data intelligible cross-borders (Knaack 2018). Unlike other aspects of derivatives regulation, trade reporting did not involve a trade-off between financial stability and competitiveness, rather it posed a coordination problem (i.e. the need to use the same formatting, which resulted in a 'network externality')[1] (Knaack 2018).

The first issue that cropped up in the post-crisis regulatory debate on trade reporting was whether to establish one global trade repository, and, if that was the case, in which jurisdiction, and subject to which governance rules. Here, the risk of creating a 'monopoly' had to be weighed against the easing of data aggregation under 'one roof', so to speak. Alternatively, there could be a multiplicity of trade repositories, one in each of the main jurisdictions, which would increase reporting costs and complicate data aggregation. The choice between one global trade repository or several domestic trade repositories also had implications for the public authorities and the financial industry. In fact, the first option would have led to choosing the US-based Depository Trust & Clearing Corporation (DTCC) as 'the' global trade repository, strengthening its market position and giving the US authorities relatively easy access to its data, as compared to foreign authorities. The second option would have allowed jurisdictions to develop trade repositories on their territory and under their supervision (interview, December 2018).

The second issue in the regulation of trade reporting concerned the conditions for regulators' access to data and cross-border data exchange, due to the potentially sensitive commercial information dealt with. Two competing rationales were at stake: financial stability, which required data sharing among regulators cross-borders, and domestic legal barriers to data sharing—notably, in the US and the EU—which obstructed the exchange of information across borders. The Dodd-Frank Act and the enacting regulation

[1] Network effects occur when the value of a product or service increases according to the number of actors using it.

required US trade repositories to make data available to US regulators, but US regulators were allowed to reject data requests from foreign counterparts. This became a bone of contention in the context of the Greek crisis in 2010, when European regulators unsuccessfully sought information about the credit derivatives market from the US-based trade repository ran by the Depository Trust & Clearing Corporation (DTCC), the Warehouse Trust. In retaliation, the EU rules on trade reporting, which were adopted afterward, included similar provisions regarding the possibility to reject data requests from foreign counterparts (Buckley et al. 2012).

The third issue in the regulation of trade reporting concerned the format of data reporting, with reference to which three main aspects stood out. The Legal Entity Identifier (LEI) was a standard reference code that was to provide a universal method of identifying entities, including both financial and non-financial firms, that were counterparties in OTCDs transactions, or other financial transactions. Each entity would be registered and assigned a unique code that would be associated with a set of reference data (e.g. basic elements, such as name and address, or more complex data, such as corporate hierarchical relationships). While the LEI would assign a unique identification number to each counterparty engaged in a financial transaction, a Unique Product Identifier (UPI) would convey information about the financial product traded, and a Unique Transaction Identifier (UTI) would convey information about the specific transaction (CPSS-IOSCO 2012b). Thus, the international standards for the format of data reporting, aggregation, and accessibility were inextricably intertwined with the international standards for LEI, UPI, and UTI.

A global LEI was intended to address coordination problems and deal with network externalities, without, prima facie, distributive implications (Knaack 2018). A coordination problem emerges when the interests of participants coincide and each participant has an incentive to do something that chimes in with what the others do—to this end, participants need to coordinate their actions. A global LEI offered collective benefits to users and the broader public. Hence, the creation of a LEI had the support of the financial industry, as elaborated below. However, there were two sources of market failure (FSB 2012). The first was a problem of collective action and coordination in getting an agreement on a particular identification scheme. The second reflected the problem of launching a network. At the outset, the incentives for potential early movers to acquire a LEI were low. Thus, the initial approach that relied on voluntary adoption and market incentives proved to be insufficient (interview, December 2018). The LEI was a public good, offering collective benefits that were not captured by market incentives alone. In several aspects, the public interests and the private sector interests were aligned, but not always. For example, there were incentives for suppliers of the LEI to exploit their privileged position (FSB 2012). For all these reasons, international standards for LEI were needed. However, the problem was that (different) domestic rules on LEI were adopted in key jurisdictions prior to international standards (Knaack 2018), which made subsequent international harmonization more difficult.

International Standards for Derivatives Trade Reporting

At the Pittsburgh summit in 2009, the G20 Leaders (2009b) agreed that OTCDs contracts should be reported to trade repositories. At the outset, the FSB (2010) recognized that 'One beneficial solution would be to establish a single global data source to aggregate the information from trade repositories.' However, it also recognized that the issue of the number and location of trade repositories, as well as the number and location of CCPs, was beyond the scope of its remit. The matter was complicated by the fact that there was jurisdictional competition whereby the national authorities were keen to promote the establishment of trade repositories in their territory, so as to be able to regulate and supervise them, getting (or denying) access to their data. This jurisdictional competition intersected with market competition among trade repositories, as discussed below. Furthermore, initially, international standard-setters did not consider the harmonization of trade reporting requirements as a priority and, therefore, devoted limited efforts to it.

Given the slow progress made on trade reporting since the crisis, the G20 Leaders (2011), prompted by the US authorities (as elaborated in the following section), asked the CPSS and the IOSCO to work with FSB 'to carry forward work on identifying data that could be provided by and to trade repositories, and to define principles or guidance on regulators' access to data held by trade repositories'. The G20 also supported the creation of a global LEI, which would uniquely identify parties to financial transactions. It asked the FSB to take the lead by preparing recommendations for the 'appropriate governance framework', 'representing the public interest' for a global LEI (G20 2011).

In 2012, the CPSS-IOSCO (2012b) issued a report on *Data Reporting and Aggregation Requirements*, which specified the minimum requirements for reporting data to trade repositories and for reporting by trade repositories to regulators, as well as the types of acceptable data formats. The document also discussed issues concerning authorities' access to data, and the dissemination of selected data to the public, while taking into account confidentiality constraints. Finally, the report recommended the establishment of a system of LEIs for the aggregation of OTCDs data, arguing that it would constitute a 'global public good'. As one policymaker put it, 'with hindsight, this report was rather optimistic, but, as time went by, the challenge of harmonizing data reporting requirements became clear' (interview, February 2019).

An additional international standard-setter, outside the financial sector, got involved: the International Organization for Standardization (ISO), which was composed of representatives from various national standards organizations. What was interesting about the ISO, specifically, the Technical Committee on Financial Services Technical Committee that worked on the LEI, is that its members were not financial regulators, but rather 'general' standard-setters. Thus, the US was represented by the American National Standards Institute; the UK by the British Standards Institution; and Germany by the German Institute for Standardization. In 2012, the ISO issued the Standard 17442 on the LEI, which set the legal entity reference data that were the most essential elements of identification. The LEI code itself was 'neutral, with no embedded intelligence or country codes that could create unnecessary complexity for users'.[2] Three key principles characterized the LEI: it was a global standard; a single, unique identifier was assigned to each legal entity; and it was a public good, available free of charge to all users. The ISO 17442 standard specified the minimum reference data that would be supplied for each LEI.

The FSB sought to impart some political momentum by establishing an Expert Group, which comprised representatives from members of the FSB and 'key non-members from the global regulatory community with a major stake in the initiative' (FSB 2012), first and foremost, the CFTC and the ESMA.[3] In 2012, the FSB published a report (2012) *A Global Legal Entity Identifier for Financial Markets*, which set out fifteen global, high-level principles and thirty-five recommendations for the development of a unique identification system for parties to financial transactions. It recommended a three-tier structure for the global LEI system, which was subsequently endorsed by the G20 Leaders (2012) at the Los Cabos Summit.

The Global LEI Foundation, which was established in 2013, managed the Central Operating Unit, which provided a centralized database of the LEIs on

[2] https://www.gleif.org/en/about-lei/iso-17442-the-lei-code-structure

[3] The Group also benefited from the input and advice of an Industry Advisory Panel of more than 30 experts.

its website. From 2015 onwards, new institutions that wished to become LEI issuers needed to be accredited by the Global LEI Foundation, which monitored their compliance with the standards of the Global LEI system. The LEI Regulatory Oversight Committee, which comprised more than seventy public authorities from more than fifty jurisdictions, was to oversee the foundation. Local Operating Units were established worldwide. By the end of 2018, over 1.2 million entities from over two hundred countries had obtained LEIs from more than thirty operational issuers accredited by the Global LEI Foundation. The main use of the LEI was for the reporting and aggregation of data on OTCDs, as recommended by the CPMI-IOSCO, even though not all jurisdictions made the use of LEI compulsory. It was compulsory in the US and the EU.

The US was a pace-setter in the establishment of a global LEI. Specifically, the CFTC sought to harmonize the LEI, UTI, and UPI, which were portrayed by the Commissioner of the CFTC as the 'The Rosetta Stone of Swaps Data'[4] (O'Malia 2014). With reference to the LEI, the CFTC noted that the 'optimum effectiveness of LEIs for achieving systemic risk protection and transparency . . . would come from a global LEI created on an international basis through an international voluntary-consensus standards body, such as the ISO', which was the route subsequently followed in international standard setting. The establishment and use of a global LEI system were also endorsed by the EU (e.g. Coeuré 2015b, 2017a, Ross 2017).

The politically sensitive issue of authorities' access to data was mentioned, but ultimately side-stepped, in the CPSS-IOSCO (2012b) *Report on OTC Derivatives Data Reporting and Aggregation*. Afterwards, given the increasing number of trade repositories worldwide and the transatlantic dispute on this matter, the FSB asked the CPSS-IOSCO to take forward the work on the authorities' access to trade repositories data. In 2013, the CPSS-IOSCO (2013) issued the *Authorities' Access to Trade Repository Data*. The report outlined a 'data access model', whereby trade repositories would provide data requested by the authorities, subject to legal restrictions and confidentiality considerations. In order to avoid cross-border problems, the document suggested that regulators should put in place agreements so as to address relevant legal obstacles. The report also noted that since the data on OTCDs was held in multiple trade repositories, some form of data aggregation was needed in order to get a global view of the OTCDs market.

[4] The term 'rosetta stone' has been used to represent a crucial key in the process of decryption of encoded information.

This issue was subsequently taken up by the FSB (2014a) *Feasibility Study on Aggregation of OTC Derivatives Trade Repository Data*, so as to impart some 'political drive' to this matter (interview, February 2019). The report, prepared by a study group set up by the FSB and composed of members of the CPSS, the IOSCO, and macroprudential and microprudential supervisors, compared three basic options for aggregating OTCDs trade repository data: a 'physically centralized' model; a 'logically centralized' model; and the collection and aggregation of raw data from trade repositories by the authorities themselves. It concluded that the first and second aggregation options were highly preferable, but the third option was the only available, even though it did not meet all the authorities' data needs. The report also noted that for data aggregation it was critical to complete the standardization of important data elements, including the LEI, the UPI, and the UTI. The FSB asked the CPMI and the IOSCO to develop global guidance on data harmonization (FSB 2014a).

The international harmonization of trade reporting requirements was given new momentum by the US, which acted as a pace-setter internationally. The CTFC argued that 'the urgency for a holistic view of the financial markets, without borders, was underscored by how the financial crisis caught the world by surprise. Data that could have identified systemic risk was fragmented across regulators and nations. Risk knows no boundaries. Our ability to monitor it shouldn't have any either' (O'Malia 2014). The CTFC had the political support of the US Treasury, which was very influential in the FSB. In a congressional hearing, the Undersecretary of the US Treasury, Mary Miller (2014), noted that:

> One area that will require significant international cooperation is the task of ensuring not only that all derivatives transaction are reported to trade repositories, but that the information collected can be used for the purposes it was intended: bringing transparency to our derivatives markets and helping regulators and market participants develop more insight into the types and levels of exposure throughout the financial system. A great deal of work still needs to be done to ensure that the data reported by industry and collected by regulators will be as useful as possible, or we will be at risk of not achieving that goal. The data are fragmented, with many different trade repositories, within and across jurisdictions, collecting different kinds of information in different ways, keeping us from putting all of that information together to develop a full picture of the market. We need to roll up our sleeves and address any obstacles to making these data useful for market participants and for regulators who are monitoring financial stability.

In late 2014, the CPMI-IOSCO established a Working Group for the Harmonisation of key OTCDs data elements and the establishment of UPI and UTI. The Harmonisation Group acknowledged that the responsibility for issuing requirements for the reporting of OTCDs transactions to trade repositories fell within the remit of the relevant national authorities (CPMI-IOSCO 2015). It also stayed clear of issues discussed by other international workstreams. The FSB, in particular, planned work on legal and regulatory changes that would be needed to implement a global aggregation mechanism that would meet the data access needs of regulators. In other words, there was a 'division of work' in international standard setting. The CPMI-IOSCO dealt with the more 'technical part' of data formatting and aggregation, and the FSB with the more 'political' part that involved the regulatory changes needed to make it possible and the governance structure for the management of UTI and UPI (interview, February 2019).

After public consultation, the CPMI-IOSCO (2017a) issued *Guidance Harmonisation of the Unique Product Identifier (UPI),* which was to identify OTCDs products that the authorities required to be reported to trade repositories. The following year, the FSB (2018c) issued *Governance Arrangements for the Unique Product Identifi*er *(UPI).* In parallel, the CPMI-IOSCO (2017b) issued *Technical Guidance Harmonisation of the Unique Transaction Identifi*er (UTI), which discussed the definition, format, and usage of the UTI. Since there was no agreement among jurisdictions about what should be reported, the broad term 'reportable transaction' was used in the report to cover any transaction that must be reported to a trade repository (interview, February 2019). At the same time, the FSB (2017b) issued *Governance Arrangements for the Unique Transaction Identifier (UTI),* subsequently designating the ISO as the responsible body for maintaining the UTI data standards. Finally, the CPMI-IOSCO (2018a) issued *Technical Guidance on the Harmonisation of Critical OTCDs Data Elements (other than UTI and UPI).* Afterward, the FSB (2019b), in consultation with the CPMI-IOSCO, designated the Derivatives Service Bureau—a subsidiary of the Association of National Numbering Agencies that monitors national numbering agencies for compliance with various standards on behalf of the ISO—as the service provider for the UPI system and sole issuer of the UPI code. The FSB also decided that UPI reference data would be set as international data standards to be maintained by the ISO (for an overview of international standards for derivatives trade reporting, see Table 5.1 and Figure 5.1).

To sum up, data reporting to trade repositories was controversial for a variety of reasons. To begin with, given the initial failure to develop international standards, various jurisdictions defined differently which transactions were reportable and the format of reporting. Thus, a transaction that was reportable under one jurisdiction was not necessarily reportable under another jurisdiction, or it needed to be reported in a different way. Moreover,

Table 5.1 International standards for the reporting of derivatives trades to repositories

International standard-setting body	Date of issuance	Standards (framework, guidance, etc.)
CPSS-IOSCO	2012	Data Reporting and Aggregation
FSB	2012	Global LEI Governance
ISO	2012	LEI code
CPSS-IOSCO	2013	Authorities' Access to Trade Repository Data
FSB	2014	Feasibility Study of Data Aggregation
Global LEI Foundation	2015	Establishment of Global LEI system
CPMI-IOSCO	2017	Guidance on UTI
CPMI-IOSCO	2017	Guidance on UPI
FSB	2017	Governance of UTI
ISO & GLEI	2017	Technical work
FSB	2018	Governance of UPI
CPMI-IOSCO	2018	Guidance on other Critical Data

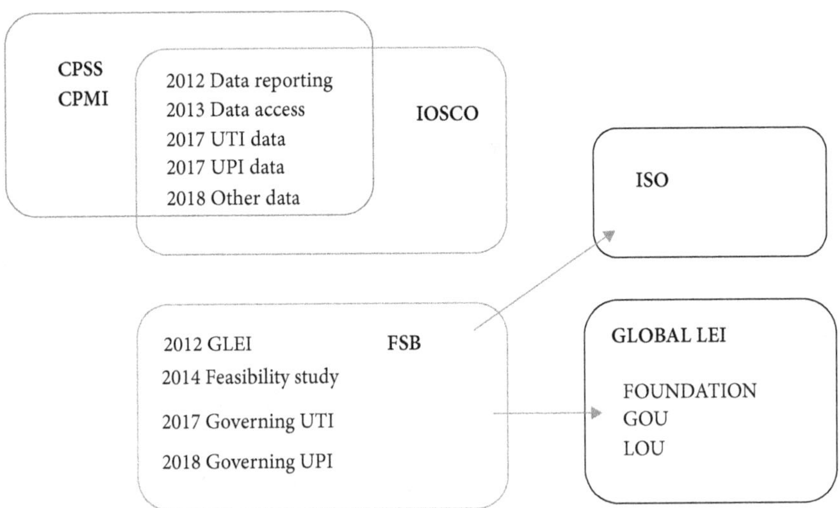

Figure 5.1 Post-crisis international standard setting for trade repositories (adapted from Quaglia and Spendzharova 2020b)

some jurisdictions required that both counterparties to a transaction reported the transaction ('double-sided reporting'), while other jurisdictions required only one of the counterparties to report the transaction ('single-sided reporting'). In the US, it was single-sided reporting, whereas the EU required dual-sided reporting, which resulted in the generation of two UTIs. In addition to the reporting of OTCDs transactions, the EU also required the reporting of exchange-traded derivative transactions; however, the US did not.

Furthermore, concerns about financial stability—in particular, regulators' ability to access data—were intermixed with commercial preoccupations, namely, competition among trade repositories and the promotion of domestic trade repositories. Jurisdictions were reluctant to grant each other access to trade repositories data. Even where memoranda of understanding were agreed on in order to facilitate cross-border data sharing, data were difficult to aggregate because they had a different format. At the same time, the diversity of data reporting requirements in various jurisdictions increased compliance costs for the financial industry. International harmonization would have implied switchover costs for industry, which, however, complained about the costs of complying with different national reporting rules due to the lack of international standards.

As a consequence of this fragmentation, the public authorities lacked aggregate data and a global view of derivatives markets, which was the main rationale for introducing trade reporting requirements post-crisis. No authority was able to examine the entire global network of OTCDs data. As one regulator noted 'while jurisdictions sought to agree on trade reporting requirements, the world moved forward' (interview, February 2019). However, gradually, international standards for LEI, UPI, and UTI were issued and specific governance systems for these data were established. There was also partial harmonization of other trade reporting data. Cross-border data sharing was agreed upon in principle, but remained limited de facto. Thus, in order to keep up the pressure for reform, FSB decided to periodically monitor the removal of legal barriers to authorities' access to data of trade repositories across jurisdictions (see FSB 2018c).

State-Centric Explanation of Standard Setting for Trade Reporting

The US was a first-mover in regulating derivatives trade reporting at the domestic level, followed by the EU. These jurisdictions were belated pace-setters in promoting precise, stringent, and consistent standards for trade reporting. These jurisdictions had aligned preferences to a certain extent, in that they both considered trade reporting as a way of better monitoring derivatives markets to improve transparency and safeguard financial stability, given the role that OTCDs had in the building up of the international financial crisis. The implications of unilateral regulatory action for the competitiveness of the domestic derivatives industry were limited, and, actually, domestic rules could encourage the development of domestic trade repositories. However, unilateral action could not address the network externalities deriving from the lack of international standards. These negative externalities became clear once domestic rules were issued and the data collected in various jurisdictions were difficult to aggregate in order to provide a meaningful picture of the global derivatives markets (Knaack 2018).

In the US, the CFTC, which was the regulatory agency in the lead on this issue, adopted domestic rules on trade reporting in 2011, recognizing the importance of this type of data. As Commissioner O'Malia (2013) put it '"The price of light is less than the cost of darkness"... this quote really speaks to the power of data and analytics and the foregone opportunities if you fail to either capture or effectively utilize the data... regulators must improve their own capacity and capability to intake data as well as the development of analytical tools to identify and monitor risk'. The CFTC was one of the first regulators to flag the problem concerning data formatting and aggregation. 'We have data challenges all over the place... the data submitted is not usable in its current form... none of our computer programs load this data without crashing.... Each reporting party has its own internal nomenclature to compile its data and, therefore, even when market participants submitted the correct information to trade repositories, the language they use is different' (O'Malia 2014).

When serious difficulties with data aggregation and access emerged, the US authorities stepped up their regulatory action internationally by promoting international standards. The CFTC's rules issued in 2011 prescribed, inter alia, the use of LEI, UTI, and UPI, all tools that were subsequently 'uploaded' onto international standards. On one hand, the CFTC promoted the international harmonization of the format for data reporting. Dan Bucsa (*Risknet*, 7 October 2017), a senior official at the CFTC and co-chair of the CPMI-IOSCO Harmonisation Group, argued that a global framework for trade reporting data would allow regulators to make better use of the information collected. On the other hand, the CFTC was keen to preserve domestic regulatory autonomy, pointing out that the harmonization of trade data was not the same thing as 'complete standardization of domestic legal regimes' (*Risknet*, 7 October 2017). The US was able to be a pace-setter internationally because it had market power, a domestic regulatory template, and subject-specific expertise. The US authorities led some of the key transgovernmental committees and working groups, as detailed in the penultimate section.

The EU was slower than the US in developing domestic rules on trade reporting because the EU policy-process is generally cumbersome, but also because neither the EU nor its member states had existing trade repositories. The EU and its member states were keen to develop EU-based trade repositories for two reasons. The first reason was to challenge the market dominance of the US-based Depository Trust & Clearing Corporation (DTCC), the largest trade repository in the world. The second reason was to make sure that EU regulators could get access to data without facing legal hurdles. The EU adopted rules for trade reporting in 2012. Afterward, the EU, like the US, faced major problems concerning data aggregation, so the EU supported the US's effort to set international standards in this field. The Executive Director of the ESMA, Verena Ross (2014), pointed out the need to improve the quality of trade reporting data. The member of the Executive Board of the ECB, Benoît Cœuré (2015b), stressed the 'large remaining data gaps in the field of derivatives, where the ability to monitor the size of derivatives markets and the interconnections between financial market infrastructure participants is key if we are to successfully assess the risks across them, especially when considering the global nature of these markets and the fragmentation of the financial market infrastructure landscape worldwide. Data are widely available, but they are fragmented and reported in a non-harmonized way.'

Other jurisdictions, notably, those in Asia, promoted the setting up of domestic trade repositories after the crisis. Since these jurisdictions were aware of the challenge of data aggregation (see, for example, the Hong Kong Monetary Authority 2015), they did not act as foot-draggers at the international level. However, the sequencing of domestic rules first, followed by international standards later, made international harmonization more difficult than it would have been otherwise, that is, in a sequencing starting with international standards issued prior to domestic rules. Once trade repositories proliferated in a variety of jurisdictions, each subject to its own set of rules, also regarding the format of data reporting and aggregation, it became difficult to agree ex-post on international rules that could potentially challenge domestic rules, and would, therefore, involve adjustment (i.e. compliance) costs (Knaack 2018).

The main jurisdictions had an interest in promoting the consistency of various sets of rules on trade reporting. Yet, the fragmentation of regulatory competences at a domestic level and the limited domestic coordination did not facilitate the management of regime complexity internationally. A variety of domestic regulatory authorities—central banks and securities market supervisors—were involved. In the US, there were the Federal Reserve, the CFTC, and the SEC. In the EU, the authorities involved were the ECB, the ESMA, the Commission, the national central banks, and the national securities market regulators of the member states. The fragmented allocation of responsibilities at the domestic level had implications for the external representation of the US and the EU in international standard-setting bodies. On the one hand, the large number of US and European officials in the key working groups increased the influence of these jurisdictions and enabled them to have a comprehensive view of multiple standard-setting processes. On the other hand, as one regulator noted 'often the only venues in which domestic regulators dealing with trade reporting met for joint discussions as well as to coordinate their actions were international standard-setting bodies' (interview, February 2019).

In the CPSS-IOSCO Task Force, the US had four representatives from the CFTC, four from the SEC, one from the Federal Reserve of New York and two from the Federal Reserve Board of Governors. For the EU, the ECB was present, together with central bankers and/or securities market regulators from France, Germany, the UK, Italy, Spain, and the Netherlands. In the CPMI-IOSCO Harmonisation Group, the US had five representatives from the CFTC, five from the SEC, and one from the Federal Reserve. On the EU side, there was the ECB and national central banks and/or securities markets regulators from France, Germany, the UK, Italy, and the Netherlands. In the FSB Aggregation Feasibility Study Group, the US was represented by two officials from the CFTC, one from the Treasury, three from the Federal Reserve Bank of New York and one from the Federal Reserve Board. On the EU side, there was the ECB and national central banks and/or securities market regulators from France, Germany, the UK, Italy, and the Netherlands. As one regulator remarked, 'it was a crowd'.

Transgovernmental Explanation of Standard Setting for Trade Reporting

A variety of transgovernmental networks of domestic financial regulators contributed to harmonizing trade reporting requirements, including rules on data formatting and authorities' access to data. The process of coordination among international standard-setting bodies was particularly convoluted because these were new issues in the regulatory agenda at the national and international levels, and various sets of regulators, as well as private standard-setters, were involved. A deliberate division of work took place among international standard-setting bodies. The FSB had an overall coordination role, acting as a transmission mechanism between the political authorities gathered in G20 and sectoral regulators in international standard-setting bodies. It also dealt with the more political issues. The CPMI-IOSCO did technical work, which was taken over by the FSB when governance issues were discussed, or when technical discussions reached an impasse. An international standard-setter outside the financial sector, the ISO, carried out some of the more specialised work concerning LEI, UPI, and UTI, building on its past track record in regulating data standards.

Thus, the CPSS-IOSCO's work (2012b, 2013) on data format, aggregation and sharing among authorities was followed by the FSB's work (2014a, 2017b), whereby the FSB's intervention was intended to break the deadlock that plagued the work of the technical standard-setters, that is to say, the CPSS and the IOSCO (interview, February 2019). Similarly, the CPSS-IOSCO (2012b) started the policy discussion on the global LEI, with a particular focus on the minimum reference data, whereas the FSB (2012) dealt with governance issues of the global LEI system, which was politically sensitive (interview, February 2019). The ISO standard on LEI dealt with the more specialised parts of the standard-setting process by regulating the code structure. Subsequently, the global LEI system was established. Following similar regulatory dynamics, the CPMI-IOSCO (2017a,b) provided technical guidance with reference to UTI and UPI, whereas the FSB (2017b, 2019b) discussed governance issues. The ISO, then, became involved, given that the FSB (2018c) and the Global LEI Foundation (2017) posited that ISO standards should be used, where available.

International standard-setting bodies were instrumental in bringing together different views among regulators. For example, securities markets regulators and central bankers had somewhat different priorities. 'Securities markets regulators were eager to take the lead in international standard setting for trade reporting because they were in the process of establishing their own database, defining statistical aggregates, whereas central banks already had a consolidated experience in this matter, and had their own aggregated data gathered by the BIS' (interview, February 2019). These transgovernmental networks also had different regulatory outlooks, which had to be reconciled in order to set international standards. For instance, 'when the CPSS-IOSCO

Working Group began to discuss liquidity, the members of the group realized after five minutes that they had different ideas about liquidity: securities markets regulators meant market liquidity, whereas central bankers had in mind funding liquidity, that is to say, cash and deposits. Hence, we concurred that the first step was to agree on a common definition of liquidity and gather some metadata' (interview, February 2019). Furthermore, the heavy involvement of the CFTC, which had limited pre-crisis experience in international standard setting (Ryan and Ziegler 2015; Posner 2018), in various working groups contributed to its socialization at the international level, smoothing out some of its initial positions on trade reporting and improving its willingness to engage with foreign counterparts over time (interview, December 2018).

At the same time, there were political limits to the effectiveness of transgovernmental networks in promoting the international harmonization of trade reporting. For instance, the FSB (2014a: 1) noted that the establishment of an international trade repository (to be precise 'a centralized aggregation mechanism') was the best solution for dealing with problems of cross-border data sharing and aggregation. Furthermore, privately, several regulators acknowledged that a 'global trade repository would have been the first best solution in purely economic terms' (interview, December 2018). However, this option was not politically feasible because various jurisdictions were keen on promoting their domestic trade repositories and wanted to retain jurisdictional control of trade reporting data. Afterward, the FSB sought to put pressure on jurisdictions to remove domestic barriers to cross-border data sharing through periodical progress reports on this matter. Since the problem persisted (see FSB 2018c; DTCC 2018), the FSB (2019a: 39) relaunched the idea of a 'global aggregation mechanism for trade reporting of OTC derivatives data', and began working on a costs-benefits analysis as well as potential governance structures.

In order to address the challenges of cooperation between multiple international standard-setting bodies and promote the consistency of regulatory outputs, several mechanisms were used. First, task forces and working groups with mixed membership were set up by the CPSS-IOSCO and the FSB. These groups were jointly chaired by different authorities from each of the two parent committees. In 2010, the CPSS-IOSCO set up a Task Force that was co-chaired by a central bank in Europe (Banque de France) and two securities markets regulators, respectively, in the US and India. In 2012, the CPSS-IOSCO Working Group on Trade Repositories Data Access by authorities was set up. The group was co-chaired by a central bank in Europe (Banque de

France) and a Canadian securities markets regulator; its membership included central bankers and securities markets regulators. In 2014, the CPMI-IOSCO set up the Harmonisation Group to develop guidance regarding the definition, format, and usage of key OTCDs data elements, including UTI and UPI. In the Harmonisation Group, one chair came from the CPSS (the ECB) and one from the IOSCO (the CFTC); one was a central banker and the other a securities markets regulator; one was from the EU, to be precise the euro area, the other from the US; and the membership of the Group included a mix of central bankers and securities markets regulators.

The FSB, which included members from the CPSS, the BCBS, the IOSCO, set up working groups with mixed membership. An Expert Group on the LEI was set up in 2012 and comprised representatives from the members of the FSB and 'key non-members from the global regulatory community with a major stake in the initiative', notably, the CFTC and the ESMA (FSB 2012). The FSB also set up a Working Group on Aggregation Feasibility Study Group, co-chaired by a central bank (the ECB) and a securities market regulator (the CFTC). Finally, the FSB set up a Working Group on UTI–UPI Governance, which was co-chaired by the ECB and the CFTC. As observers, it also included the co-chairs of CPMI-IOSCO Data Harmonisation Working Group as well as other members of that group. The coordination mechanism of institutional deference was also used, thus, the CPSS/CPMI-IOSCO and the FSB deferred to the ISO for the most technical parts of international trade reporting requirements.

Within transgovernmental networks, regulators of the main jurisdictions, which were actively involved in all of the working groups dealing with interlinking issues concerning trade reporting, were mindful of the need to move forward with all of them. For instance, the Executive Director of the ESMA, Verena Ross (2017), remarked that 'the LEI constitutes an example of where we have genuinely achieved a common global data standard. . . . The LEI global success story should encourage us to move ahead with the specification and global agreement around other key data standards—such as the UPI and UTI.' Similarly, the member of the Executive Board of the ECB, Benoit Coeure (2017), noted that after LEI it was critical that harmonization of important data elements be completed, in particular through the establishment of UTI and UPI. However, it was challenging for the main jurisdictions to coordinate domestically. For instance, in the CPSS-IOSCO Task Force and the CPMI-IOSCO Harmonisation Group, the US had about a dozen officials from five different regulatory authorities and the EU had about ten officials from six member states plus the ECB.

Industry-Led Explanation of Standard Setting for Trade Reporting

Trade reporting had limited distributional implications for the financial industry, although it indirectly fed into the competitive struggle among trade repositories. Initially, there was competition between the existing trade repositories (mainly, the Depository Trust & Clearing Corporation—DTCC) and the main stock exchanges, which were keen on establishing new trade repositories, so as to provide the services of trading, clearing, settlement, and reporting 'under one roof', so to speak (Knaack 2018). Subsequently, business competition developed among trade repositories, each of which was eager to expand or protect its market shares, often with the support of the public authorities in the respective jurisdictions (interview, December 2018). Domestic rules on trade reporting were instrumental to that end. By 2018, there were 224 trade repositories operating in member jurisdictions of the FSB (2018c).

At the outset, trade reporting requirements were not expected to be very costly for industry to implement and were designed in a way that did not undermine the profitable informational advantage of dealer banks (Knaack 2018). Therefore, early on, there was no opposition from the financial industry to the introduction of post-crisis trade reporting requirements. Yet, the costs for the financial industry increased once different domestic reporting requirements proliferated across jurisdictions, which affected the preferences of various parts of the industry. By and large, the financial industry sought to limit the precision and stringency of post-crisis trade reporting requirements so as to make them less expensive for the industry by limiting the amount of information that traders had to report to repositories and limit the disclosure of sensitive information by trade repositories to regulators.

However, the main dealer banks and other cross-border traders also favoured greater international harmonization of reporting requirements. In fact, reporting costs were particularly high for the dealer banks and other cross-border traders, which had to report according to different rules across jurisdictions. For this reason, the main international trade associations, such as the ISDA, the Global Financial Markets Association (GFMA), the Securities Industry and Financial Markets Association (SIFMA), etc. were vocal supporters, first, of a global trade repository and, failing that, of international reporting standards as a way to harmonize domestic regulations. It is worth reporting at length an extract of the ISDA's (2011c) response to the CPSS-IOSCO consultation because it not only summarizes the preferences of the dealer banks, but also sheds light on the preferences of other industry stakeholders:

> We believe that fragmentation of trade repositories will introduce operational complexity, undermine risk reduction and impose unnecessary costs. . . . we believe that the solution needs to be global, utilized by all participants. We are concerned that a shared, global regulatory aim – understanding how and where derivatives business may be creating systemic risk – underpinning efforts towards the establishment of an effective trade repositories infrastructure, is being undermined, in many instances by the pursuit of local (national or regional) regulatory mandates. We observe that in some instances, the reasons for this relate to systemic risk and regulatory control (regulators wishing to hold the relevant data in their jurisdiction). In others, this is for commercial reasons (promotion of the interests of a potential local trade repositories service provider). . . . Our preference is for 'one trade repository per asset class', or ideally, 'one trade repositories for all asset classes'.

Among trade repositories, Depository Trust & Clearing Corporation (DTCC) (2011a), which was the oldest and largest trade repository in the world, was the best placed to gain a monopolistic position, if jurisdictions decided to set up a global trade repository. Therefore, not surprisingly, it favoured a 'centralized global data aggregator model'—hence, the establishment of a global trade repository—as opposed to a 'federated model' and asked for more international harmonization (DTCC 2011a). The DTCC shared the ISDA's and the dealer banks' preferences concerning the establishment of one leading trade repository worldwide. Indeed, the ISDA and the DTCC established ad-hoc cooperation on the matter. In 2011, the ISDA selected the DTCC's Trade Information Warehouse as the preferred supplier of a global data repository for interest rate derivatives, equity-based derivatives, and commodity-based derivatives (over time, the DTCC gained the ISDA's approval in all five asset classes). In the same year, the DTCC created a regulator's portal through which regulators were able to access detailed position reports from a global data set.[5] Over thirty different regulators worldwide linked to the DTCC's portal, including regulators in the US and the EU.

The dealer banks, mainly represented by the ISDA (2011c), favoured a global trade repository and asked for more harmonization, so as to avoid

[5] http://www.dtcc.com/news/2011/march/01/dtcc-launches-portal-to-give-global-regulators-access-to-cds-data

fragmentation, which would result from national rules and local mandates concerning trade repositories. This association argued that 'a reduction in the number of trade repositories will benefit the industry and regulatory community'. Although the ISDA raised concerns about data confidentiality, it suggested that a global memorandum of understanding among regulators would mitigate data confidentiality risks and ensure that 'confidentiality concerns were not used as the sole motivation for establishing a trade repository where no independent business reason existed for such an entity'. Furthermore, the ISDA (2011c) and the Securities Industry and Financial Markets Association (SIFMA) (2011) strongly supported the development and implementation of a standard LEI and worked with other financial associations to that end. Indeed, a group of trade associations, led by the Global Financial Markets Association (GFMA), solicited service providers to propose a LEI system, before the public authorities re-launched the project in 2012.

Unlike the dealer banks and their associations, smaller trade repositories, mainly established post-crisis, opposed the creation of a global trade repository that would take over part of their business. The REGIS TR (2011), a trade repository established post-crisis in the EU by the Bolsas y Mercados Españoles and Clearstream, was against 'monopolistic solutions', like the one proposed by the DTCC and the ISDA. However, it also pointed out the need for international cooperation, noting that 'most trade repositories will apply to become registered under multiple jurisdictions; so if all jurisdictions act independently, the process of fulfilling all the requirements of all regimes will be quite burdensome and, very likely, will imply an increase in the costs for both the industry and the supervisors' (REGIS TR 2011). Consequently, REGIS TR encouraged regulators 'to reach a global consensus in order to provide a level playing field for trade repositories operating globally'.

Trade repositories also worried about data confidentiality. The Chicago Mercantile Exchange (CME) (2013), which owned a large trade repository, warned against 'potential unrestricted access of regulators to trade repositories data' and supported the 'determination of the minimum level of data access that authorities could require in support of their particular mandates'. The CME argued that regulators should share the information they received from trade repositories with other authorities on an ongoing basis. The Depository Trust & Clearing Corporation (DTCC) (2013b) argued that a trade repository should conduct its own due diligence of the data requested by regulators to ensure that the requested information was not 'disproportionate'. It also raised the concern that even if a data set was anonymized, it would be possible to discern counterparty identities. This 'fingerprinting' could enable regulators to access information for purposes that were beyond the mandate under which the data was accessed. These concerns about confidentiality and data anonymization were taken on board in the drafting of the international reporting standards outlined in the previous section.

Unlike, for example, the case of the elemental regime for the recovery and resolution of CCPs, which are discussed in the next chapter, the buy-side of the financial industry had preferences that were primarily aligned with the sell-side (dealer banks). The International Capital Market Association (ICMA) (2013), which brings together private and public sector issuers, financial intermediaries, asset managers, and other investors, stressed the need for international standards for trade reporting. Echoing widespread concerns in the financial industry, the association noted that:

> Reporting data is a costly exercise for firms and this cost escalates as reporting burdens proliferate. In considering the relatively new sphere of trade repository it is clear that there are significant risks [that] multiple different demands will be placed upon firms, across financial products, markets and geographies. Whilst each of these individual demands may be well-motivated, there is an understandable concern that, absent some coordination, this could prove inefficient to firms and leave public authorities with a sea of data which still fails to meet their actual needs. At the same time, there is clearly an opportunity to coordinate the development of new demands in a way which alleviates burdens on firms and amplifies benefits for public authorities.

Similarly, regional and national banking associations, as well as individual banks, worried about the costs of reporting and data confidentiality. The European Banking Federation (EBF) (2011) asked that any initiative on data reporting should make a cost-benefit assessment of reporting new data, pointing out that 'data standardization processes, despite their many advantages, are also likely to result in substantial compliance costs for the industry'. Deutsche Bank (2011), a large German dealer bank, argued that the additional data requirements would lead to the generation of substantial volumes of data, which would not ultimately allow regulators to obtain a clear picture of risk concentration. The requirement to report a substantial quantity of new data would impose 'large operational and technological burdens on both market participants and the receivers of the information'.

The financial industry, especially transnational associations and large dealers, repeatedly pointed out the need for international harmonization of trade reporting in several regulatory venues (e.g. the CPSS/CPMI, the IOSCO, the FSB and vis-à-vis the domestic authorities). The industry also engaged in private sector governance of legal identifiers, which was de facto instrumental in promoting international regulatory consistency because 'regulators partly borrowed from private sector practices, rather than starting tabula rasa' (interview, February 2019). Indeed, early on, the main trade associations stepped in by developing industry-led initiatives in the absence of international rules. To begin with, the Depository Trust & Clearing Corporation (DTCC), in conjunction with another major industry player, SWIFT, was selected in 2012 by the CFTC to provide an Interim LEI for OTCDs trading in the US. Thus, the DTCC and SWIFT provided an interim global LEI solution, until the launch of the international LEI system. Furthermore, in order to comply with the reporting requirements issued by the CFTC in 2012, derivatives traders had to obtain a UTI. Thus, the ISDA worked closely with industry stakeholders and with the CFTC in order to develop private-sector practices for UTI. The ISDA's UTI standard became widely used by market participants, and was accepted by various regulators (ISDA 2015a). Thus, private actors played a role in setting trade reporting standards before the G20 stepped up the international harmonization effort—afterward, public standard-setting bodies became more prominent.

Conclusion

In terms of regime complexity, the elemental regime on trade reporting encompassed rules on data format, aggregation, access as well as rules on entity, product, and transaction identifiers. It consisted of 'several interlocking reforms' (interview, December 2018) and could, therefore, be regarded as a regime complex in its own right. A state-centric account has considerable analytical leverage in explaining the setting of precise, and consistent international standards for trade reporting, first and foremost, on legal entities, products, and transaction identifiers. The US was a belated pace-setter, with the support of the EU. There were no foot-dragging jurisdictions. To be precise, there was consensus on the need to have mandatory reporting of derivatives trades, but not on the way to do it. Initially, this issue was given limited priority by international standard-setters, which had not previously worked on this matter. Thus, international standards were adopted only after domestic regulation had been issued in several jurisdictions. This delay made subsequent international harmonization more difficult (Knaack 2018;

Newman and Posner 2018) and, indeed, it remains limited with reference to critical data (other than LEI, UTI, and UPI) and data access.

Transgovernmental networks acted as an intervening variable in international standard setting for trade reporting. They promoted coordination among the alphabet soup of public and private standard-setters (CPSS/CPMI, IOSCO, FSB, ISO, OTCD Forum, OTCD Regulators Group, LEI Foundation, ISDA, SWIFT, etc.) and sought precision, and consistency for international rules on data formatting, access, LEI, UTI, UTI, etc. A variety of coordination mechanisms (e.g. joint working groups, institutional deference) were deployed to that end. The FSB imparted some political drive to the process of data sharing and dealt with governance issues, which were sensitive, whereas most of the technical work on data harmonization was done by the CPSS/CPMI-IOSCO, the ISO and, later on, by the LEI system. The new rules on trade reporting also highlighted the need to strengthen the regulation of trade repositories and CCPs, which are discussed in the following chapter.

The financial industry acted as an intervening variable in shaping trade reporting standards. On the one hand, the opposition of trade repositories *and* their respective national authorities to the establishment of a global trade repository took that option—which was favoured by most dealer banks and other cross-border derivatives traders—off the table. On the other hand, the dealer banks and other large traders mobilized in favour of the international harmonization of reporting rules. The industry became increasingly vocal about the costs of trade reporting resulting from different domestic rules across jurisdictions, and, therefore, lobbied for international harmonization. The financial industry, notably, the ISDA, SWIFT, the Depository Trust & Clearing Corporation (DTCC), also engaged in private-sector governance on these matters, working closely with regulators, which partly built on some of the private sector practices.

6
International Standards for CCPs

Financial market infrastructures for clearing, settling and reporting financial transactions form the 'backbone' of the financial system (Russo 2013). They include central counterparties (CCPs), central securities depositories (CSDs), trade repositories, payment, and securities settlement systems. After the crisis, following the mandatory central clearing of derivatives, CCPs became crucial nodes of the financial system because they had the potential to concentrate systemic risk (Bernanke 2011; Tucker 2011). Thus, new rules to improve the resilience, recovery, and resolution—which were referred to as the three 'Rs'—of CCPs were necessary. International rules for the resilience of CCPs were set first, followed by rules for the recovery and resolution of CCPs. Initially, the rule for the resilience of CCPs had limited granularity and the division of work among various international standard-setting bodies dealing with different aspects of CCPs regulation was unclear. Subsequently, the Joint Work Plan (FSB, BCBS, CPMI, IOSCO 2015) clarified the division of work and relatively more precise, stringent, and consistent rules for the resilience, recovery, and resolution of CCPs were issued in 2017, followed by guidance on supervisory stress testing in 2018.

The US and the UK were pace-setters internationally and partial first-movers domestically. Their preferences were shaped by the need to safeguard financial stability and protect the international competitiveness of their clearing industry. The EU had preferences that were, by and large, aligned with those of the US. However, the EU was mainly a fence-sitter internationally and a late-mover domestically, especially concerning the recovery and resolution of CCPs, because it lacked domestic regulatory capacity and the member states had somewhat heterogeneous preferences on important issues. Other jurisdictions, notably those on the fringe, were fence-sitters internationally and late-movers domestically, waiting for international rules to be set first because many of these jurisdictions set up domestic CCPs only after the crisis.

A variety of transgovernmental networks of domestic financial regulators were involved in international standard setting and deployed formal and informal coordination tools in order to promote regulatory consistency within the elemental regime on CCPs. This was important because the rules for the

The Politics of Regime Complexity In International Derivatives Regulation. Lucia Quaglia, Oxford University Press (2020).
 DOI: 10.1093/oso/9780198866077.003.0001

resilience of CCPs were designed to avoid the need to resort to recovery and resolution, and most of the tools used in the recovery of CCPs were also used in the resolution of CCPs. At the same time, financial interest groups mobilized in several international regulatory venues with a view to shaping the specific content of the new standards according to their preferences, mainly based on the distributional effects of the rules, that is, the expected costs and benefits. The heterogeneous interests of private actors concerning the tools for the recovery and resolution of CCPs partly cancelled out their respective influence on regulatory outcomes. At the same time, the mobilization of the industry in a multiplicity of international regulatory venues contributed to rule consistency.

This chapter first discusses some key issues concerning the regulation of the resilience, recovery, and resolution of CCPs. It, then, examines the CPSS-IOSCO's work on the resilience of CCPs, followed by a discussion of the CPSS/CPMI-IOSCO's work on the recovery of CCPs and the FSB's work on the resolution of CCPs. Subsequently, the analytical leverage of the state-led, the transgovernmental and the industry-led explanations is assessed against the empirical record. The chapter concludes by examining regulatory consistency within the elemental regime on the resilience, recovery, and resolution of CCPs, and its interlinkages with other elemental regimes on derivatives.

Key Issues in Regulating CCPs

Clearing is the process by which a 'clearing house', also called a 'central counterparty' (CCP), acts as a middleman for both the buyer and the seller of a financial instrument. As explained in Chapter 4, clearing through CCPs reduces and mutualizes counterparty credit risk and allows the 'multilateral netting' of transactions between market participants, which simplifies outstanding exposures (Murphy and Senior 2013). Clearing is important for financial stability given the huge volume of trades in derivatives that are conducted daily (Genito 2019). It is also a lucrative financial activity for those financial centres capable of attracting this business. The resilience of CCPs concerns their ability to withstand financial stress and avoid failure. Recovery, which occurs if resilience fails, involves the use of private sources of funding to keep CCPs operating. Resolution, which occurs if recovery fails, concerns the orderly wind-down of CCPs.

The resilience of CCPs partly depends on the rules set in place to deal with the different types of risk—credit, liquidity, business, and operational risks—to which CCPs are exposed (CPSS-IOSCO 2012a). It also depends on the level of risk in the system and that of the participants. The resilience of a CCP is improved by stringent credit risk requirements, that is to say, the amount of minimum financial resources that a CCP should have in order to be able to cover the default of a certain number of participants. According to the so-called 'cover one', a CCP should have financial resources to cover the default of the largest participant. According to 'cover two', a CCP should have enough resources to cover the default of the two largest participants. There should also be provisions for uncovered credit losses, that is to say, losses that go beyond the amount of financial resources that CCPs are required to hold. The 'rule-book' of CCPs[1] should indicate how to allocate uncovered losses through the 'default waterfall' and serve as a starting point for the recovery of CCPs.

Although recovery and resolution are strictly interconnected, there are important differences: they have distinct objectives, tools, and decision-making authorities. The objective of recovery is to restore the CCP to financial health, whereas the objective of resolution is to wind it down in an orderly manner without impairing its critical functions. However, both recovery and resolution share the objective of preserving financial stability and ensuring the continuity of critical functions. Recovery is carried out by the CCP, according to its rulebook, to which members of the CCP have to sign up. It is a contractual arrangement that is binding for participants, regardless of their jurisdiction. Resolution is carried out by the resolution authority. The recovery plan is prepared by the CCP and is then reviewed by the supervisory authority. The resolution plan is prepared by the resolution authority (FSB 2017a). Yet, the distinction between 'recovery and resolution is blurred for CCPs' and the 'tools which are ostensibly for resolution are effectively forms of recovery' (Singh and Turing 2018).

The CCP's rulebook indicates the default waterfall, which refers to the financial tools available to the CCP to cover losses arising from the default of a clearing member and the order in which these resources will be used. In case of default of a clearing member, the CCP first uses the resources of the defaulter (initial margins, and contributions to the default fund, explained below). Then, a tranche of CCP's capital (the so-called 'skin in the game') is used. It is a pre-defined tranche of a CCP's own funds that is typically positioned before additional losses are mutualized and after the resources of the defaulting member (ISDA 2015a). 'The amount of skin in the game is not

[1] The CCP's rulebook is a private contract between the CCP and its members. This contract defines the rights, obligations, and tools available to the CCP in the event of a clearing member's default.

calibrated with a view to constituting a significant amount of loss-absorbing resources. Rather, it is mainly designed to make sure that the incentives of CCPs are aligned with those of clearing members. In the past, CCPs were utilities, they were owned by their members, so their incentives were mutually aligned. Post-crisis, CCPs were for-profit entities, no longer owned by their members. Hence, the incentives of CCPs and clearing members were no longer aligned' (interview, January 2019).

Then, in the default waterfall of CCPs, there is the use of mutualized resources, that is, the default fund contributions of the clearing members and further calls on clearing members for unfunded default fund contributions. At the end of the default waterfall, the recovery plan kicks-in, setting the tools for replenishing financial resources. First, there are tools to allocate uncovered losses caused by member default: cash calls on participants, and position-based loss allocation tools, such as margin haircutting.[2] Initial margins are collected by the CCP to protect it and its members against the potential future default of a clearing member. The initial margin covers the obligations of the participant that posted it. Variation margins are funds that are collected by the CCP and paid out to reflect current exposures resulting from actual changes in market prices (Lockwood 2018). Margin haircutting could be limited to direct participants, or could be applied to the margin of all participants (direct and indirect). Another tool is the termination of unmatched contracts (known as 'tear-up') that could not be sold in an auction (CPSS-IOSCO 2012a). Finally, there are resolution-only tools that are mainly borrowed from the rules on bank resolution. These are: the sale of a CCP's entire business or the critical functions to a viable competitor; the creation of a publicly controlled 'bridge' CCP; the write-down of capital and debt instruments (bail-in); and the allocation of losses among clearing members.

What is distinctive in the case of CCPs is that some instruments used in recovery (e.g. cash calls, variation margin haircutting, the tearing up of contracts) can also be used in resolution, but the tools used in recovery are regulated by the CCP's rulebook (a private contract) and are deployed by the CCP, whereas resolution is regulated by statutory law and takes place under the aegis of the public authorities. As one interviewee (December 2018) put it, 'it does not make sense to separate recovery and resolution for CCPs, it is a continuum and, actually, for the most part, it is recovery because resolution is

[2] Margins are the cash or the securities that must be deposited by the clearing members as collaterals for a given position cleared through the CCP. Through 'haircutting', the value of an asset is calculated as the market value of the asset reduced by a certain percentage (the 'haircut').

the very last option for CCPs.... [T]he resolution authorities use tools lifted from the CCPs' rulebooks (e.g. tear up the contract), thus, resolution can be seen as an extension of recovery.' A CCP's recovery plan has implications for its resolution plan. Resolution, which is triggered by the supervisory authorities and then managed by the resolution authorities, could occur before the CCP's recovery tools have been exhausted. The line between recovery and resolution is not fixed and is likely to vary from jurisdiction to jurisdiction, according to the domestic regulatory framework. Consequently, 'recovery takes place in the shadow of resolution' (CPSS-IOSCO 2013).

A controversial issue is the use of CCPs equity (capital) and clearing members' resources in the recovery and resolution of CCPs (Peters 2019). In many CCPs, early on in the default waterfall, the CCP would bear losses with a view to limiting moral hazard. Some jurisdictions require a 'skin in the game' for CCPs, that is to say, the commitment of a given amount of the CCP's own financial resources in the event of a member default.[3] However, the amount of the CCP's own resources is unlikely to be sufficient to cover losses, which would then need to be allocated to participants, albeit maintaining appropriate incentives for owners to ensure that CCPs do not engage in excessive risk-taking (FSB 2018b). Yet, clearing members, gathered in the ISDA, especially, the large dealer banks, and buy-side participants are unhappy with this approach. They argue that it is unfair that it is the members—not the profit-seeking clearing company and its shareholders—that have to pay for the recovery and resolution of CCPs.

Other important issues in regulating the recovery and resolution of CCPs concern the following: use of taxpayer money, which is regarded as acceptable by some jurisdictions (for example, Canada), but not by others (such as the US); access to central bank liquidity, which is in place in some jurisdictions, but not in others; recovery-related powers of CCPs, which CCPs want as broad as possible; the resolution-related powers of the public authorities, which differ across jurisdictions; and allocation of financial losses, which, in turn, depends on the tools used in recovery and resolution and their sequencing. More generally, there is the need to prevent moral hazard, which would ensue from permitting various parties to take on extra risk for which, ultimately, they are not responsible. In other words, it is necessary to calibrate incentives and align responsibility and control (ISDA 2015b). 'It is all a question of incentives,

[3] For instance, CCPs in the EU are required to place 25% of their total minimum capital ahead of non-defaulting clearing members within the default waterfall. Furthermore, CCPs in Europe have to maintain minimum capital requirements of EUR 7.5m or, in aggregate, sufficient to ensure an orderly winding down (at a minimum six months of operating costs) (Huhtaniemi and Peters 2017).

everything in clearing is structured around incentives', as the chairman of the Chicago Mercantile Exchange (CME), Sunil Cutinho, put it (*Tradenews*, 25 November 2014).

A final issue that is explicitly discussed with reference to rules on resolution concerns the principle of 'no creditor worse off than in liquidation', including the 'counterfactual scenarios' to be used for this assessment and the possibility of compensation, if the intervention of the resolution authorities cause a deviation from the no creditor worse off principle. The expectation is that upon entry into resolution, any outstanding contractual obligations set out in the internal rulebook of the CCP (including outstanding recovery measures) should be honoured first. However, there may be exceptions, if the resolution authority determines, subject to the no creditor worse off safeguard and appropriate compensation measures, that other resolution actions are more appropriate. The question is, then, how to define the counterfactual scenario in order to calculate compensation (Huhtaniemi and Peters 2017).

The elemental regime on the three Rs fed into the regime complexity of post-crisis derivatives regulation in several ways. The most obvious interlinkage was the fact that the CPSS-IOSCO's (2012a) *Principles for Financial Market Infrastructures* set the prudential rules designed to strengthen the resilience of financial market infrastructures, including CCPs, so as to prevent them from getting into trouble, which would then trigger recovery, regulated by CPMI-IOSCO (2014, 2017c) and resolution, regulated by FSB (2014b, 2017a). Consequently, the stricter the prudential rules for CCPs (for example, the amount of financial resources to deal with various types of risk), the less likely it would be that CCPs would need to undergo recovery and resolution. In turn, the CPMI-IOSCO (2014, 2017c) rules on recovery overlapped with the FSB's (2014a, 2017a) rules on resolution and vice versa. Indeed, some of the instruments used for the recovery of CCPs are also used for their resolution and the resolution plan is often a continuation of the recovery plan (interviews, December 2018).

The resilience of CCPs partly depends on margin requirements. Furthermore, clearing members have to pay a contribution to the CCPs default fund. The more stringent the rules on margins and contributions to the default fund, the stronger the resilience of the CCPs, and the greater the resources available for the recovery and resolution of the CCPs. However, this also makes clearing more expensive for direct and indirect participants. All this could discourage central clearing, which was one of the key objectives of the post-crisis reform of derivatives markets. Furthermore, margin requirements for cleared derivatives had to be consistent with those for uncleared OTCDs in order to prevent regulatory arbitrage by structuring derivatives contracts in such a way as to elude the obligation for central clearing. Thus, the rules on CCPs margins were interlinked with the rules on margins for uncleared OTCDs, discussed in the penultimate chapter.

Another area of regulatory interlinkages concerned the elemental regime on CCPs and the elemental regime on banks (which was mainly the responsibility of the BCBS) because of the 'CCP-bank nexus', whereby given the potential 'destabilizing feedback loops, the risks of CCPs and banks should be considered jointly, rather than in isolation' (Faruqui et al. 2018). The Chairman of the Federal Reserve, Powell (2015) remarked that 'it is often noted that CCPs made it through the recent financial crisis without direct government assistance. But many of their major clearing members did receive such assistance. CCPs must now plan for a world in which these large firms will fail and be resolved without government support.... One effective way to make a CCP safer is to make its member banks safer.' Recent work by international standard-setters (FSB-BCBS-CPMI-IOSCO 2018b) mapped the interlinkages between CCPs and clearing members, the most important of which tended to be systemically important banks.

International Standards for the Resilience of CCPs

Following the post-crisis regulatory reforms mandating derivatives clearing through CCPs, several observers warned that 'CCPs will be the next AIG' (*Financial Times*, 1 May 2015). Andrew Bailey (2014), Deputy Governor of the Bank of England, pointed out the need for 'robust risk standards for CCPs, implemented consistently across jurisdictions'. In turn, the Chairman of the Federal Reserve, Ben Bernanke (2011), hoped that 'the regulatory agencies in the US, and those in other major countries, can adopt a single set of enhanced risk-management standards that will apply to all systemically important financial market utilities globally'. The starting point for the adoption of new post-crisis standards for the resilience of CCPs were the CPSS-IOSCO (2004) *Recommendations for CCPs*.

As one financial regulator remarked, 'after the international financial crisis, there was the need to move away from recommendations to something stronger in order to underpin the international clearing system. It was the first time that there was so much focus on this group of international standard-setters, namely, the CPSS and the IOSCO' (interview, June 2018). One option would have been to re-issue institution-specific standards (e.g. on

CCPs, payment and settlement systems), updating pre-crisis regulation. The other option would have been to have these different standards consolidated into one single document. This second option was eventually chosen, so it was a 'self-imposed complexity because it was not easy to issue standards suitable for various types of financial market infrastructures, such as CCPs, trade repositories, payment and settlement systems and so on' (interview, November 2018).

In April 2012, the CPSS-IOSCO issued the *Principles for Financial Market Infrastructures* (approximately 200 pages). The *Principles* included the pre-existing rules on payments and settlement systems, as well as recommendations for CCPs and trade repositories. This wide coverage partly explains the limited granularity of these standards. The CPSS-IOSCO (2012b) also developed an *Assessment Methodology* that was designed to be used both by the authorities and the infrastructures in order to facilitate the monitoring of compliance with the *Principles*. In addition, the IMF and the World Bank were to employ the *Methodology* in the context of their Financial Sector Assessment Program (Russo 2013). The *Principles* contained specific rules on credit risk, margins, and collaterals, liquidity risk, and general business risk.

In order to deal with credit risk, CCPs were required to maintain financial resources that were sufficient to cover the default of the clearing participant that would cause the largest credit exposure to the CCP. CCPs with 'more-complex risk profile' or that were 'systemically important in multiple jurisdictions' should maintain additional financial resources to cover the default of the two participants that would potentially cause the largest aggregate credit exposure (CPSS-IOSCO 2012a: 1). The previous CPSS-IOSCO *Recommendations for CCPs* (2004) only required the coverage of the largest single exposure. This move from the so-called 'cover one' to 'cover two' was advocated by the UK, with some support from the US, given the fact that these two jurisdictions had global CCPs. Cover two was resisted by jurisdictions, such as those in Asia, but also in some EU countries, which had small, mainly domestic CCPs, and which argued that it would be costly to move from cover one to cover two (interview, June 2018). The lining up of jurisdictions on this matter depended on the type of CCPs that they had. A compromise was, therefore, reached in the *Principles for Financial Market Infrastructures*: cover one for simple (mainly domestic) CCPs, clearing equities; and cover two for big CCPs, clearing OTCDs (James and Quaglia 2020a).

CCPs were required to have risk-based margins, whereby the initial margin methodologies should not only consider 'normal' market conditions (as required by the CPSS-IOSCO (2004) *Recommendations*), but also extreme events. In comparison to the CPSS-IOSCO (2004) *Recommendations*, the

CPSS-IOSCO (2012a: 43) *Principles* were more prescriptive about the methodology for calculating margins, for example, establishing that 'initial margin should meet an established single-tailed confidence level of at least 99 percent with respect to the estimated distribution of future exposure'. New rules were introduced concerning the segregation and portability of the positions of a participant's customers. Collaterals requirements were strengthened, CCPs were to enforce haircuts on collaterals and be aware of concentration limits. There were no specific rules on segregation, portability, and collaterals in the CPSS-IOSCO (2004) *Recommendations*.

As for liquidity risk, CCPs were required to maintain sufficient liquid resources in all relevant currencies to settle securities-related payments. In contrast to the requirements on credit risk, a CCP should only 'consider' maintaining additional liquidity resources sufficient to cover the default of the one or two largest participants, depending on whether, respectively, the CCP was domestic or systemically important, whereas the coverage of the one or two largest exposures was compulsory for credit risk. This difference was due to the fact that a requirement for liquidity risk was significantly more demanding than the same requirement for credit risk (Russo 2013). The CPSS-IOSCO (2004) *Recommendations* had no provisions on liquidity. One interviewee (June 2018) noted that the 'Bank of England and the Federal Reserve stressed the liquidity risk of CCPs, whereas, previously, the focus was on credit risk, but central banks tend to pay attention to liquidity'. In order to cover the general business risk, a financial market infrastructure should hold liquid net assets funded by equity equal to a least six months of current operating expenses (CPSS-IOSCO 2012a: 88), so that it could be able to continue its operations if it incurred general business losses.

Concerning the responsibilities of the authorities, the *Principles* (2012) deliberately did not discuss whether central banks or securities regulators should be responsible for the supervision of CCPs because various jurisdictions had different institutional frameworks in place at the national level. The CPSS-IOSCO standards left open who was the competent authority. Consequently, the central bank's oversight function, which mainly concerned system-wide financial stability, ran in parallel to the supervision of individual CCPs and, at times, created tensions, with the risk of placing multiple requirements on CCPs (interview, September 2018). The CPSS-IOSCO (2012a) *Principles* deliberately remained agnostic concerning CCPs access to central bank liquidity because different jurisdictions had heterogeneous preferences on this matter (e.g. Mersch 2017; Powell 2017) as well as different domestic institutional arrangements, as explained in the following section.

In international regulatory fora, the pace-setters seeking to trade up the rules on CCPs resilience were the US, the UK, and, to a more limited extent, the EU and the member states that had large CCPs (notably, France and Germany) (James and Quaglia 2020a). Policymakers in these jurisdictions were prompted by the need to protect the stability and competitiveness of their domestic clearing system, as elaborated below. Paul Tucker (2011), Deputy Governor of the Bank of England, defined the CCPs as 'system risk managers' as well as 'super-systemic', especially those clearing globally-traded instruments. The Chairman of the Federal Reserve, Ben Bernanke (2011), pointed out that 'increased reliance on clearing houses to address problems in other parts of the system increases the need to ensure the safety of clearing houses themselves. As Mark Twain's character Pudd'nhead Wilson once opined, if you put all your eggs in one basket, you better watch that basket.' The ECB supported the trading up of international standards for the resilience of CCPs. However, the ECB also pursued a distinctive euro area agenda on clearing, arguing that 'as a rule, the core infrastructures for the euro should be located in the euro area. When they are not located in the euro area, they should comply with the CPSS-IOSCO *Principles*, and with central bank-relevant policies, so as to preserve the integrity of the currency. Moreover, they should be subject to effective oversight by euro area authorities' (Cœuré 2012).

In terms of timing and sequencing, the CPSS-IOSCO standards were issued in 2012, shortly after the US had adopted some domestic rules on CCPs. The EU was in the process of finalizing its legislation, the EMIR. At any rate, the CPSS-IOSCO standards lacked the level of granularity that could have helped to prevent or settle the regulatory disputes that emerged between the US and the EU (Posner 2018). In particular, there were transatlantic disagreements on the requirement that non-US CCPs handling US trades should register with the CFTC and undergo joint supervision by the CFTC, as well as disagreements concerning the different margin requirements for CCPs in the US and the EU (Knaack 2015; Pagliari 2013b). These regulatory disputes risked the fragmentation of the global derivatives markets and were of particular concern to the main cross-border dealers and the global CCPs, as elaborated in the concluding chapter.

International Standards for the Recovery of CCPs

International standards for the recovery and resolution of CCPs were controversial because, potentially, taxpayer money could be involved. There was no specific international or national legislation on these matters; and, more generally, there was a 'knowledge-gap' (interview, November 2018). Hence, the discussion concerning these issues was delayed and, deliberately, the *Principles* stated that they did 'not directly address issues relating to the design and implementation of resolution and insolvency regimes for financial market infrastructure' (CPSS-IOSCO 2012a: 11). The *Principles* only established that a CCP should have default rules and procedures that enabled it to continue to meet its obligations in the event of a participant default. A CCP should also publicly disclose key aspects of its default rules and procedures in its rulebook. Once international standards to improve the resilience of financial market infrastructures were set, the regulatory debate moved on to discuss the recovery and resolution of financial market infrastructures, first and foremost, CCPs.

Initially, the recovery and resolution of financial market infrastructures were discussed by the CPSS-IOSCO (2012c), which for consultation issued a *Report on Recovery and Resolution of Financial Market Infrastructures*. The report put forward a number of questions concerning the methods, the scope, and the loss allocation arrangements. It also discussed how the recovery and resolution of financial market infrastructures related to the FSB's (2011) *Key Attributes of Effective Resolution Regimes for Financial Institutions*. Afterward, given the potential fiscal implications of resolving CCPs, finance ministry officials took an interest in this matter. This, combined with the fact that the FSB had already issued the *Key Attributes for the Resolution of Financial Institutions* in 2011 (FSB 2011), meant that the discussions concerning the resolution of CCPs were taken over by the FSB (2014b), whereas recovery continued to be discussed by the CPMI-IOSCO (2014).

The US and the UK were pace-setters in international standard setting for the recovery and resolution of CCPs, prompted by concerns about financial stability. As early as 2011, Paul Tucker of the Bank of England warned that if a CCP 'went bust', the result would be 'mayhem' that would be 'as bad as, conceivably worse than, the failure of large and complex bank.... We, therefore, need effective resolution regimes for CCPs.' The US and the UK were also partial first-movers, unilaterally, at the domestic level. The extension of the resolution regime from banks to CCPs that took place in the US and the UK partly informed the international regulatory debate on these issues. This approach was softly criticized by some observers, for example, the IMF (Singh and Turing 2018), which argued that 'the classic approach to resolving a bank' had 'little chance of success with a CCP', which were not banks. Therefore, the 'toolkit which has been assembled for resolving banks is of limited use for troubled CCPs. Furthermore, CCP resolution may have to take place much more rapidly than the resolution of a bank.'

In 2014, the CPMI-IOSCO issued a *Report on Recovery for Financial Market Infrastructures*, including CCPs, which was slightly revised in 2017. This report was intended to provide guidance on the recovery planning process and the content of the recovery plans, as well as a menu of tools for recovery. Given the fact that jurisdictions and the financial industry had different preferences on the recovery and resolution tools, the report specified that

> The inclusion of a tool in the report does not mean that it should necessarily be used by a financial market infrastructure. Moreover, some jurisdictions may not allow financial market infrastructures to use all the tools listed in this report, or may limit certain tools to specific types of FMIs. Moreover, a financial market infrastructure may have or seek to design additional or alternative tools to include in its recovery plan .... The triggers for entry into resolution may vary from jurisdiction to jurisdiction. Some tools may be used for either recovery or resolution. However, some jurisdictions may reserve certain tools for exclusive use by the resolution authorities.
>
> (CPMI-IOSCO 2014: 3)

In 2017, the CPMI-IOSCO (2017c) issued *Resilience and Recovery of Central Counterparties (CCPs): Further Guidance on the Principles for Financial Market Infrastructures*, which was designed to provide clarity and granularity concerning the implementation of the *Principles* with reference to CCPs. The *Guidance* included more details about how to put recovery into practice: the definition of the internal procedures that CCPs should follow; their sequencing; the rebuilding of depleted financial resources; and the testing of recovery plans. It also discussed new items, namely, the amount of CCPs' skin in the game and the possibility for CCPs to issue bail-in-able debt.

International Standards for the Resolution of CCPs

In parallel to the CPSS/CPMI-IOSCO's discussion on the recovery of financial market infrastructures, the FSB carried out work on the resolution of financial market infrastructures. In 2014, the FSB (2014b) reissued the *Key Attributes of Effective Resolution Regimes for Financial Institutions*, incorporating guidance on their application to non-bank financial institutions in four new Annexes. *Annex 1 Resolution of Financial Market Infrastructures*, including CCPs, was developed by the FSB in conjunction with the CPMI and the IOSCO. It was a start, but more detailed provisions were necessary, and the FSB continued its work of standard setting. In 2016, the FSB issued a discussion note on *Essential Aspects of CCP Resolution Planning*, specifically focusing on the resolution of CCPs. A range of comments was received from the private actors in the financial industry for and against the use of different tools, expressing heterogeneous preferences on whom losses should or should not fall in resolution, as elaborated below.

In July 2017, the FSB issued *Guidance on Resolution and Resolution Planning for Central Counterparties (CCPs)*, which complemented the FSB *Key Attributes of Effective Resolution Regimes* (2011, 2014b) by providing guidance on implementing the *Attributes* in the resolution of CCPs. The *Guidance* covered: the policy objectives for CCPs resolution; the powers of the resolution authorities; the indicators for entering a CCP into resolution; the use of loss allocation tools in resolution; the no creditor worse off safeguard; resolution planning, including resolvability and cross-border cooperation, also through crisis management groups for systemically important CCPs. According to the no creditor to worse-off safeguard, clearing members, equity holders, and creditors should have a right to compensation if the resolution authority departed from the loss allocation under the CCP's rulebook, or if they did not receive in resolution, at a minimum, what they would have received in the case of liquidation. The resolution authority should also have the power to compensate clearing members that contributed financial resources to resolution in excess of their obligations under the CCP's rules. The means of compensation envisaged were equity or debt instruments.

In the preparation of this document, the main issues discussed by members of the FSB concerned: the timing of entry in resolution (whether this should be at a presumptive point during the CCP's recovery process or not) and the sequencing of resolution tools (whether these should follow a fixed sequence or allow more flexibility) (Huhtaniemi and Peters 2017). The 'Anglo-Saxons were keen to use the CCPs rulebook for recovery and resolution, embedding recovery and resolution in the contractual relations between the CCPs and their members, with the use of a clear toolkit and a fixed chain of events that could give certainty to stakeholders.... This would limit the flexibility of tools available to the resolution authorities. Also, these jurisdictions tended to rule out resolution, focusing only on recovery.' In contrast, 'continental member states wanted to base resolution on legislative texts, not contractual relations, giving more powers to the public authorities through the use of a flexible toolkit' (interviews, February 2019). The second issue concerned the principle of no creditor worse off than in liquidation, specifically, the counterfactual scenarios to be used for this assessment and the possibility of compensation, if the intervention of the resolution authorities caused a deviation from the no creditor worse off principle. The consensus was to use the CCP's rulebook and assess the deviations from it.[4]

In the preparation of the *Guidance* by the FSB (2017a), some controversial issues were deliberately left open, notably, the financial resources to support the resolution of CCPs and the treatment of CCPs equity in resolution (interview, February 2019). Subsequently, the FSB (2018b), in collaboration with the CPMI-IOSCO, issued for consultation a discussion paper on *Financial Resources to Support CCP Resolution and the Treatment of CCP Equity in Resolution,* evaluating whether existing tools were adequate for resolving CCPs as well as possible approaches to the treatment of CCPs equity in resolution. The main issues were to what extent, and at which stage of resolution, should CCPs equity be used to absorb losses. This matter juxtaposed the interests of the CCPs, which wanted equity to be used to absorb losses as late as possible and as little as possible, to those of the other participants, which held the opposite preferences. Furthermore, the preferences of the public authorities were not entirely aligned within jurisdictions. For instance, the resolution authorities, notably the FDIC, wanted CCPs equity to be subject to full write down in the case of resolution, whereas some supervisory authorities, such as the CFTC and the SEC, wanted to have some safeguards for CCPs equity (interview, January 2019).

Once the international standards for the resilience, recovery and resolution of CCPs were issued (for an overview of these standards see Table 6.1), the regulatory discussions considered the implementation of the new rules. The US and the UK continued to be pace-setters internationally. According to David Bailey (2014) of the Bank of England, there were areas in which 'international standards could benefit from additional guidance. . . . For example, one clear area of the current international standards that could be further developed to strengthen CCPs' resilience relates to stress testing requirements . . . otherwise, it may be difficult for participants to fully compare the level of stress that CCPs can withstand.' Similarly, Jerome Powell (2014) of the Federal Reserve noted that 'it is time for domestic and international regulators to consider steps to strengthen credit and liquidity stress testing

[4] There were also discussions concerning the (different) tools to be used for losses deriving from the default of participants and losses not deriving from participants default (e.g. operational failure of CCPs).

Table 6.1 International standards for the resilience, recovery and resolution of CCPs

International standard-setting body	Date of issuance	Standards (framework, guidance, etc)
CPSS-IOSCO	2012	Principles for Financial Market InfrastructuresAssessment Methodology
CPSS-IOSCO	2012	Report on Recovery and Resolution of Financial Market Infrastructures
CPSS-IOSCO	2014	Report on Recovery for Financial Market Infrastructures
FSB	2014	Key Attributes of Effective Resolution Regimes for Financial Institutions + Annex 1 Resolution of Financial Market Infrastructures
CPMI-IOSCO	2017	Resilience and Recovery of CCPs: Guidance on Principles for Financial Market Infrastructures
FSB	2017	Guidance on Resolution and Resolution Planning for CCPs
CPMI-IOSCO	2018	Framework for Supervisory Stress Testing of CCPs
FSB-BCBS-CPMI-IOSCO	2018	Analysis of Central Clearing Interdependencies

conducted by CCPs.... [B]oth clearing members and regulators need a more systematic view of what stress tests are performed...there are also important questions about the comparability of stress scenarios, assumptions, and results'. In 2018, after public consultation, the CPMI-IOSCO (2018b) issued the *Framework for Supervisory Stress Testing of Central Counterparties*. The framework made clear that it was designed to support the authorities for the purpose of 'evaluating broad, macro-level impacts across multiple CCPs, rather than assessing the adequacy of resources at specific CCPs, which is typically an objective of microprudential stress testing' (CPMI-IOSCO 2018b). Therefore, for microprundential stress testing, national regulators remained free to use their own (often different) models.

Another issue that later on entered the international regulatory agenda, and well illustrates regime complexity, was the interdependency of CCPs and banks as a result of post-crisis reforms that forced much of the OTCDs market into central clearing. A joint study conducted by the FSB, the BCBS, the CPMI, and the IOSCO (2018b) revealed that many of twenty-six CCPs examined across fifteen jurisdictions had relationships with the same financial entities. Concentration was high with 88% of financial resources, including initial margin and default funds, held by ten CCPs. Of the 307 clearing members included in the analysis, the largest twenty accounted for 75% of financial resources provided to CCPs. More than 80% of the CCPs surveyed were exposed to at least ten global systemically important banks. The study stressed the 'CCP–bank nexus' (FSB, BCBS, CPMI, IOSCO 2018b), discussing the endogenous interactions between CCPs and banks in periods of stress and concluding that given the 'potentially destabilizing feedback loops, the risks of banks and CCPs should be considered jointly, rather than in isolation' (this point is further discussed in the concluding chapter).

State-Centric Explanation of Standard Setting for the 3 Rs of CCPs

The US and the UK were pace-setters in promoting international standards for the resilience, recovery, and resolution of CCPs. These jurisdictions have leading international financial centres that trade and clear massive volumes of derivatives and have several globally active CCPs and dealer banks in their territory.[5] Consequently, after the crisis, policymakers in these countries were keen to tighten up the regulation of CCPs in order to safeguard domestic financial stability. Domestic rules would not suffice to this end because CCPs were established in many jurisdictions after the crisis and were used by US and UK derivatives dealers. Hence, the US and the UK wanted to avoid negative externalities deriving from the potential failure of loosely regulated CCPs abroad as well as preserving the competitiveness of the financial industry in the US and the UK, given the fact that stringent regulation means higher costs for CCPs, clearing members and end-users (James and Quaglia 2020a). Many CCPs were for-profit entities owned by exchanges—they were not public utilities—hence they jostled for a slice of clearing business in the post-crisis regulatory context (interview, January 2019). Andrew Gracie (2015), senior official at the Bank of England, explained that the CPMI-IOSCO's work on CCPs resilience was 'important not only in its own right, but also to provide the market—the users of CCPs—with the tools and incentives to monitor resilience and drive effective risk management in CCPs themselves. To

[5] The main CCPs worldwide are the London Clearing House (LCH) in the UK, the Depository Trust & Clearing Corporation (DTCC), the Chicago Mercantile Exchange (CME) Clearing, the Intercontinental Exchange Clear (ICE) CCPs, which are all based in the US, but also operate with subsidiaries in the UK. Collectively, these CCPs account for most of the clearing activity globally. However, the list of CCPs that are recognized as systemically important in more than one country also includes CCPs outside the US and the UK, such as Eurex Clearing in Germany; Bolsas y Mercados Españoles (BME) Clearing in Spain; Cassa di Compensazione e Garanzia in Italy; EuroCCP in the Netherlands; Hong Kong Futures Exchange Limited (HKFE) Clearing Corporation in Hong Kong.

encourage *competition* between CCPs on *resilience*, not *cost*' (emphasis in *italics* added).

Moreover, the rules on the resilience of CCPs have implications for the rules on the recovery and resolution of CCPs, which also have considerable cross-border implications, potentially resulting in negative externalities in the leading financial centres. As Paul Tucker (2011) explained:

> The largest CCPs are systemically relevant at a global level, important for financial stability in multiple jurisdictions due to the nature of their business and the composition of their members and users. They serve multiple markets, having dozens of clearing members from different countries and clearing products in multiple currencies. A patch-work of approaches to recovery and resolution would risk regulatory arbitrage and competitive distortion and so, whilst the fiscal backstop against the unsuccessful resolution of a CCP is ultimately a national one, it is best that the answer on how to avoid this backstop ever being used is developed at a global level.

Similarly, the chairman of the Federal Reserve, Ben Bernanke (2011), noted that 'Coordination among regulators, both within and between countries, is especially important in light of the increasing interdependencies among financial market utilities [CCPs] around the world.' For all these reasons, the US and the UK had incentives to act as pace-setters, promoting post-crisis international standards for the resilience, recovery, and resolution of CCPs. Moreover, the US and UK were well-placed to take the lead because of their market power, that is, the size of their financial sector and the fact that they were leading international financial centres. These jurisdictions also had considerable expertise in these matters: they were exposed to thinking by industry experts and did a lot of work in this domain post-crisis with a view to developing domestic rules (Helleiner 2014; James and Quaglia 2020a). Moreover, senior US and UK officials chaired key international committees and working groups dealing with the regulation of CCPs, as detailed below.

At the domestic level, the US and the UK were partial first-movers in that they developed domestic rules on CCPs resilience and extended the rules on bank resolution to CCPs prior to or in parallel with international standards. In the US, specific provisions on CCPs were included in the Dodd-Frank Act (2010) and subsequent enacting regulation. The CFTC issued rules on derivatives clearing organizations (the term used for CCPs clearing derivatives in the US) in 2011–12 and the FDIC, which was the resolution authority for banks, was appointed as the resolution authority also for CCPs. The resolution regime for CCPs in the UK, which was introduced by the Financial Services Act (2012), was inspired by that in the banking sector, and in fact, the Bank of England became the resolution authority also for CCPs. Yet, even in these jurisdictions, the domestic regulatory debate ran in parallel and intersected with the international debate, especially on the recovery and resolution of CCPs. Indeed, the authorities in both the US and the UK (see, for example, Bank of England 2012) openly acknowledged that they would need to revise domestic rules after the adoption of international standards.

The EU and its member states, which were in the process of setting up or substantially expanding CCPs on their territory, also faced a trade-off between domestic financial stability and the international competitiveness of the clearing industry. A senior ECB official, Daniela Russo (2013), argued that international standards were warranted because 'the membership, product and currency coverage of financial market infrastructures and their related financial risk implications have become increasingly cross-border in nature. Furthermore, interdependencies between financial market infrastructures have also grown significantly.' With reference to the recovery and resolution of CCPs, a member of the Executive Board of the ECB, Benoît Cœuré (2018), remarked that 'the disorderly failure of a major CCP would be disastrous. Many CCPs are globally systemic, responsible for clearing global markets and with participants from across the world.' Thus, the EU supported the pace-setting efforts of the US and the UK at the international level.

However, the EU was unable to take the lead internationally, despite the size of its financial market because the EU lacked expertise and domestic regulatory templates on these matters, which weakened its negotiating position in international regulatory fora. Domestically, the EU was a late-mover: it adopted rules on CCPs resilience in 2012, which were partly based on international standards, as openly acknowledged in the preamble of the EMIR, but were much more detailed. The European Commission proposed a directive on CCPs recovery and resolution as late as 2017, only after the CPMI-IOSCO (2017c) and the FSB (2017a) had adopted their *Guidance*, so as to ensure consistency between the international rules and the prospective EU rules. The adoption of the proposed legislation was subsequently slowed down by the negotiations concerning the supervision of CCPs, which was part and parcel of the revision of EMIR (the so-called EMIR 2), which, in turn, was affected by Brexit.

Furthermore, whereas most of the supervisory competencies on CCPs remained at the national level, the Commission, the ESMA, and the ECB were keen to increase EU-level supervision and expand their respective competences on CCPs. The ESMA and the ECB were eager to acquire new power concerning, respectively, the supervision and the oversight of EU and non-EU CCPs. The ECB also called for the relocation of non-euro area CCPs to the euro area on financial stability grounds (it was the so-called 'location policy'). Indeed, the Bank worried about the fact that UK-based CCPs, which cleared large amounts of euro-denominated instruments, were not supervised by the authorities of the euro area (i.e. the ECB). Yet, the ECB would have to provide liquidity in euro to non-euro area CCPs in case of emergency. For this reason, a member of the Executive Board of the ECB, Eddie Mersch (2018), underscored that 'liability and control need to be well aligned. The ECB must be able to monitor and control the risks posed by CCPs.' This issue came prominently to the fore in the context of Brexit because the UK, where the bulk of euro-denominated derivatives are cleared, would become a third country, and would no longer be subject to EU regulation (James and Quaglia 2020a,b).

The member states resisted the centralization of the supervision of CCPs at the EU level, be it with the ESMA or the ECB. The member states also had somewhat heterogeneous preferences about the recovery and resolution of CCPs. For example, policymakers in France and Germany were reluctant to accept the haircutting of margins as a resolution tool, whereas Italian policymakers supported it on the grounds that it provided an additional tool to the authorities (interview, February 2019). European countries, other than France and Germany, were somewhat less engaged in the international standard-setting process because many CCPs in the EU were set up after the CPSS-IOSCO (2012a) *Principles* had been agreed upon and, at any rate, there were only nine CCPs at that time in the euro area. Member states that had global CCPs were the UK, France, Germany, Italy, Spain, and the Netherlands. But only two CCPs, Eurex (Germany) and LCH.Clearnet (France), cleared OTCDs in the EU. Thus, France and Germany were the most active in the international regulatory debate as well as in the UK–EU negotiations on euro clearing in the context of Brexit (see James and Quaglia 2020a,b).

Other jurisdictions, especially those in Asia, were fence-sitters internationally and late-movers domestically. International standards concerning the three Rs of CCPs were not particularly penalizing for jurisdictions on the fringe. It is true that that the move from 'cover one' to 'cover two' for credit risk—which was one of the main post-crisis regulatory reforms—was less difficult for global CCPs (like the ones in the UK and the US), which had many large customers (the dealer banks), than for small domestic CCPs, whose members were domestically focused banks (James and Quaglia 2020a). However, some EU member states and the US also had small domestic CCPs, not only jurisdictions in Asia. Eventually, a compromise solution was found in the CPSS-IOSCO working group that drafted the *Principles*, as explained above. Furthermore, jurisdictions on the fringe lacked subject-specific expertise and domestic regulatory templates, not least because, prior to the financial crisis, these jurisdictions did not have domestic CCPs. Hence, international standards were instrumental in informing the domestic regulation of newly established CCPs in these countries. For example, the Monetary Authority of Singapore extended the resolution regime for banks to CCPs in 2012 and, following the work of the CPMI-IOSCO and the FSB, the Authority consulted on recovery and resolution rules for CCPs. In Hong Kong, the regulation of CCPs recovery and resolution lagged behind and remained at an earlier stage than for banks (IMF 2019).

Did the 'great powers' (Drezner 2007) play a role in promoting consistency across the elemental regime on CCPs? It is true that the US, the UK, and, to a lesser extent, the EU were the main drivers of post-crisis international standards for CCPs. For instance, these jurisdictions chaired some of the key committees. The CPSS-IOSCO Steering Group on the resilience of CCPs was co-chaired by the Federal Reserve, the SEC, and the FSA of Japan, whereas the Editorial Team was co-chaired by the SEC and the ECB. The CPMI-IOSCO Working Group on the recovery of CCPs was co-chaired by the CFTC and the ECB. The Chair of the FSB Resolution Steering Group was the Chair of the European Single Resolution Board. Yet, the empirical evidence suggests that the main jurisdictions faced several hindrances in coordinating the activities of international standard-setters.

To begin with, when international standards were set, no jurisdiction had a fully fledged domestic regulatory template on the recovery and resolution of CCPs. Hence, national policymakers did not have (pre-set) preferences deriving from existing domestic regulatory frameworks. Furthermore, a multiplicity of domestic regulatory authorities was involved in the US and the EU, with different competences and regulatory outlooks. On the US side, the CPSS-IOSCO Working Group that prepared the *Principles* included officials from the CFTC, the SEC, the Federal Reserve Board of New York, the Board of Governors of the Federal Reserve. The FDIC was involved in the FSB Working Group on resolution. On certain issues, the preferences of domestic regulatory agencies were not aligned. The Federal Reserve primarily paid attention to matters of concern for central banks, notably, the liquidity resources of CCPs and their access to central bank liquidity (interview, January 2019). The CFTC and the SEC, which supervise different types of CCPs, at times, had uneasy relations at the domestic and international levels, as pointed out, for example, by the Report of the US Treasury (2017), which recommended that these agencies should work more closely together, so as to minimize 'rule overlaps'. The FDIC, which is the resolution authority for CCPs, also had its own institutional preferences, clearly expressed when tools for CCPs resolution were discussed, supporting the wiping out of CCPs capital, which was, instead, resisted by the CFTC. For the US Treasury, the priority in setting the rules on the recovery and resolution of CCPs was to rule out taxpayer support. Several interviewees pointed out that the US positions very much depended on which domestic authority took the lead in a given regulatory venue, or on a certain matter (see also Lavelle 2019).

The EU's internal and external coordination concerning the elemental regime on three Rs of CCPs was also problematic. To begin with, the EU did not have domestic regulatory templates on the recovery and resolution of CCPs, and EU legislation was proposed as late as 2017. The European Commission, the ECB, the ESMA, and the member states had heterogeneous preferences concerning the supervision, recovery, and resolution of CCPs (James and Quaglia 2020a,b). Moreover, the fact that the main member states were involved in the international standard-setting process, together with the EU authorities, did not improve the external coordination of the EU. For example, the CPSS-IOSCO Working Group, which was co-chaired by the ECB, also included officials from the Commission and the ESMA (as observers) and from eight member states (UK, France, Germany, Italy, Spain, the Netherlands, Belgium, and Sweden). Previous research points out the absence of a cohesive position of the EU internationally, if the EU lacks a domestic regulatory template to upload (Quaglia 2014b) and both the EU authorities and the national authorities are present in the same international venues (Mügge 2011a). The UK position was better coordinated because the Bank of England was in the driving seat (albeit the FSA was also involved), but, then, the issue of CCPs regulation and supervision became entangled in the Brexit negotiations and the tug of war on the clearing of euro-denominated instruments.

Transgovernmental Explanation of Standard Setting for the 3 Rs of CCPs

International standard setting for the resilience recovery and resolution of CCPs started basically from scratch because there were no pre-existing international rules, albeit domestic rules were in the process of being discussed in the US and the EU. Transgovernmental networks of regulators in standard-setting bodies contributed to ironing out disagreements among jurisdictions, for example, concerning cover one or cover two for credit risk, the use of statutory or contractually based tools for resolution, and the counterfactual scenarios to be used to assess the 'no creditor worse off than in liquidation'. International fora were also instrumental in reconciling the priorities of various networks of regulators, which had different competences and regulatory outlooks. To begin with, central bankers do 'oversight' of CCPs, which is system-wide, informal, based on 'moral suasion'. Securities regulators do 'supervision', which focuses on individual CCPs and is a formal process based on rules and litigation. In the discussion concerning the tools for the recovery and resolution of CCPs, the different views of central bankers and securities markets regulators had to be brought together. For example,

> the suspension of clearing in case of CCPs resolution was fine for financial stability – that was the concern of central bankers, which also paid attention to the stability of clearing members, mostly dealer banks. But, for securities market regulators – which focused on markets and products – the suspension of clearing was difficult to accept because certain OTCDs were subject to mandatory clearing via CCPs. Securities markets regulators tend to pay less attention to pro-cyclical effects and systemic repercussions of their choices, they focus on the individual CCP and its stability, not that of the system. Central banks pay attention to pro-cyclical effects and to how the problems of CCPs affect clearing members (banks) (interview, January 2019).

Another example was the allocation of the costs of recovery and resolution: 'securities markets regulators sought to protect the final investors, thus securities markets regulators paid attention to the losses suffered, for example, by pension funds and collective investment funds, etc. These were indirect clearing members, which had different interests from direct clearing members (large banks). Banking supervisors, instead, were more interested in the effects of CCPs recovery and resolution on banks, most of which were direct clearing members' (interview, January 2019). These discussions played out in the CPSS/CPMI-IOSCO Working Group on recovery and the FSB Working Group on resolution.

It was a process of trial and error, not least because it was a new area of financial regulation. One interviewee (December 2018) remarked that 'certain resolution tools were prescribed for CCPs by copying what was done for banks, without really thinking whether these tools were transferable or not, and whether they could work or not for CCPs.... Several resolution tools that are used for banks do not provide financial resources (i.e. liquidity) to keep the

CCPs going, and therefore are not suitable to be applied to CCPs. . . . To keep ailing CCPs afloat, you need liquidity. The non-liquidity tools would not work for CCPs. So far, they have never been used once for CCPs, but they have been widely used for banks. That is part of the problem: there is limited technical knowledge in and practical experience of the recovery and resolution of CCPs. That is true at the international, EU and national levels.' Over time, regulatory discussions taking place in the CPSS/CPMI-IOSCO and the FSB contributed to developing a more rounded understanding of specific tools for CCPs recovery and resolution.

Nonetheless, on certain issues that were controversial, either from a political or a bureaucratic point of view, no agreement was reached and/or the standards issued remained rather general. For instance, capital requirements for CCPs and the amount of their skin in the game, initially, were not discussed by international standard-setting bodies. On the one hand, regulators were keen to point out that, unlike banks (which mainly rely on capital), CCPs had three main lines of defence: margins, default fund contributions, and CCPs' own resources (capital) (Domanski et al. 2015). On the other hand, over time, the FSB (2018b) sought to move this discussion forward with a view to setting international rules, for instance, on the treatment of CCPs equity in resolution.

Other times, the standards were deliberately rather general, as in the case of CCPs' access to central bank liquidity. On this matter, various jurisdictions (and central banks therein) had heterogenous preferences as well as different domestic institutional arrangements. In the euro area and in the UK, CCPs had access to central bank liquidity. The ECB and the Bank of England announced their willingness to backstop CCPs under a limited set of circumstances. Moreover, in France and Germany (but not in the UK or Italy), CCPs had a banking license, so they had access to central bank liquidity like 'normal' credit institutions. Yet, CCPs did not have access to central bank liquidity in all jurisdictions. In the US, CCPs that were designated as systemically important had access to the Federal Reserve, but not the other CCPs. Central bankers themselves had different views on this matter. The Chairman of the Federal Reserve, Ben Bernanke (2011), pointed out that the 'existence of emergency credit facilities for financial market utilities could give rise to moral hazard'.

In contrast, the ECB (Mersch 2018) was upfront about the need for CCPs to get access to central bank liquidity, arguing that 'in extreme situations, liquidity shortfalls could foster contagion and lead to CCPs and banks becoming distressed. This could mean the ECB needs to provide liquidity to systemic CCPs or to their members to ensure that payment systems continue to function smoothly and that monetary policy can be transmitted effectively' (see also Mersch 2017). The Bank of England favoured some constructive ambiguity. Deputy Governor, Paul Tucker (2013), argued that 'central banks will ensure that there are no technical obstacles in the way of their providing liquidity to a solvent and viable CCP at short notice. Central banks are absolutely not committing to provide such support. Private sector liquidity absolutely must be the first port of call, and so CCPs should not rely on central bank funds in their liquidity planning.' Given the different preferences, the CPMI-IOSCO *Report* (2014) and *Further Guidance* (2017c) remained agnostic on this issue.

Transgovernmental networks in standard-setting bodies also played an important role in promoting regulatory consistency and managing regime complexity because there were several interlinkages concerning the resilience, recovery, and resolution of CCPs. In order to promote international regulatory consistency, a variety of coordination tools were deployed (see Quaglia and Spendzharova 2020a). The most important formal mechanism was the work plan to enhance the resilience, recovery, and resolution of CCPs, which the G20 Finance Ministers and Central Bank Governors tasked the FSB, the BCBS, the IOSCO, and the CPSS/CPMI to agree upon. Although the joint work plan in 2015 was agreed on by all the committees, it was issued by the FSB plenary. So, the FSB had a leading role (interview, January 2019).

The work plan stated that: the CPMI-IOSCO should remain the primary forum for international cooperation on the regulation, supervision, and oversight of CCPs, including recovery, given the 'the substantial existing CPMI-IOSCO expertise on CCP resilience'. The FSB Resolution Standing Group was to be the focal point for work on the resolution of CCPs, in close cooperation with the CPMI-IOSCO. This arrangement was also intended to enable regulators to consider the impact of CCPs resolution on banks and other financial institutions. The BCBS would remain the primary forum for the international coordination concerning bank exposures to CCPs, given 'the depth of the BCBS's expertise on issues of bank supervision and regulation'. Following the issuance of the work plan, the coordination between international standard-setters and their regulatory outputs improved. The Joint Chairs' Report in 2017 confirmed that the initial work plan had largely been completed, albeit drawing attention to 'several points of interaction between CCP recovery and resolution in order to ensure the consistency between their respective policies'.

Other tools that were used in order to address the challenges of coordination between various transgovernmental networks dealing with the resilience, recovery, and resolution of CCPs and promote the consistency of their regulatory outputs were joint working groups with mixed membership. Hence, the

CPSS-IOSCO set up a Steering Group that coordinated the review of standards for financial market infrastructures, and an Editorial Team that implemented the review. The co-chairs of the Steering Group and the Editorial team came from both parent committees, hence they were central bankers and securities markets regulators of major jurisdictions. The other members of these groups were a mix of central bankers and securities markets regulators. The FSB, which took the lead in coordinating among the three bodies, included members from the CPSS/CPMI, the BCBS, and the IOSCO. Furthermore, a joint study group of the BCBS, the FSB and the IOSCO was established in 2015 to analyse interdependencies between CCPs and major clearing members (banks).

Finally, the tool of cross-referencing each other's standards used to promote consistency. For example, the CPMI-IOSCO *Recovery of Financial Market Infrastructures* (2014: 1) states that 'this report is consistent with the *Key Attributes of Effective Resolution Regimes for Financial Institutions* of the FSB'. It also points out that 'this report is intended to provide supplemental guidance to the CPSS-IOSCO (2012a) *Principles for Financial Market Infrastructures* regarding recovery planning' (CPMI-IOSCO 2014: 4). The FSB (2014b: 68) *Key Attributes of Effective Resolution Regimes for Financial Institutions, Annex 1: Resolution of Financial Market Infrastructures* makes clear that 'The scope of the guidance is aligned with that of the CPSS-IOSCO *Principles for Financial Market Infrastructures* (2012a)'.

Industry-Led Explanation of Standard setting for the 3 Rs of CCPs

International standard setting for the resilience of CCPs did not have major distributional implications for the financial industry. CCPs, derivatives dealers and end-users were broadly supportive of the CPSS-IOSCO (2012a) *Principles.* The main financial associations actually asked for more fully fledged international rules that would facilitate cross-border business. The Institute of International Finance (IIF) (2010) pointed out the need to move rapidly to a 'complete set of fully developed international standards' in this area because the US and the EU were in the process of adopting their own rules on the matter, which could lead to market fragmentation. Similarly, the ISDA (2011b) called for 'an effective harmonized international framework for financial market infrastructures'. Furthermore, the main trade associations, namely, the International Swaps and Derivatives Association (ISDA), the Clearing House and Institute of International Finance (IIF) (ISDA et al. 2013b), the

Investment Management Association (IMA) (2013a), as well as regional and national banking associations (e.g. EBF 2013a; FBF 2013a) pointed out the need for bespoke international rules on CCPs, which were very different from other types of financial market infrastructures.

Recovery and resolution had major distributional implications for different parts of the financial industry, which had competing interests. The main sets of players were: the CCPs, the direct participants, namely, the clearing members (mainly, dealer banks) and the indirect participants, that is, the buy-side (such as investment funds and pension funds) and the end-users of derivatives, which accessed CCPs via clearing members. The crux of the matter concerned how losses should be allocated among CCPs, direct participants, and indirect participants. Each group was keen to shift the costs of recovery and resolution onto the other groups. Briefly, CCPs were critical of the skin in the game (i.e. the use of CCPs' capital to cover losses) and wanted direct and indirect participants to contribute to the recovery of CCPs in order to avoid resolution. Direct participants supported CCPs' skin in the game and wanted indirect participants to contribute to the recovery of CCPs in order to avoid resolution. Indirect participants favoured CCPs' skin in the game, opposed their contribution to CCPs' recovery and resolution, and favoured resolution, instead of recovery. Hence, CCPs, direct participants and indirect participants, respectively, had aligned preferences across jurisdictions and mobilized in a variety of international regulatory venues in order to articulate their interests. Their preferences partially 'canceled out' each other, and partially contributed to watering down the content of international standards, which remained rather general regarding key distributional issues. For example, international standards did not prescribe a specific cap for the exposure of direct participants to CCPs, or whether indirect participants should share losses or not.

With reference to the work on recovery, CCPs sought to shape the content of the proposed rules in a way that would be favourable to them. Thus, the European Association of Clearing Houses (EACH 2013a) supported retaining a balance between the 'automatic implementation' of the recovery tools and the 'discretion' of CCPs. The EACH (2016) strongly supported the sharing of losses as widely as possible, not ruling out loss allocation to indirect participants as well as direct participants. The CCP12 (2016), which represents a group of CCPs in various jurisdictions, pointed out the need 'to balance the goal of ensuring proper risk management incentives for the CCP and ensuring proper default management incentives for the non-defaulting clearing members.... If set inappropriately, CCPs' skin in the game can dampen the clearing members' incentives to participate in the recovery'.

Similarly, the main US-based CCP and the largest in the world, the Depository Trust & Clearing Corporation (DTCC) (2013a), believed that the CPSS and the IOSCO should avoid 'specific loss allocation rules' and a 'one-size-fits-all approach'. Financial market infrastructures should have 'sufficient discretion' to act during the recovery phase. It stressed that given the ability of financial market infrastructures to adopt legally binding rules to allocate losses arising from a participant's default on an ex-ante basis (the rulebook), 'recovery tools would be as effective, if not more so, as resolution tools for allocating losses'. The Depository Trust & Clearing Corporation (DTCC) (2016) was critical of pre-defined rules on CCPs' skin in the game. The largest CCP in the EU, the London Clearing House (LCH) (2013), and the largest CCP on the Continent, Eurex (2013), pleaded in favour of having a variety of tools available for recovery, and some 'discretion' and 'flexibility' in using them, drawing a clear distinction between recovery and resolution.

The dealer banks in a joint response issued by the ISDA, the Clearing House and the Institute of International Finance (IIF) (2013), called for limited liability for clearing participants with respect to their CCP exposures, stressing that any loss allocation mechanism should apply equally to all clearing participants. In a subsequent joint response, the ISDA, the Association for Financial Markets in Europe (AFME), the Asia Securities Industry & Financial Markets Association (ASIFMA), the Clearing House, the Futures Industry Association (FIA), the Global Financial Markets Association (GFMA), the Institute of International Finance (IIF), the ISDA, and the Securities Industry and Financial Markets Association (SIFMA) (2016a) noted that CCPs' skin in the game varied greatly across CCPs. Many clearing members supported requiring a standardized amount equal to a percentage of the default fund (e.g. 10%) and a second tranche of 'appropriately sized' skin in the game in the default waterfall of CCPs.

The indirect members sought to shape the recovery rules in a way that would be favourable to them. The Alternative Investment Management Association (AIMA)—Managed Funds Association (MFA) (2013), whose members were mostly indirect participants of CCPs, stressed that the regulatory focus should be on resilience, that is to say, preventing the failure of CCPs ex-ante through financial resource requirements and risk management rules. Moreover, given the fact that clients would be impacted by a CCP failure, they would need to have meaningful representation on the governing bodies of CCPs. These associations were concerned that regulators appeared to focus on 'CCP recovery and continuity at any cost, whereas, in certain circumstances, a prompt wind-down of a failing CCP, with the immediate return of clients' assets, would be preferable to a prolonged and costly CCP recovery'. If this was not possible, a CCP should allocate losses in a way that such losses did not fall disproportionately on clients. The Alternative Investment Management Association (AIMA) (2016) noted that it was important that the CCP itself was exposed to the loss of its own funds as part of the default waterfall, so that its interests would be in line with those of the participants.

The Investment Association (2016) (formerly, the Investment Management Association, IMA), which represented end-users, supported clear resolution measures, not open-ended recovery attempts. The association pointed out that initial and variation margins of clearing members' clients should be protected from haircutting. Along similar lines, Blackrock (2016b), a large investment management company that was a vocal indirect participant, criticized initial and variation margin haircutting because they were tools that enabled the CCP to allocate losses to its customers. It concluded that 'there is no precedent for users of a service, who pay fees to access a service, to also be responsible for keeping that service in business after it has failed in its core mission, which for a CCP is the provision of credit risk mitigation'.

With reference to the work on CCPs resolution, the CCPs, the direct participants and the indirect participants sought to shape the content of the proposed rules in their favour. CCPs stressed that resolution should only commence after the recovery plan had been exhausted (EACH 2017). According to the Chicago Mercantile Exchange (CME) (2017), which also owned a large CCP, recovery should have priority over resolution, which should be the last resort. CCPs opposed writing down the equity of a financial market infrastructure prior to other steps and called for the bail-in to be limited to participants (EACH 2017). CCPs strongly rejected the idea of compensating participants with equity (e.g. Eurex 2017).

Direct participants argued in favour of a clear boundary between recovery and resolution (ISDA et al. 2016b). Should a CCP enter resolution, the resolution authority should respect the default waterfall and the arrangements made by the CCP with its participants (the rulebook). The loss allocation rules should not be determined by the CCP alone. Instead, they should be discussed with the authorities and the clearing members. Several participants argued that equity should bear losses beyond the skin in the game of CCPs and that there should be a cap on the exposures of the clearing members to CCPs in recovery and resolution. Clearing members asked for as much disclosure as possible, whereas CCPs cautioned against disclosing elements of the resolution plan. Participants supported resolvability assessments and powers for the resolution authorities to require changes to CCP rulebooks, whereas CCPs resisted these powers.

The Alternative Investment Management Association (AIMA)—Managed Funds Association (MFA) (2013), which mainly represented indirect participants that accessed CCPs via dealer banks, stressed the need to prevent the failure of CCPs ex-ante. The Investment Management Association (IMA) (2013a) pointed out that loss allocation to direct and indirect participants should be considered as a resolution tool, not recovery and, therefore, the resolution authorities alone should have the power to enforce it. Furthermore, the losses eventually incurred by the government should be recovered from CCPs' shareholders, and only as a last resort from clearing members (IMA 2013a; EBF 2013a). The position of Blackrock was indicative of the position of several indirect participants. Blackrock (2014) argued in favour of a rapid and complete winding-down of the failing CCP and timely repayment of margins to participants. Blackrock (2016a), like other indirect participants, opposed the haircutting of collaterals of indirect participants.

The financial industry carried out considerable work on the recovery and resolution of CCPs—this work fed into the work carried out by regulators, as this was a new area of regulation for them. In 2013, the ISDA published a technical paper, *CCP Loss Allocation at the End of the Waterfall* (ISDA 2013c), which analysed the various recovery tools and strategies that could be used at the end of the default waterfall, and which became a point of reference for the public authorities. Subsequently, the ISDA (2015b) issued a *CCP Default Management, Recovery and Continuity: A Proposed Recovery Framework.* JPMorgan Chase, a large dealer bank, issued a proposal calling for users of CCPs, as well as the CCPs themselves, to contribute to a fund that could be used to bolster a failing CCP. CCPs already had a default fund that was mostly funded by the members themselves, but JPMorgan wanted CCPs to have more skin in the game. The proposal drew support from some industry groups, but was opposed by CCPs. Blackrock wrote several papers on these issues. In 2014, it noted that, whereas in the banking sector regulators sought to eliminate the problem of 'too big to fail' for large banks by increasing capital requirements to enhance the resiliency of banks and set rules for bank resolution, in the case of the central clearing mandate, regulators focused primarily on assuring that a CCP could be recovered rather than resolved (Blackrock 2014). In a later paper, Blackrock (2016b) argued that efforts to protect the financial system from the failure of a CCP should also endeavour to protect the ultimate customers of CCPs, namely, end-investors.

The financial industry mobilized extensively on international standard-setting for CCPs, seeking access across all relevant regulatory venues. Thus, private actors tried to influence every venue dealing with CCPs, advocating their preferences in the CPSS/CPMI, the IOSCO, the FSB, and the BCBS. Several financial associations and individual companies submitted similar responses to the consultations carried out by the CPSS/CPMI-IOSCO on recovery and those carried out by the FSB on resolution. Indeed, financial industry responses often cross-referenced each other, meaning that they referred to previous responses sent by the same interest group to the same international standard-setting body over time, but they also referred to the similar responses that each interest group sent to several standard-setters at the same time.

As a consequence, financial groups contributed to promoting international rule consistency concerning the elemental regime on the 3 Rs of CCPs and other elemental regimes on derivatives. For example, when international standards for CCP resilience were discussed, the ISDA (2011b) pointed out that the standards for CCPs overlapped with many other regulatory initiatives, including Basel III issued by the BCBS. Indeed, CCPs are 'qualifying CCPs' for Basel III exposure purposes, only if they comply with the CPSS-IOSCO (2012a) *Principles*. Consequently, ISDA urged 'these standards to be developed by CPSS-IOSCO in an active dialogue with the BCBS'. The ISDA also 'strongly urged the CPSS-IOSCO to develop principles that address financial market infrastructures resolution. As an international standard-setter, the CPSS-IOSCO is uniquely placed to provide needed leadership and clarity on a critical subject, which also has potential cross border aspects.'

Conclusion

The CPSS-IOSCO (2012a) *Principles for Financial Market Infrastructures* were intended to improve the resilience of financial market infrastructures, especially CCPs. Subsequent international standards issued by the CPSS/CPMI-IOSCO and the FSB, respectively, dealt with the recovery and resolution of CCPs. The state-centric approach has considerable explanatory power in accounting for international standard-setting for CCPs. After the crisis, the US (Helleiner 2014; Knaack 2015) and the UK (James and Quaglia 2020a) were keen to tighten up rules on CCPs, hence they acted as pace-setters at the international level. They were well placed to do so because they had vast derivatives markets, several global CCPs, many dealer banks as well as considerable expertise. These jurisdictions had the support of the EU, which, like the US and the UK, was keen to protect financial stability as well as prevent regulatory arbitrage. With reference to the elemental regime on the resilience, recovery, and resolution of CCPs, there were no major disagreements among the 'great powers', whose preferences were, by and large, aligned. Furthermore, regulators in these jurisdictions were alerted to the interlinkages among these sets of standards. However, on certain important issues, such as the amount of CCPs' skin in the game, or CCPs' access to central bank liquidity, the preferences of the great powers were heterogeneous, thus no international rules were set, or they remained deliberately general. Other jurisdictions, including those on the fringe, were fence-sitters, but not foot-draggers.

Transgovernmental networks of domestic regulators facilitated international standard setting and were instrumental in promoting regulatory consistency and managing regime complexity. In order to facilitate the coordination of their respective (often, overlapping or interlinked) work, international standard-setting bodies used a variety of tools. Given the difficulty of regulatory coordination on these issues at the domestic level,[6] transgovernmental networks did a good job of promoting the precision, stringency, and consistency of various standards for the 3 Rs of CCPs. It is true that international standards for CCPs sometimes lacked granularity, for example, concerning CCPs margin models. Other controversial issues that were not discussed concerned the extraterritoriality of domestic rules. The different margin models used in the US and in the EU, and the extraterritoriality of their respective domestic rules, became very controversial in the 'tug of war' between the US and the EU (Knaack 2015; Newman and Posner 2018; Pagliari 2013b).

However, the CPSS/CPMI-IOSCO's and the FSB's documents became more granular over time (see, for example, the CPMI-IOSCO *Guidance* in 2017c and the FSB *Guidance* in 2017a), and sought to harmonize supervisory stress testing for CCPs (CPMI-IOSCO 2018b). They also set out to tackle controversial issues that had previously been side-stepped (such as financial resources to support CCP resolution and the treatment of CCP equity in resolution, see FSB 2018a) and/or issues that emerged as time went by (such as the interdependencies between banks and CCPs, see FSB, BCBS, CPMI, IOSCO 2018b).

The financial industry did not oppose post-crisis rules on CCPs, but private actors mobilized in order to shape the content of the new rules so that they

[6] There was considerable bureaucratic turf fighting on CCPs regulation and supervision at the domestic level in the US and the EU. In the US, it took seven years (from the approval of Dodd Frank Act in 2010 to the issuing of the Treasury Report in 2017) and the intervention of the Treasury to clarify that the FDIC was the authority responsible for the resolution of CCPs. In the EU, the review of EMIR brought into the spotlight the bureaucratic rivalry among EU regulatory authorities (ECB, ESMA, Commission) as well as national ones (James and Quaglia 2020b).

would be in line with their preferences, that is to say, the expected distributional implications of the new rules. Unlike in the case of other international financial standards, such as capital requirements for banks (see Lall 2012; Young 2012), the preferences of the financial industry were not aligned within jurisdictions. On the contrary, the preferences of CCPs tended to be similar across jurisdictions, like those of the direct and indirect participants. Private actors mobilized in several international regulatory venues and by doing so they also highlighted the interlinkages among various elemental regimes on derivatives and the need for regulatory consistency. The following chapter discusses the elemental regime on capital requirements for bank exposures to CCPs, and the regime complexity resulting from the interlinkages between rules on CCPs and rules on banks, which were direct and indirect members of CCPs.

7

International Standards for Bank Capital Exposures to CCPs and Derivatives

During the international financial crisis, several banks had to be bailed out by their respective governments in many countries. Afterwards, there was a need to increase capital requirements for banks, so as to make them more resilient to financial shocks. One of the commitments taken by the G20 leaders at the Pittsburgh summit in 2009 was to set 'internationally agreed rules to improve both the quantity and quality of bank capital and to discourage excessive leverage' (G20 2009b). The post-crisis elemental regime on bank capital for derivatives—specifically, the credit valuation adjustment (CVA), the leverage ratio, and bank exposures to CCPs—was nested into the broader bank capital regime and was interlinked with the elemental regimes on derivatives trading and clearing. In 2010, the BCBS agreed on key elements of the Basel III Accord that set capital requirements for internationally active banks. Further work on certain elements of Basel III was undertaken between 2011 and 2017, when the so-called Basel IV Accord was eventually agreed upon.

With reference to the CVA, the leverage ratio and bank exposures to CCPs, like other parts of Basel III, the US and the UK were pace-setters internationally, promoting relatively precise, stringent and consistent rules. However, they were not first-movers domestically because they waited for international standards to be agreed upon. These jurisdictions favoured higher capital requirements to safeguard financial stability, but were concerned about the competitive implications of unilateral regulatory action for their financial industry. The EU (minus the UK), in principle, agreed on the need for higher capital requirements for banks. In practice, however, the EU worried about setting the bar too high, given that EU banks were undercapitalized and provided most of the credit to the real economy. Hence, the traditional dilemma between financial stability and financial industry competitiveness was a 'trilemma' in the EU, which was also mindful of the impact of capital rules on economic growth (Howarth and Quaglia 2016).

Several transgovernmental networks of domestic financial regulators were involved because, although the new capital rules were formally issued by the

The Politics of Regime Complexity In International Derivatives Regulation. Lucia Quaglia, Oxford University Press (2020).
 DOI: 10.1093/oso/9780198866077.003.0001

BCBS, the committee was aware of the impact of its rules on derivatives trading and clearing. Thus, the BCBS worked extensively with the CPSS/CPMI and the IOSCO. International bank capital requirements, including those concerning derivatives trading and clearing, were heavily contested by the financial industry because of the distributional implications (i.e. expected economic costs) of the new rules. Yet, the financial industry was unable to prevent this reform, it was only able to partially shape the content of the new standards by making them less stringent than initially proposed. Private actors also urged regulators to consider capital reforms in conjunction with other post-crisis standards, so as to avoid a regulatory 'overkill' and improve consistency across elemental regimes on derivatives.

Key Issues in Bank Capital Requirements and Derivatives

The first post-crisis reform to be discussed with reference to bank capital requirements and derivatives was the credit valuation adjustment (CVA), which was an adjustment to the fair value (or price) of derivatives in order to account for counterparty credit risk. During the financial crisis, banks suffered significant counterparty credit risk losses on their OTCDs portfolios. The majority of those losses came not from counterparty defaults, but from fair value adjustments on derivatives. The value of derivatives fell because counterparties were less likely than expected to meet their obligations. For example, the total CVA losses on monoline insurers in the US amounted to 54 billion dollars from 2006 to 2011 (ISDA 2011a). Under the Basel II market risk framework, banks were required to hold capital against the variability in the market value of derivatives on their trading book, but there was no requirement to capitalize against variability in the CVA (BCBS 2011). As Viljanen (2015) put it, 'CVA losses were a blind-side hit' for the BCBS and for pre-crisis banking regulation more generally. In order to address this regulatory gap, the BCBS introduced the CVA variability charge as part of the Basel III Accord. The purpose of the CVA capital charge was to capitalize the risk of future changes in the CVA. Thus, when entering into bilateral OTCD transactions, banks were required to hold capital to protect against the risk that the counterparty defaulted, as well as the CVA risk. The contentious point was how to calculate the CVA.

The second post-crisis reform of bank capital requirements that had implications for derivatives markets was the leverage ratio. Basel III introduced a minimum 'leverage ratio', which was a non-risk-based ratio and was calculated by dividing the Tier 1 capital of the bank (mainly equities) by the bank's average total consolidated assets (the sum of the exposures of all assets and non-balance sheet items). One of the factors that contributed to the international financial crisis was the building-up of excessive on- and off-balance sheet leverage in the banking system. In many cases, banks built up excessive leverage, while maintaining strong risk-based capital ratios (BCBS 2013a). At the peak of the crisis, the banking sector had to reduce its leverage in a manner that amplified downward pressure on asset prices. The Basel III reforms introduced a simple, transparent, non-risk based leverage ratio to act as a supplementary measure (a backstop) to risk-based capital requirements in order to capture the on- and off-balance sheet leverage of banks. The objectives were to avoid differing methods of calculating risk-weighted assets used by banks, and create a level playing field globally (Banque de France 2017).

The contentious points were, first, the acceptance of the leverage ratio and then its calculation. With reference to the leverage ratio's treatment of derivatives, two aspects attracted much attention, as elaborated in the following sections. First, whether derivatives collaterals received by a bank from a counterparty should be netted against derivatives exposures when the bank calculated its exposure measure. The second aspect concerned the leverage ratio treatment of derivatives cleared on behalf of clients. The crux of the matter was how banks' provision of derivatives clearing services should be calculated and included in the leverage ratio. If the value was set too high, banks would have a disincentive to provide clearing services for clients to access CCPs, which was one of the key objectives of post-crisis regulatory reforms of derivatives markets. If the value was set too low, it could endanger the resilience of banks, that is to say, their ability to withstand financial shocks.

The third issue concerning capital requirements and derivatives was bank exposures to CCPs, which included both trade exposures and contributions to the default funds of CCPs (which were discussed in Chapter 5). Prior to Basel III, derivatives received an exposure value of zero, but the financial crisis highlighted the need for banks to capitalize for counterparty credit risk. Moreover, there was a need for banks to capitalize their exposure to CCPs' default funds, which consisted of contributions made by clearing members and were designed to protect CCPs from losses caused by the default of a clearing member. Capital for bank exposures to CCPs should be lower for more resilient and better-managed CCPs (the so-called 'qualifying CCPs'), which posed fewer risks to banks that were clearing members. The underlying rationales of this reform were to incentivize banks to use CCPs for clearing, but also to make the financial system more resilient to failures of CCPs by increasing capital for bank exposures to CCPs. However, if capital requirements were set too high, there would be a disincentive for banks to clear through CCPs (*Risknet*, 6 June 2013, 27 January 2011). Consequently, the key issues were how to calculate bank exposures to CCPs, and the definition of a 'qualified' CCP and a 'non-qualified' CCP to which full capital charges would apply.

International Bank Capital Requirements and Derivatives

The Basel III Accord *Global Regulatory Framework for More Resilient Banks and Banking Systems* was agreed upon in late 2010 and was the cornerstone of the international regulatory response to the financial crisis. The accord was designed to set capital requirements for internationally active banks worldwide. Capital requirements have traditionally been regarded as the main instruments to ensure the stability of the banking sector and, hence, financial stability tout court. In 1988, the BCBS issued the Basel I Accord (Kapstein 1989, 1992; Simmons 2001), which was updated by the Basel II Accord in 2004 (Tsingou 2008; Underhill and Zhang 2008; Wood 2005). Over time, these 'soft' international rules were incorporated into (legally binding) national legislation in more than a hundred countries (Quillin 2008). The BCBS put forward concrete proposals on Basel III in the wake of the financial crisis in December 2009. Other documents (for example, on the countercyclical capital buffer) were issued for consultation throughout 2010. A general agreement was reached in July 2010 and a final agreement was eventually signed in December (BCBS 2010a). Compared to Basel II, Basel III was negotiated in record time—less than two years—due to the political salience imparted to it by the international financial crisis. The Basel III rules were to be phased in gradually from 2013 until 2019. The accord and its subsequent revisions had major implications not only for the banking sector, but also for derivatives markets.

A first set of post-crisis capital rules were intended to capture the risk of changes to the CVA for various financial instruments, first and foremost, derivatives. In 2010, Basel III set two approaches for calculating the CVA capital charge, namely, the 'advanced CVA risk capital charge' method and the 'standardized CVA risk capital charge' method. The advanced approach was available only to banks that had the approval to use the Internal Model Method for calculating exposure at default for counterparty credit risk capital calculation. In the standardized approach, a regulatory formula was used to calculate the CVA risk capital charge (BCBS 2010a). Both approaches did not cover an important driver of the CVA risk, namely, the exposure component of the CVA. Several banks hedged against CVA variability, but the Basel III framework did not recognize these hedges (*Finriskalert*, 16 December 2015).

In 2015, the BCBS *Review of the Credit Valuation Adjustment Risk Framework* proposed some revisions to the existing capital rules in order to take into account the exposure component of the CVA risk, together with its hedges. This review was partly triggered by the fact that the EU and the US disagreed on interpretation of the Basel III provisions on the CVA,[1] and the financial industry (especially, in the US) complained about the uneven implementation of the CVA rules worldwide (*Financial Times*, 24 April 2013), as elaborated in the following sections. Hence, the BCBS decided to review this issue. The revision of the CVA framework was also designed to make it more consistent with the approaches used in the market risk framework of the trading book, which was also under review by the BCBS. The CVA was a fair-value adjustment to the price of a fair-valued instrument. Therefore, the capital charge that related to it should be consistent with the capital charge for market risk (BCBS 2015). In 2016, the BCBS (2016a) issued a revised version of *Minimum Capital Requirements for Market Risk in the Trading Book*, which covered derivatives exposures in the trading book. In 2017, all these changes were included in *Basel III: Finalising Post-crisis Reforms* (BCBS 2017), which was dubbed by some observers as Basel IV.

The main objectives of the revised CVA framework were an improved assessment of the CVA risk, including related hedges; the consistency of regulatory requirements for the CVA risk with the revised framework for market risk; and the consistency of the regulatory CVA risk calculation with the CVA calculation for accounting purposes (KPGM 2018). Key elements of the revised CVA standards were that banks would not be allowed to use an internal model to calculate capital requirements for the CVA risk; and the existing 'standard' and 'model-based advanced' methods were replaced by a 'basic approach' and a 'standardized approach'. In comparison with the first consultation of the BCBS on the CVA, in July 2015, the final standards adopted in 2017, together with other revisions of the Basel III framework, adjusted the methodology and updated the calibration of risk weights. The revised framework was due to come into force in 2022, at the same time as the revised framework for market risk.

[1] In 2014, the BCBS (2014a) found the EU to be 'materially non-compliant' with Basel III. Part of the non-compliance stemmed from the EU's interpretation of Basel III provisions on CVA, as transposed in EU legislation, the CRD IV (see Quaglia 2019).

A second controversial aspect of Basel III that had implications for derivatives markets was the *leverage ratio*, which required banks to have a set percentage of common equity relative to total assets. In June 2013, the BCBS published for consultation the *Revised Basel III Leverage Ratio Framework and Disclosure Requirements*. The revisions to the framework concerned primarily the denominator of the leverage ratio, that is to say, the exposure measure. With reference to derivatives, the proposed rules did not allow the netting of collaterals received by banks and prescribed the grossing up of their exposure measure for collaterals provided—hence, the new measures would be costly for banks. A related issue, which was also contested by banks, concerned the leverage ratio treatment of client cleared derivatives. In parallel with the consultation on the proposal, the BCBS undertook a quantitative impact study of the estimated effects of the proposed rules.

Given the criticisms raised by the financial industry during the consultation and the results of the quantitative impact study conducted by regulators (*Financial Times*, 14 January 2014), several amendments were made prior to releasing the final standard, *Basel III Leverage Ratio Framework and Disclosure Requirements*, in January 2014 (BCBS 2014b). To begin with, in order to avoid the double-counting of exposures, a clearing member's trade exposures to qualifying CCPs associated with client-cleared derivatives transactions could be excluded if the clearing member did not guarantee the performance of a qualifying CCP to its clients. Furthermore, the variation margin associated with derivatives exposures could be used to reduce the leverage ratio's exposure measure. Finally, certain commitments would be weighted using a credit conversion factor, in some cases reducing the incremental balance sheet impact. Previously, all commitments were weighted at 100% (BCBS 2014b).

Further adjustments to the definition and the calibration of the leverage ratio were made afterward. Therefore, a consultative paper was published in April 2016 (BCBS 2016b). Some of the proposed revisions to the leverage ratio concerned the measurement of derivatives exposures, whereby the crux of the matter was the treatment of initial margin posted by clients to banks accessing CCPs to clear on the behalf of clients. Market participants criticized the fact that collaterals posted as initial margins by clients to clearing members (banks) were not permitted to reduce the clearing members' exposures. Hence, the leverage ratio treatment of client initial margins could adversely impact on the ability of clearing members to provide clearing services. Banks, CCPs, exchanges, and large users of derivatives lobbied hard to change the proposed rules (*Financial Times*, 25 July 2016, 6 April 2016, 26 August 2015).

In 2017, the BCBS finalized a set of Basel III reforms. The revisions sought to improve the calculation of risk-weighted assets and the comparability of banks' capital ratios by enhancing the robustness and risk sensitivity of the standardized approaches for credit risk, CVA risk and operational risk. The new rules constrained the use of internal models.[2] A leverage ratio buffer was introduced to limit the leverage of global systemically important banks, and the existing Basel II output floor was replaced with a more robust risk-sensitive floor based on the committee's revised Basel III standardized approaches (BCBS 2017).

In June 2019, the leverage ratio was revised with reference to clearing services, specifically, the treatment of the leverage ratio capital requirements for derivatives that a bank centrally cleared on behalf of its clients. The revisions were informed by the BCBS's review of the impact of the leverage ratio on banks' provision of clearing services as well as lobbying from the financial industry (*Financial Times*, 9 July 2019). The review included the assessment of quantitative and qualitative information collected by the committee and a joint evaluation conducted by the FSB, the BCBS, the CPMI, and the IOSCO (2018a) of the effects of post-crisis reforms on the incentives to centrally clear derivatives. The BCBS (2019) revised the leverage ratio treatment of client cleared derivatives, permitting initial and variation margins received from a client to offset the replacement cost and potential future exposure for client cleared derivatives. This revision was intended to balance 'the robustness of the leverage ratio as a non-risk based safeguard against unsustainable sources of leverage with the policy objective set by the G20 Leaders to promote central clearing of standardized derivatives contracts as part of mitigating systemic risk and making derivatives markets safe' (BCBS 2019).

International Standards for Capital Requirements for Bank Exposures to CCPs

Besides the CVA and the leverage ratio, the third set of post-crisis bank capital rules that had implications for derivatives markets was the capitalization of bank exposures to CCPs, in light of the greater use of CCPs following mandatory clearing and the systemic importance of CCPs after the crisis.

[2] For instance, by placing limits on certain inputs used to calculate capital requirements under the internal ratings-based approach for credit risk and by removing the use of the internal model approaches for the CVA risk and for operational risk.

In December 2010, the BCBS, building on work conducted by the BCBS-CPMI-IOSCO Task Force on CCPs, proposed that trade exposures of banks to 'qualifying CCPs' should receive a 2% risk weight, whereas, previously, it was zero. To calculate the exposure amount, banks could use the same model that they used under the bilateral framework for OTCDs. If collaterals were posted in a way that was bankruptcy remote from the CCP, the risk weight applied to collaterals was 0%. In addition, the bank's default fund exposures to a CCP should be capitalized according to a method that estimated risk arising from such a default fund, based on a CCP's financial resources and its 'hypothetical capital requirements'. The BCBS (2010b) noted that this hypothetical capital was to be used solely for the purpose of calculating the capital required for a bank's default fund exposures to a CCP. It also noted that 'CCP capital adequacy is determined by a CCP's overseer and the hypothetical capital discussed herein is not intended to be a basis for assessing the adequacy of a CCP's financial resources'.

In July 2012, the BCBS (2012) issued the *Interim Capital Requirements for Bank Exposures to CCP*. The Committee's framework for capitalizing exposures to CCPs was consistent with the CPSS-IOSCO (2012a) *Principles for Financial Market Infrastructures* (discussed in Chapter 6). If a CCP was supervised in a manner consistent with the *Principles* (hence, it was a 'qualifying CCP'), exposures to such a CCP would receive a preferential capital treatment. Banks were to apply a risk weight of 1250% to their default fund contributions to a 'non-qualifying' CCP. For qualifying CCPs, banks were to apply a risk weight determined according to a risk-sensitive formula that considered the size and quality of a qualifying CCP's financial resources, the counterparty credit risk exposures of such CCP, and the application of such financial resources via the CCP's loss bearing waterfall (BCBS 2012). If a bank acted as a clearing member of a CCP for its own purposes, a risk weight of 2% was to be applied to the bank's trade exposure to the CCP with reference to OTCDs and exchange-traded derivatives (BCBS 2012). However, the 2% risk-weight would be calculated on the basis of a member's cleared exposures, not the trade it cleared on behalf of clients, unless the member also guaranteed the trade against CCP default losses (Gregory 2014). This clarification was welcomed by the dealer banks because it meant that banks offering clearing services as intermediaries for non-members would not need to hold capital against non-guaranteed customer trades (*FX Week*, 6 August 2012).

Afterward, the BCBS, in collaboration with the IOSCO and the CPSS/CPMI, set out to improve the interim capital requirements for bank exposures to CCPs. In fact, the impact studies carried out by regulators showed that calculating the hypothetical level of default resources using the existing approach—combined with the nature of the formulae for determining the capital charge—meant that capital charges on member contributions to default funds varied significantly across CCPs. In many cases, the charges were very small, and in some cases, they were very large, and higher than for bilateral transactions (BCBS 2013a). Moreover, low capital charges did not meet the objective of ensuring adequate capital held against CCP exposures, while very high charges undermined the incentives for banks to use CCPs. There were also concerns that the interim rules could disincentivize qualifying CCPs and their members from increasing member contributions to CCPs' default funds, hence reducing the resilience of CCPs (BCBS 2013a). In order to address these issues, a Joint Working Group on CCPs was formed by the BCBS, the IOSCO and the CPSS/CPMI and the 'revised policy framework represented a blending of the perspectives from each of the group's constituencies' (BCBS 2014d).

In 2013, the BCBS, in collaboration with the CPSS-IOSCO, issued a new consultative document on *Capital Requirements for Bank Exposures to CCPs*, with a view to revising the interim rules. The proposed changes were to affect only exposures to qualifying CCPs, not the capital treatment of non-qualifying CCPs. The BCBS recognized that the primary source of risk in a CCP came from the possibility of a member default on the trades cleared by the CCP, and the potential inadequacy of the margins and the pre-funded default fund contribution posted to the CCP by the defaulter to cover its default. The creation of a default fund did not create new risks for the system, rather it mutualized and distributed losses. The interim approach ignored the fact that as default resources increased, the probability of a loss falling on trade exposures decreased because the default fund was more likely to be able to absorb all the losses incurred. The Committee, therefore, proposed a more risk-sensitive approach to the capital treatment of trade exposures to a qualifying CCP, whereby the risk weight applied to trade exposures would depend on the level of pre-funded default resources available to the qualifying CCP, relative to a reference level of pre-funded resources (BCBS 2013a).

The most controversial issue was to determine the appropriate reference level for default resources. The CPSS-IOSCO (2012a) *Principles* and the BCBS (2013b) *Non-internal Model Method for Capitalising Counterparty Credit Risk Exposures* (NIMM) set out two different ways of calculating the reference level, which reflected, respectively, the different views of securities markets regulators and banking regulators. According to the CPSS-IOSCO *Principles*, the financial resources of CCPs (including contributions from the CCP itself and from its members) should be sufficient to cover the default of either the one, or, in some cases, the two participants that would potentially cause the largest aggregate credit exposure to the CCP in extreme, but plausible, market conditions (see Chapter 6). This method was identified as the 'Cover*' default fund. The BCBS (2013b) proposed, instead, the non-internal model method for capitalizing counterparty credit risk exposures, which was identified as 'NIMM' and was intended to better capture the effects of collateral and netting, improving the risk sensitivity by differentiating between margined and unmargined trades (*Risknet*, 6 June 2013).

The BCBS sought to evaluate the suitability of NIMM through a quantitative impact study that assessed, inter alia, how NIMM compared with the Cover* calculations. The Committee proposed to use the larger of the Cover* requirement and the hypothetical level of default resources calculated by using NIMM to ensure that a prudent amount of capital was held by bank clearing members (BCBS 2013b). NIMM would effectively be a floor on the Cover* requirement for the purposes of calculating the bank capital requirements of clearing members.[3] To sum up, the crux of the matter concerned the method of calculating exposures to default funds, namely, Cover*, which was favoured by the CPSS-IOSCO, or the NIMM, which was favoured by the BCBS. The financial industry favoured NIMM because it was more risk-sensitive and was, therefore, likely to lead to a lower estimation of capital requirements.

The final policy framework for *Bank Exposures to CCPs* (BCBS 2014d) retained many of the features from the interim framework including the scope of application, the treatment of trade exposures to qualifying CCPs and the capital requirements for bank exposures to non-qualifying CCPs. The final standards differed from the interim requirements by including: a single approach for determining the capital requirements for bank exposures to qualifying CCPs (NIMM, which was renamed as the standardized approach for counterparty credit risk), so the Cover* was eliminated; and there was an explicit cap on the capital charges applicable to a bank's exposures to a qualifying CCP. Banks were to apply a risk weight to their default fund contributions determined according to a risk-sensitive formula that considered the size and quality of a qualifying CCP's financial resources, the counterparty credit risk exposures of the CCP, and the application of financial

[3] The BCBS (2013b) expected that in most cases the Cover* default fund would be larger than the hypothetical default fund requirement calculated under NIMM. However, using the Cover* requirement alone could create an incentive for qualifying CCPs to calculate the Cover* requirement in order to reduce the capital charges faced by their bank clearing members so as to gain a competitive advantage.

Table 7.1 International standards for capital for bank exposures to CCPs and derivatives

International standard-setting body	Date of issuance	Standards (framework, guidance, etc)
BCBS	2010	Global Regulatory Framework for More Resilient Banks and Banking Systems (Basel III)
BCBS*	2012	Interim Capital Requirements for Bank Exposures to CCP
BCBS	2014	Basel III Leverage Ratio Framework
BCBS*	2014	Revised Capital Requirements for Bank Exposures to CCPs
BCBS	2016	Minimum Capital Requirements for Market Risk in the Trading Book
BCBS	2017	Basel III: Finalising post-crisis reforms (Basel IV)
FSB-BCBS-CPMI-IOSCO	2018	Analysis of Central Clearing Interdependencies
BCBS	2019	Leverage ratio treatment of client cleared derivatives

* These standards were issued in close cooperation with the CPSS/CPMI-IOSCO.

resources via the CCP's loss bearing waterfall in the case of clearing member defaults (BCBS 2013a) (for an overview of international standards for capital for bank exposures to CCPs and derivatives see Table 7.1).

State-Centric Explanation of International Standard Setting for Bank Capital Requirements

The US and the UK acted as pace-setters in promoting relatively precise, stringent, and consistent post-crisis international capital requirements for banks. In the wake of the crisis, the Secretary of the US Treasury, Timothy Geithner, pointed out that 'the top three things to get done are capital, capital and capital' (*Washington Post*, 25 March 2010). Daniel Tarullo (2011b) of the Federal Reserve Board argued that strong capital standards were central to the overall reform agenda for financial regulation because 'the crisis confirmed that capital standards had been wholly inadequate: the required capital levels were much too low, particularly trading book capital requirements', including those concerning derivatives. Like his US counterparts, the Executive Director of the Bank of England, Andy Haldane, argued that 'with hindsight, the capital assigned to certain categories of high-risk and off-balance-sheet transactions by Basel rules was far too low' (Alessandri and Haldane 2009) and praised the leverage ratio, arguing that 'it should be placed on an equal footing with capital ratios' (Haldane 2012). Similarly, the so-called Turner Review published by the British FSA (2009) called for an increase in 'the quality and quantity of capital... significantly above existing Basel rules... a maximum gross leverage ratio... and liquidity regulation and supervision'.

The US and especially the UK had a very internationalized banking sector—meaning that they were home and host to large cross-border banks. Hence, they were very exposed to negative externalities resulting from undercapitalized foreign banks that had limited resilience to financial shocks. During the international financial crisis, US authorities had to bail out several US banks and the Federal Reserve had to provide a substantial amount of emergency funding to the subsidiaries and branches of foreign undercapitalized banks operating in the US. Foreign subsidiaries and branches, in turn, transferred part of that funding to their parent companies in Europe (McDowell 2012). In the UK, the three largest domestic banks had to be bailed out by the government using taxpayer money. In terms of externalities, about 40% of the banking sector was foreign-owned in the UK, the majority of which was owned by banks headquartered outside of the EU.

Hence, domestic unilateral action (i.e. national capital rules) would not suffice to deal with negative externalities in the US and the UK. International harmonization was needed. A member of the Board of Governors the Federal Reserve, Daniel Tarullo (2011a), advocated a revision of international capital standards in order to promote international financial stability, arguing that 'weaknesses in one group of internationally active banks could quickly be transmitted globally' (Tarullo 2011a). Mark Carney (2014), Governor of the Bank of England, noted that 'the UK's financial sector can be both a global good and a national asset—if it is resilient.... Reforms of domestic banking are far from sufficient for a global hub like London. Now is the time for a greater focus on what's needed for resilient international banking and robust global markets. This will require sustained international engagement.'

Furthermore, the adjustment costs deriving from tighter international capital and liquidity standards were low in the US and the UK. The massive government-led recapitalization of ailing US and UK banks during the crisis left them relatively well-capitalized afterward. In terms of domestic regulatory templates, US banks already complied with the leverage ratio, which had been in place in the US since the 1990s. Furthermore, capital markets in the US provided the bulk of funding to the real economy. Similarly, the banking sector, especially wholesale investment banking in the City of London, did not provide substantial funding to the real economy. Hence, the impact of new international capital requirements on economic growth in the US and the UK was expected to be lower than in continental Europe (Howarth and Quaglia 2016).

The EU was in favour of tightening up capital requirements for banks, albeit not to the same extent as the US and the UK. Mario Draghi, President of the ECB, in his former capacity as chairman of the FSB, called the loopholes in Basel II 'one of the major factors of the crisis' (Draghi 2008). Yet, continental countries were less exposed to negative externalities than the US and the UK, and were, instead, subject to higher adjustment costs resulting from higher capital requirements. As for externalities, most of the EU cross-border banking was intra-EU (i.e. to and from other EU countries) and, on average, foreign penetration by non-EU headquartered banks was below 10% in the EU as a whole. In 'core' EU countries, such as France and Germany, foreign (EU and non-EU) bank penetration was the lowest in the EU (Schoenmaker 2013). As for the adjustment costs to more stringent international capital standards, these costs were high for banks in continental Europe, which were significantly undercapitalized. Furthermore, banks provided most of the credit to the real economy in continental Europe, thus, stricter capital rules would be detrimental to economic growth.[4] Hence, continental countries in the EU faced a trilemma concerning financial stability, the international competitiveness of their financial industry and economic growth (Howarth and Quaglia 2016).

In the negotiations of Basel III, the US and the UK supported a restrictive definition of capital, higher levels of capital, as well as the leverage ratio. In contrast, France and Germany—which were the main member states in the euro area—were keen to have a broader definition of capital, lower capital requirements and no leverage ratio because this would reduce the adjustment costs of their banks to the new rules. For example, the former governor of the Banque de France argued that the riskiness of the activities of 'traditional' European universal banks was lower than that of (largely Anglo-Saxon) investment banks and that this feature would not be captured by a crude leverage ratio (*Financial Times*, 26 October 2010). The outcome of the international standard-setting process, the Basel III Accord, was a compromise. It tightened up the definition of what counted as capital, but left some national

[4] A 2011 IMF study suggested a particularly significant impact of the proposed Basel III rules upon bank lending in Germany and a comparatively small drop in the UK, with France somewhere in between (Cosimano & Hakura 2011).

flexibility; it increased capital requirements, but by less than what had been proposed by the US and UK; and it set up a leverage ratio.

The EU, under the impulse of elected officials in continental countries (Young 2014) and in the European Parliament (Greenwood and Roederer-Rynning 2015), implemented Basel III with significant modifications. To no avail, the UK Chancellor and other seven European finance ministers published a letter criticizing the efforts of the European Commission, France, and Germany to water down the application of the Basel III Accord in the EU. In fact, the EU was found by the BCBS (2014a) to be 'materially non-compliant' with several provisions of the accord. In particular, the EU's counterparty credit risk framework provided an exemption from the Basel's CVA capital charge for certain derivatives exposures. EU banks were allowed to exclude exposures to pension funds, sovereigns, and qualifying non-financial end-users. These CVA exemptions were introduced to avoid both collateral and CVA costs for non-financial corporates and pension funds, and to limit disruptions in EU sovereign debt markets (*Mondaq*, 27 November 2013).

In the negotiations of Basel IV, the EU worried about the impact of the proposed rules on continental banks (*Bloomberg*, 11 June 2017). France and Germany, together with the Netherlands and Denmark, were the most critical towards the proposed rules (*Financial Times*, 1 September 2016). The EU member states, gathered in the Council of Ministers (2016), stressed that the BCBS should take account of the impact on 'different banking models' and avoid creating 'significant differences for specific regions of the world'. Along similar lines, the European Parliament (2016) underscored the need 'to promote the level playing field at the global level by mitigating—rather than exacerbating—the differences between jurisdictions and banking models, and by not unduly penalizing the EU banking model'.

Having opposed the leverage ratio during the Basel III negotiations, the EU supported a revision of the leverage ratio in the Basel IV negotiations in order to make it less punitive for banks. The effects of the leverage ratio on the availability of banks willing to access CCPs in order to provide clearing services to their customers were compounded in the EU, which lagged behind the US in introducing the leverage ratio. Some dealer banks through which indirect participants accessed CCPs had little capacity on their balance sheets.[5] This problem was worsened by the fact that, whereas the US rules provided

[5] Work carried out by the Banque de France and the Autorité de Contrôle Prudentiel et de Résolution (2018) confirmed that considerable attention was paid by clearing members to the impact of client clearing on banks' capital requirements and profitability.

exemptions from clearing for small banks with less than $10bn in assets, the EU rules did not (*Financial Times*, 25 July 2016). The UK also called for a recalibration of the ratio. Mark Carney (cited in *Market Voice*, 8 March 2016), Governor of the Bank of England, pointed out that, partially as a result of the regulatory reforms introduced, many small financial firms that typically used derivatives for hedging purposes encountered difficulties in gaining access to clearing. As for implementation, the European Commission put forward a legislative proposal in order to make the leverage ratio binding in the EU by including it in the so-called Pillar 1 as late as 2018.

Jurisdictions on the fringe, first and foremost in Asia, supported higher capital requirements post-crisis, albeit they were not active participants of the negotiations on Basel III, having joined the BCBS only in the wake of the crisis. Afterward, China over-complied with Basel III when it implemented this standard domestically, also because Chinese banks were well capitalized after the crisis, hence they faced low adjustment costs (Knaack 2017). The Deputy Managing Director of the Monetary Authority of Singapore, Ong Chong Tee (2017), praised the higher capital requirements introduced post-crisis. However, he advocated the revision of the leverage ratio because it impaired the capacity of clearing members to offer client clearing services, noting that the ratio 'may have created an unintended impact on the market's incentives and overall ability to centrally clear, which will be inconsistent with the objectives of the central clearing'.

However, jurisdictions were not monolithic actors. Often, there were different domestic views, even among regulators, on post-crisis bank capital requirements that had implications for derivatives. In the US, the FDIC was the staunched supporter of the leverage ratio, which had been introduced as part of the FDIC Improvement Act in 1991. With reference to Basel IV and further revisions of the leverage ratio, the FDIC opposed the relaxation of the methodologies for calculating bank exposures concerning derivatives. The Chairman of the FDIC, Martin Gruenberg (2018), noted that 'this simple approach has served well in addressing the excessive leverage that helped deepen the financial crisis'. A senior official of the FDIC, Thomas Hoenig (2015), criticized 'efforts in the US, and internationally at Basel, to weaken the leverage ratio treatment of cleared derivatives, and possibly all derivatives', pointing out, instead, the 'substantial risks' that 'derivatives posed to the broader economy'. He also stated, 'I am concerned that calls to weaken leverage capital requirements for derivatives are being taken seriously by some regulators.' In contrast, the CFTC worried about the availability of banks willing to provide clearing services to their clients to access CCPs, and the costs of these services (Giancarlo 2017).[6] The Federal Reserve and the OCC also called for a recalibration (downward) of the ratio (*Financial Times*, 12 April 2018). Indeed, the recalibration of the leverage ratio was one of the Federal Reserve's highest-priority (Quarles 2018).

In the EU, during the negotiation of Basel III, there was a division between the UK (which sided with the US) and France and Germany (Howarth and Quaglia 2016). There were also different views between financial regulators, who were keen for the EU to implement the international rules that regulators had agreed upon in Basel, and elected officials, who were more exposed to lobbying by the financial industry and firms in the real economy (Greenwood and Roederer-Rynning 2015; Young 2014). Interestingly, a similar divide between elected officials and regulators had emerged in the US with reference to the domestic compliance with Basel II, which was not implemented in the US prior to the crisis (Herring 2007). As for the negotiations on Basel IV, the EU was less internally divided, as compared to Basel III, mainly because on several (but, by no means, all) issues the preferences of the member states, including the UK, were not very dissimilar (James and Quaglia 2020a).

Transgovernmental Explanation of International Standard Setting for Bank Capital Requirements

Transgovernmental networks of domestic regulators in standard-setting bodies contributed to ironing out disagreements among jurisdictions and within jurisdictions by reaching a workable compromise on Basel III and its revision, Basel IV. Although on key issues, such as the level of capital requirements and the leverage ratio, the main jurisdictions had different preferences, regulators were able to reach an agreement in the Basel by sometimes papering over controversial issues (see Howarth and Quaglia 2016; Lall 2012; Young 2012). However, these issues were reopened when international rules were implemented at the domestic level, as in the case of Basel III in the EU (Quaglia 2019). Likewise, Basel II was not implemented in the US because of the opposition of elected officials and domestic banks (Herring 2007). These episodes highlight the limits of transgovernmental networks when dealing with rules that are politically salient.

[6] A study of the CFTC pointed out the decreasing number of banks willing to access CCPs on behalf of their customers, as elaborated in the penultimate section. Furthermore, according to CFTC estimates, allowing for initial margin offset in the calculation of the leverage ratio would reduce banks' own funds by only 1%, while reducing the cost of clearing services by 70% (Giancarlo 2017).

International fora were also instrumental in reconciling the priorities of various networks of regulators, which had different compositions, competences, and regulatory outlooks. Thus, banking regulators in the BCBS mainly worried about the resilience of banks and the banking sector. Securities markets regulators in the IOSCO prioritized central clearing by not penalizing clearing members and their customers, which cleared through CCPs. The first instance of this dilemma, and the need to reconcile different regulatory outlooks, concerned bank exposures to CCPs, whereby banking regulators and securities markets regulators used different ways of calculating the hypothetical capital for CCPs. Thus, the BCBS favoured the NIMM model, whereas the IOSCO preferred the Cover* model. These different views were brought together by the Task Force composed by members of the BCBS, the IOSCO, and the CPSS/CPMI, which set the rules on bank exposures to CCPs. Although it was not the main reason, one of the reasons why the leverage ratio was substantially revised less than two years after it had been set by the BCBS was the fact that those rules, agreed upon by banking regulators on their own, did not take sufficiently into account the effects of the new rules on central clearing.

Another instance of the need to reconcile different views among regulators within jurisdictions was the revision of the leverage ratio with a view towards making it less stringent in the treatment of derivatives exposures. The decline in the number of clearing members was a matter of concern for the derivatives regulators, such as CFTC, which highlighted the withdrawal of several banks from clearing. Indeed, many large banks, including State Street, Bank of New York-Mellon, Nomura, RBS, and Deutsche Bank, exited the business. By contrast, a senior official of the FDIC (a banking regulator), Hoenig (2018), criticized the effort underway to try to relax the leverage ratio's treatment of initial margin because banks that acted as clearing agents for their clients also guaranteed their clients' exposures to CCPs without limit. Therefore, removing initial margins from the exposure calculation of the ratio would trigger a 'reduction in private capital', which would 'necessarily be underwritten by the FDIC, the Federal Reserve, and, then, the taxpayer.... The US should not engage in this race to the bottom.'

Transgovernmental networks promoted regulatory consistency through a variety of coordination tools. Formal tools included *institutional deference* and the *cross-referencing* of standards. Thus, the BCBS decided to define the CCPs that complied with the CPSS-IOSCO (2012a) *Principles* as 'qualifying CCPs' for Basel III exposure purposes, adopting a preferential capital treatment for qualifying CCPs exposures, as compared to non-qualifying CCPs exposures, on the grounds that the former CCPs would be more resilient than the latter. Another tool was the conduct of *joint studies*, notably by the one by BCBS, the CPMI, the IOSCO, and the FSB (2018a) on *Incentives to Centrally Clear Over-The-Counter Derivatives,* which assessed the combined effects of the various regulatory reforms concerning derivatives markets post-crisis. Finally, there were informal coordination tools, such as phone calls, exchanging draft proposals etc. Furthermore, often the same regulators sat in various working groups in various capacities—it was like a 'carousel' (interview, February 2019).

However, it was a process of learning by doing by regulators in transgovernmental networks, hence, standards had to be 'adjusted' over time, mainly because of interlinkages among elemental regimes on derivatives. The regulators of the main jurisdictions, which were actively involved in all international bodies and, therefore, had a comprehensive overview of post-crisis reforms, were aware of the need to promote regulatory consistency and 'adjust' international standards if negative spillovers across sets of rules occurred. That was the case, for example, of the capital rules on bank exposures to CCPs, and the leverage ratio.

According to Mark White (2013), the Chair of the Working Group on bank exposures to CCPs, the BCBS's move to mandate higher capital requirements for CCP exposures was the result of a 'realization by regulators that the political push to clear OTCDs through CCPs had to be balanced by proper capitalization of the risks that arose from such exposures'. He noted that there had been a 'steep learning curve' among banking regulators about the implications of the central clearing reform: 'banks haven't always properly tracked their exposures to CCPs in the past because they haven't been material and no capital was required. But, in the future, they are going to be material, so we want to make sure they are properly monitored and capitalized'. At the same time, regulators in the BCBS recognized that requiring the capitalization of bank exposures to CCPs would impact the behaviour of CCPs and were aware of the need to consider a variety of CCP-related issues—not just bank capitalization (interview, April 2019). Therefore, the BCBS worked extensively with the CPSS/CPMI-IOSCO. The BCBS focused on the adequacy of bank capitalization and the resilience of the banking system, whereas the CPSS/CPMI-IOSCO focused on the resilience of CCPs.

Similarly, the revision of the leverage ratio took place by trial and error and was spurred by the regulators of the main jurisdictions that were active in transgovernmental networks. Governor Mark Carney of the Bank of England urged the BCBS to reconsider the treatment of derivatives trades in the leverage ratio, noting that although the leverage ratio did not normally allow collaterals to reduce exposures, an exception was warranted to allow initial margins to reduce leverage exposures for centrally cleared client trades (*Financial Times*, 5 July 2016). Vicky Saporta, Executive Director of the Bank of England, acknowledged the effects of capital rules on clearing and the need to 'make adjustments . . . to unintended consequences' (*Reuters*, 4 July 2018). Work carried out by the Banque de France and the Autorité de Contrôle Prudentiel et de Résolution (2018) confirmed that the demand for clearing had increased as a result of regulation on mandatory clearing and higher margins for uncleared derivatives, but also that a high leverage ratio discouraged banks from providing client clearing services. The joint study by the BCBS, the CPMI, the IOSCO, and the FSB (2018a) on *Incentives to Centrally Clear Over-The-Counter Derivatives* made a similar point. For all these reasons, as well as the intensive lobbying from the financial industry, the leverage treatment of derivatives exposures for centrally cleared client transactions within the leverage ratio exposure measure was reviewed (downward) in 2019.

Regulators outside the core jurisdictions were also aware of the interlinkages between different sets of standards. For example, Ong Chong Tee (2017), Deputy Managing Director of the Monetary Authority of Singapore, argued that:

> Taken individually, each set of reforms has been well-considered and for good reasons. For instance, the banking capital and liquidity reforms strengthen the ability of banks to better withstand future shocks; OTC derivative reforms seek to improve transparency, prevent market abuse and reduce systemic risks. The two sets of reforms aimed at achieving a safer financial system, albeit from different angles. However, to ensure that they complement each other without creating unintended consequences, we also need to carefully examine how the different elements will interact. . . . Therefore, in the next phase of our work on the reforms, sector regulators will have to work closely towards greater consistency and coherence with the inputs of all market participants.

Industry-Led Explanation of International Standard Setting for Bank Capital Requirements

The financial industry, first and foremost banks, to no avail, opposed higher capital requirements and the leverage ratio set by Basel III. However, private financial actors succeeded in watering down some of the proposed reforms, also by forging a broad coalition with associations and firms in the real economy. Although all banks resisted precise and stringent capital requirements, the specific preferences they articulated depended on their business model and the expected costs of the new capital rules for them. For example, US and UK banks were better positioned than continental banks to meet the requirements introduced by Basel III. One senior British bank representative indicated that British banks would have preferred lower capital requirements, but also that 'they could live with the new levels set by Basel III' (interview, London, 15 March 2012). In contrast, French and German banks had pressing concerns about their ability to meet higher capital requirements and the leverage ratio (Howarth and Quaglia 2016).

The financial industry opposed the leverage ratio, even though this opposition was much weaker in the case of US banks, which were already subject to the leverage ratio domestically. With reference to the calculation of derivatives in the leverage ratio, the revisions proposed by the BCBS were seen by the financial industry as 'extremely conservative' as they 'disallowed either offsetting secured financing transactions or derivative cash collateral in this calculation' (JP Morgan 2014). A study conducted by JP Morgan (2014), expressed concerns that the new rules would inflate the denominator (the exposure measure) of the leverage ratio to such an extent that it would become the binding capital constraint for more than half of the banks surveyed in the study. The study (over)estimated that compliance with the revised leverage ratio would require banks to either raise $108 billion of additional capital, or shed $3.6 trillion of assets.

A joint letter of the ISDA, the Futures Industry Association (FIA), the Securities Industry and Financial Markets Association (SIFMA), the Managed Funds Association (MFA), the World Federation of Exchanges (WFE), the Intercontinental Exchange Clear (ICE), the Chicago Mercantile Exchange (CME), London Clearing House (LCH), and Eurex to the *Financial Times* (26 August 2015) argued that the leverage ratio should recognize segregated client margins as reducing the bank's economic exposure. The letter pointed out that the flaws in the application of the leverage ratio to cleared derivatives threatened 'to undermine the global efforts to bring more derivatives into central clearing, damage the health of the clearing ecosystem, and make it more difficult for investment managers, commodity producers, and other customers to hedge their risks.... This harms farmers seeking to manage commodity price fluctuations, commercial companies wishing to lock in prices as they distribute their goods and pension funds using derivatives to enhance workers' retirement benefits. The negative impacts on the real economy are significant' (ISDA et al. 2015 in *Financial Times*, 26 August 2015). The signatories of the letter were not only banking associations, but also CCPs, buy-siders, and end-users. Thus, this joint letter was part of a lobbying strategy to forge a broad coalition, so as to be more influential in the regulatory process.

During the BCBS's consultation on the revision of the leverage ratio, launched in April 2016, the financial industry highlighted possible adverse effects on the ability of clearing members to continue offering clearing services to third parties through CCPs. According to the industry, the leverage ratio, which was a non-risk based measure, ignored the risk-reducing effect of initial margins received by banks from their clients for derivatives cleared through CCPs. Consequently, several responses to the consultation called for, inter alia, the deduction of initial margins from the denominator of the leverage ratio. The main transnational associations, the ISDA, the Global Financial Markets Association (GFMA), the Institute of International Finance (IIF), the Clearing House, and the Japan Financial Markets Council submitted a joint response (2016) to the BCBS, which spelled out some of the main criticisms raised by the industry.

> The industry thinks that, in the context of a bank exposure created by a cleared derivative transaction, the leverage ratio framework should recognize the exposure-reducing effect of initial margins, particularly as it is not used to increase the bank's leverage. Treating initial margins for client clearing as additional leverage ratio exposure... significantly overstates it, acting against client clearing businesses, and contradicting the G20 mandate by creating an economic disincentive for clearing brokers to offer clearing services.... The lack of a specific treatment to address initial margin requirements artificially overstates leverage on a system-wide basis.

Various sets of private financial actors had different preferences concerning capital requirements for bank exposures to CCPs, although they had some common preferences in favour of 'risk-sensitive' calculations. In a nutshell, banks initially opposed the 'indirect regulation' of CCPs by raising bank capital for exposures to CCPs, and argued, instead, that CCPs should be regulated more strictly. Subsequently, banks accepted the trade exposure proposal of a 2% risk weight, but criticized the proposed high capital requirements for bank exposure to CCPs default funds—banks wanted 'risk-sensitive' (i.e. lower) capital for their contributions to CCPs default funds. CCPs accepted the trade exposure risk weight (which, nevertheless, would directly affect banks, not CCPs), but argued that the CCPs default funds (and, hence, the contributions of banks to these funds) should be calculated by using the CCPs internal model, not those proposed by the BCBS, which were more stringent. The specific preferences expressed by various parts of the financial industry largely reflected their cost-benefits analysis, that is to say, the distributional implications of the proposed rules.

The International Banking Federation (IBF) (2011) criticized the 'rationale of addressing CCPs' macro-systemic risk through the micro-prudential supervision of banks', whereas CCPs systemic risk should be addressed through appropriate regulation of CCPs, in terms of risk management standards (including margining, risk controls, and transparency), CCPs membership's standards, CCPs capital standards and emergency access to central bank liquidity. Like the IBF (2011), the European Savings Banks Group (ESBG) and the World Savings Banks Institute (2010) questioned the indirect regulation of CCPs via higher capital requirements for bank exposures to CCPs, and argued that CCPs should be regulated more strictly, given that banks had limited influence on CCPs decisions. The International Swaps and Derivatives Association (ISDA), the Asia Securities Industry & Financial Markets Association (ASIFMA), the Association for Financial Markets in Europe (AFME), the British Bankers Association (BBA), the Global Financial Markets Association (GFMA), the Institute of International Finance (IIF), the Securities Industry and Financial Markets Association (SIFMA) (2011), which submitted a joint response, believed that it was inappropriate for clearing members to capitalize their exposures to CCPs whenever they acted as a financial intermediary on behalf of a client, except if clearing members provided a guarantee of CCPs performance to clients. Hence, dealer banks proposed (and, later, achieved) that for the 'clearing member-to-CCP leg' no capital requirement should be required, unless the clearing member had guaranteed the CCP's performance to the client.

In subsequent rounds of consultation, a joint response of the International Swaps and Derivatives Association (ISDA), Global Financial Markets Association (GFMA), Institute of International Finance (IIF) (2013a) focused primarily on the proposed capital treatment of default fund contributions, which were deemed to be 'inappropriately calibrated' and 'grossly overstated'. A study conducted by these trade associations showed that the NIMM was unlikely to exceed the Cover*, and, therefore, capital requirements would be based on the Cover*, a measure of risk that was 'inconsistent with the risk-based capital framework' and resulted in capital requirements that made clearing 'uneconomical'. They, therefore, recommended the removal of the

Cover* method in favour of NIMM as the basis to quantify exposures against CCP default fund contributions. Similarly, the Futures Industry Association (FIA) (2013) worried that the Cover* requirement would substantially overstate actual exposures to qualifying CCPs default funds. Consequently, the reference level of default fund should be measured using the NIMM, instead of the Cover*. The positions of (large) individual banks (e.g. JP Morgan, Barclays, Deutsche Bank) reflected the preferences expressed by banking associations and the associations of dealer banks.

According to the CCP12 (2013), an association of about thirty CCPs, the 1250% risk weight for default fund contributions from clearing members was a 'gross over-estimation of the risk associated with qualifying CCP default funds' and would disincentivize central clearing. In relation to the proposed default fund, the major concern of CCP12 was that the Cover* was not an appropriate measure on which capital requirements should be based. Furthermore, CCP12 noted that in some jurisdictions, CCPs were required to use a 'cover two' model, whereas CCPs with the same risk profile in other jurisdictions were required to use a 'cover one' model (see Chapter 6). That made capital requirements among CCPs inconsistent, favouring CCPs located in jurisdictions with less stringent requirements. The CCP12 proposed the use of the hypothetical capital calculated with NIMM, eliminating the Cover* from the proposal. The European Association of Clearing Houses (EACH) (2013), the association of EU CCPs, first recommended the use of CCPs' internal models, arguing that CCPs had developed 'sophisticated algorithms for calculating initial margins and default funds'. Subsequently, it warned that the Cover* was not an appropriate measure and recommended that only the NIMM method be used. Similar points were made by individual CCPs (e.g. LCH, Eurex).

The financial industry was successful in shaping the content of the new capital rules that had implications for derivatives markets by making them less stringent over time. That was the case, for example, of capital requirements for bank exposures to CCPs and the leverage ratio. In fact, there were significant differences between the proposals initially put forward by regulators and the rules eventually issued. Furthermore, these rules, especially the leverage ratio, were subject to several rounds of revisions over time, which often (but, not always) re-calibrated (i.e.) existing provisions, reducing their stringency. For instance, the revision of the CVA in 2015 did not permit the use of an internal model to calculate capital requirements for CVA, but it allowed the calculation of hedges. The revision of the leverage ratio in 2014 allowed the offsetting of variation margins and excluded client cleared transactions, if the clearing members did not guarantee the performance of the CCP. In 2018, the revision of the leverage ratio permitted initial margin received from a client to offset the replacement cost and potential future exposure for client cleared derivatives. The revisions of the rules on bank exposures to CCPs eventually adopted a less onerous way to calculate such exposures.

The financial industry engaged in venue shopping in order to shape the content of international standards. Hence, private actors pointed out the costs of bank capital requirements to banking regulators in the BCBS, and the costs of margin requirements to securities markets regulators in the IOSCO. The financial industry also mobilized in order to warn regulators about the interlinkages between various standards issued by different standard-setting bodies, stressing the need for regulatory consistency. For example, the Chicago Mercantile Exchange (CME) (2011b) noted that there were a number of standard-setting bodies dealing with the regulation of CCPs, and 'decisions by any one of these bodies, individually or collectively, could have spill-over effects that could undermine the regulatory efforts'. Similarly, the Depository Trust & Clearing Corporation (DTCC) (2011b) stressed the need for the BCBS to coordinate its initiative in this field with the CPSS-IOSCO. Eurex (2011) pointed out the need to coordinate various international regulatory initiatives concerning CCPs so as to ensure consistency among: the expected requirements for CCPs (which were set by the CPSS-IOSCO); the commitments to default funds by clearing members as well as CCPs (which were set by the CPSS-IOSCO); the bank capital charges for counterparty risk on CCP and non-CCP cleared transactions (which were set by the BCBS); and the margins requirements (collaterals) for cleared and uncleared OTCDs (which were set, respectively, by the CPSS-IOSCO and the BCBS-IOSCO).[7]

Conclusions

The US was a pace-setter in promoting more precise, stringent, and consistent international bank capital requirements after the crisis. However, unlike the case of centralized trading, clearing and reporting of derivatives, this

[7] The financial industry was also concerned about regulatory inconsistency across jurisdictions, mainly deriving from the divergent implementation of international capital standards. For instance, the partial compliance of the EU with Basel rules on CVAs could provide incentives for CVA-exempted entities to use EU dealers. In March 2013, the Securities Industry and Financial Markets Association (SIFMA) sent a letter to US Treasury Secretary Jacob Lew complaining that 'the difference in the regulatory treatment of CVA in the EU runs counter to the FSB's and G20's stated objectives of promoting internationally coordinated and consistent implementation of its regulatory action plan' (*Financial Times*, 24 April 2013).

jurisdiction was not a first-mover domestically: the US waited for international standards to be set, before revising domestic rules. The EU, unlike the US and to some extent, the UK, faced a trilemma (which also involved economic growth), not only a dilemma (stability-competitiveness) and, therefore, its regulatory preferences were not closely aligned to those of the US. However, transatlantic differences mainly concerned the level of stringency of the new capital rules rather than the need to tighten up capital requirements post-crisis. Although there were no foot-draggers at the international level, foot-dragging took place at the national level during the process of domestic implementation. For instance, the EU did not comply with key aspects of Basel III, notably, the CVA. Furthermore, several jurisdictions, including the EU, but also jurisdictions on the fringe, lagged behind in the domestic implementation of Basel IV (FSB 2018c).

Networks of regulators in international standard-setting fora can be seen as an intervening variable that was instrumental in setting international standards by reconciling preferences among jurisdictions, within jurisdictions, and among regulators. Heterogenous preferences of jurisdictions, for example, on the calibration of the CVA and the use of the leverage ratio, had to be accommodated in order to set international standards. This was facilitated by the dialogue taking place in the BCBS. Transgovernmental networks also fostered rules consistency, for example, the BCBS defined 'qualifying CCPs' by deferring to the rules issued by the CPSS/CPMI-IOSCO. Furthermore, the joint assessment (the FSB, the BCBS, the CPMI, the IOSCO 2018a) of the cumulative effects of post-crisis reforms on the incentives to centrally clear derivatives, undertaken by the main international standard-setting bodies, was instrumental in recalibrating the leverage ratio.

In fact, the elemental regime on bank capital was interlinked with other elemental regimes concerning derivatives. As a senior official at the Federal Reserve noted, strong capital standards alone were not enough to contain systemic risks because OTCDs dealers were part of a global network of interconnected exposures. 'When one dealer in the network fails, as we saw in the case of Lehman Brothers, fear of losses for other dealers in the network can cause systemic stress. Capital, which covers only a fraction of exposure, cannot alone prevent this contagion' (Tarullo 2011b). Therefore, it was necessary to 'build shock absorbers' in the derivatives network, whereby non-centrally cleared derivatives should have sufficient margin requirements to prevent contagion (Tarullo 2011b). Thus, international margin requirements, which are examined in the following chapter, were agreed upon.

Despite the strong opposition of the financial industry, first and foremost by banks, new international capital requirements were adopted. Hence, the financial industry acted as an intervening variable: it was unable to prevent the new rules, but it mobilized in a variety of regulatory venues in order to partly shape their content. Private actors, which had homogenous preferences in favour of less stringent capital requirements, were successful in watering them down over time. Thus, the financial industry influenced the calibration of the CVA, the composition of the leverage ratio, and the formula to be used to calculate bank exposures to CCPs. The financial industry engaged in some venue shopping, for instance, by siding with banking regulators in the BCBS concerning the revision of the way to calculate bank exposures to CCPs. Private actors also drew attention to the need for consistency across elemental regimes on derivatives as well as their cumulative effects, particularly regarding international margin requirements, which are discussed in the following chapter.

8

International Margin Standards for Non-centrally Cleared Derivatives

After the international financial crisis, in particular, the near failure of AIG, and after the introduction of the central clearing mandate for standardized OTCDs and higher capital requirements for non-centrally cleared derivatives, there was a need to mitigate the counterparty risk potentially associated with OTCDs by setting margin requirements for derivatives non-centrally cleared through CCPs. Therefore, the G20 Leaders (2011) at the Cannes summit agreed to add margin requirements to the post-crisis reform programme and asked the BCBS and the IOSCO to develop international standards in this area. In 2013, the BCBS-IOSCO, in consultation with the CPSS and the Committee on the Global Financial System (CGFS), set up a new elemental regime on margins, which was further developed over time.

The US was a pace-setter at an international level and a first-mover at the domestic level in promoting relatively precise, stringent and consistent margins for non-centrally cleared derivatives. The dilemma between domestic financial stability and international competitiveness was particularly acute in the US, not only because of the size of its financial sector (mainly, the vast amount of uncleared OTCDs), but also because the US adopted domestic rules on margins prior to international rules, placing the US financial industry at a competitive disadvantage. The EU, including the UK, was also concerned about stability and competitiveness and, therefore, had preferences aligned to those of the US. Consequently, the EU supported the US international standard-setting efforts, but adopted domestic regulations after international rules were set. There were no foot-draggers internationally, even though several jurisdictions on the fringe were reluctant followers, as suggested by their delayed and piecemeal domestic implementation of margin requirements.

Transgovernmental networks of domestic regulators engaged in international standard setting and facilitated the ironing out of disagreements among and within jurisdictions. International margin requirements for non-centrally cleared derivatives were heavily contested by the financial industry—especially by the dealer banks (Spagna 2019)—because of the expected

The Politics of Regime Complexity In International Derivatives Regulation. Lucia Quaglia, Oxford University Press (2020).
 DOI: 10.1093/oso/9780198866077.003.0001

economic costs of the new rules. Yet, the financial industry was unable to prevent this reform, it was only able to shape the content of the new standards by making them less precise and stringent than initially proposed. Private actors also urged regulators to consider this reform in conjunction with other post-crisis standards, so as to avoid a regulatory 'overkill' for business and improve consistency across financial regimes. In terms of regime complexity, margin requirements were interlinked with the rules on mandatory clearing (Chapter 4); with the rules on the resilience of CCPs, which also set the margins for derivatives centrally cleared via CCPs (Chapter 6); and with the rules on bank capital requirements (Chapter 7), all elemental regimes concerning various aspects of derivatives markets discussed in this book.

Key Issues concerning Margins for Non-centrally Cleared Derivatives

'Following the introduction of the central clearing obligation, the expectation was that most OTCDs would be cleared through a limited number of large CCPs.[1] However, this did not happen because several OTCDs were non-standardized contracts that could not be centrally cleared. Sometimes, these contracts were deliberately designed (or re-designed) so as to avoid mandatory clearing' (interview, December 2018). The question, then, became how to regulate non-centrally cleared OTCDs in order to encourage clearing through CCPs, avoid regulatory arbitrage and protect financial stability without distorting international competition across derivatives markets. Margin requirements for derivatives non-centrally cleared through CCPs were instrumental to this end. Margin is collateral provided by counterparties to reduce credit exposure and counterparty risk. As explained in Chapter 6, there are two types of margin, initial margin and variation margin, which respectively cover the potential future exposure and the current exposure to counterparty risk. Initial margin is collateral that is posted at the outset of a derivatives transaction. Variation margin considers changes in the market value of derivatives and involves payments that are usually made daily, to ensure that mark-to-market losses from default are limited to the period since the previous payment of variation margin (Gregory 2014).

[1] Since the opportunities for netting rise with the size of the pool of trades to be netted, the expectation was that the clearing industry would consolidate into a small number of large CCPs. Yet, this did not happen because jurisdictions were keen to develop domestic CCPs.

Margin is similar to capital in that they both lock-in funds that otherwise would be available for investment. However, margin and capital are distinct in several ways. First, margin works on the basis of the principle 'defaulter-pay'. In the event of a counterparty default, margin protects the surviving party by absorbing losses using the collateral provided by the defaulting entity. In contrast, capital adds loss absorbency to the system because it is 'survivor-pay'. Second, margin is more 'targeted' and 'dynamic' than capital: each portfolio has its own designated margin for absorbing potential losses and such margin is adjusted over time. In contrast, capital is shared collectively by all the entity's activities and cannot be rapidly adjusted to reflect changing risk exposures (BCBS-IOSCO 2012).

The interlinkages between capital and margin are, however, complex. When calibrating the application of capital and margin requirements, consideration must be given to: (i) the differences in capital requirements across different types of entities; (ii) the effect that certain margin requirements may have on the capital calculations of different types of entities subject to differing capital requirements; and (iii) the asymmetrical treatment of collaterals in many capital regulations, where benefit is given for collaterals received, but no cost is incurred for the risks of collaterals posted (BCBS-IOSCO 2012). The potential benefits of margin requirements must be weighed against the liquidity impact that would result from the counterparties' need to provide liquid high-quality collaterals. Moreover, the liquidity impact of margin requirements should be considered, together with other regulatory initiatives that also have significant liquidity impacts, such as the Liquidity Coverage Ratio and the Net Stable Funding Ratio set by Basel III (BCBS-IOSCO 2012).

Prior to the crisis, variation margins were quite common for OTCDs, albeit not for end-users. In contrast, no initial margin was posted, or, at the most, there was a one-way posting of collaterals (Lockwood 2018). The rationale for the new post-crisis margin requirements was to align more closely the bilateral practices for non-centrally cleared OTCDs with practices at CCPs, which used both initial and variation margins. This quest for consistency of margins for cleared and uncleared derivatives was intended to prevent regulatory arbitrage and reduce incentives to make certain products non-standardized in order to avoid the clearing obligation (interview, December 2018). The main post-crisis innovation consisted in introducing initial margins for uncleared OTCDs. Initial margins were intended, like higher capital requirements and the central clearing mandate, to reduce systemic risk and encourage central clearing. Yet, some observers questioned why initial margins were required for non-centrally cleared OTCDs that would be more heavily capitalized under Basel III, unlike centrally cleared derivatives (Gregory 2014).

Besides the interlinkage between the elemental regimes on margin requirements and capital requirements, which is discussed towards the end of this section, some specific issues arose in the negotiation of the new international standards for margins. To begin with, there was the impact of margin requirements on liquidity because margins make use of collaterals. In order to mitigate this impact, certain types of OTCDs (for example, foreign exchange) could be exempted from margin requirements; or certain counterparties (such as non-financial end-users, or non-systemically important financial firms) could be exempted; or there could be thresholds below which no margin requirement was applied. Besides reducing the need for liquid collaterals, exemptions would also reduce the compliance costs for the counterparties involved, so different exemptions would affect different parts of the financial industry in different ways. Similarly, the range of eligible collaterals could mitigate the drain on liquidity because the broader the choice of collaterals, the lower the drain on liquidity, but then the risk was that some collaterals would not be readily available in case of need. Likewise, the possibility to rehypothecate (or reuse) initial margins could ease the impact on liquidity, but the risk was that these collaterals would not be readily available (BCBS-IOSCO 2012). A broad range of collaterals and the possibility of re-hypothecation would also reduce the costs of margins for the counterparties that had to post them.

The other major issues in setting margin requirements regarded the use and the calibration of internal or third-party models and the criteria for the calculation of haircuts because the use of different parameters would result in different margins. The concern was that different models could produce unequal margin requirements between cleared and non-cleared derivatives as well as unequal margin requirements across financial institutions that made use of internal models. More generally, the crux of the matter was to avoid inconsistencies in margin requirements between centrally cleared and non-centrally cleared derivatives, as well as inconsistencies between margin requirements across financial institutions. Finally, there was the issue of the transition period for the new rules to enter into force (BCBS-IOSCO 2012).

The elemental regime on margins for non-centrally cleared derivatives fed into the regime complexity of post-crisis derivatives regulation. Indeed, international standards for margins were interlinked with other elemental regimes, specifically: margin requirements for derivatives centrally cleared via CCPs, set by the CPSS-IOSCO; and capital requirements on derivatives traded by banks, set by the BCBS. To begin with, margin requirements for non-centrally cleared derivatives had to be consistent with margin requirements for derivatives cleared via CCPs, so as to provide the right incentives for central clearing. Hence, the former had to be higher than the latter. Policymakers in the main jurisdictions that took the lead in international standard-setting processes were aware of the interlinkages across elemental regimes and the need to promote their consistency. For instance, Paul Tucker at the Bank of England noted that 'If bilateral margin requirements are laxer than margin requirements for central clearing, there may be incentives to bypass central clearing requirements' (quoted in *Global Custodian*, March 2013). At the same time, 'reliance on modelling gives CCPs considerable discretion in setting margins' and 'competitive pressures could give CCPs incentives to shade margin requirements to the low side.... For that reason, the international authorities are establishing frameworks for setting margin requirements for, respectively, CCPs and uncleared derivatives' (Tucker 2013).

Concerning the interlinkages between capital requirements for banks and margin requirements for centrally-cleared derivatives, the governor of the Bank of England, Mark Carney (2013), explained that 'higher capital and margin requirements reduce systemic risk by creating a buffer that can absorb losses and by creating incentives to properly manage risk. Incentives provided by capital and margin requirements for non-standardized derivatives will motivate increased use of standardized products and discourage spurious customization.' However, the potential benefits had to be weighed against the liquidity impact and costs for the financial industry and end-users. The regulators wanted to curb the speculative part of uncleared OTCDs—which was smaller than the commercial part, specifically, the companies that used OTCDs for hedging—but the two parts were not easy to disentangle (interview, November 2018). On the one hand, the financial industry was 'cordially terrified by the coming collateral squeeze, created by Basel III liquidity rules, the need to post collateral to CCPs and margins in the bilateral market' (Murphy, quoted in *Global Custodian*, March 2013). On the other hand, the Bank of England reassured that 'we don't need to panic about excessive and difficult-to-meet collateral requirements—of course, we do need to watch it, and the official community is doing so very carefully.... [T]here is a lot of high-quality collateral available and the amount of it is not numerically decreasing, but actually increasing.'[2]

[2] Cited in Investment Europe, 'No need to panic about OTC collateral supply', available at https://www.investmenteurope.net/investmenteurope/news/3707581/panic-about-otc-collateral-supply-bank-england

International Margin Requirements for Uncleared Derivatives

Initially, it was believed that capital requirements for banks would be sufficient for non-centrally cleared derivatives and that credit losses could be absorbed by the increased capital requirements set by Basel III. Therefore, at first, margin requirements were not envisaged by the G20 in 2009 and 2010. However, in 2011, the G20 agreed, under the urging of the US, to add margin requirements for non-centrally cleared OTCDs to the post-crisis reform programme, and asked the BCBS and the IOSCO to develop international standards. Internationally, the US was a pace-setter on margin requirements for non-centrally cleared OTCDs. The US Treasury Secretary, Timothy Geithner, stated 'Just as we have global minimum standards for bank capital – expressed in a tangible international agreement – we need global minimum standards for margins on uncleared derivatives trades' (*Reuters*, 6 June 2011). At that time, the EU did not have domestic rules on margins, but was the only jurisdiction that had expressed the intention to adopt rules equivalent to the US proposals by introducing margin requirements for uncleared OTCDs. Thus, the EU supported the US's pace-setting efforts internationally in order to agree on precise, stringent and consistent rules on margins.

The BCBS and the IOSCO, in consultation with the CPSS/CPMI and the CGFS, formed the *Working Group on Margining Requirements* to develop a proposal on variation and initial margins for uncleared OTCDs. In July 2012, an initial proposal on *Margin Requirements for Uncleared Derivatives* was released for consultation. Additionally, a quantitative impact study was conducted by the BCBS-IOSCO in order to assess the effects of mandatory margin requirements. In February 2013, the BCBS-IOSCO released a second consultative document after considering the responses to the first consultative document as well as the results of the quantitative impact study. The first issue that was thoroughly debated throughout the negotiations was the liquidity impact of the proposed international margin requirements (interview, December 2018). Already in the first consultative paper issued by the BCBS-IOSCO in July 2012, the SEC pointed out that the proposed margins could have a much greater impact on (US) securities firms regulated under the 'net capital rule', which did not apply, for example, to EU securities firms. In turn, European regulators, who worried about the liquidity impact of Basel III for EU banks (Howarth and Quaglia 2016), were also concerned about the liquidity impact of the would-be international standards for margins.

The second issue that came up in the negotiations on international margin requirements was the scope of exemptions. Initially, the BCBS-IOSCO focused their attention on all derivatives that were not cleared by CCPs, which included five major asset classes (interest rate, credit, equity, foreign exchange, and commodity). However, foreign exchange swaps and forwards were exempted from the definition of 'swap' in the Dodd-Frank Act, and were, therefore, exempted from central clearing requirements in the US. Hence, the US authorities proposed the same exemption at the international level (Spagna 2019). The exemption was motivated by the fact that foreign exchange swaps had a short time horizon, and by the fact that some risk-mitigating measures were already in place in this sector (interview, December 2018). In fact, the Continuous Linked Settlement (CLS)[3] was a specialist US financial company that provided settlement services in the foreign exchange market with a view to mitigating the settlement risk associated with this trade (*Euromoney*, 28 September 2012). However, the EU did not have an exemption for foreign exchange swaps and EU regulators were reluctant to grant it (interview, December 2018). There was, instead, broad consensus that margin requirements should not apply to non-centrally cleared derivatives traded by non-financial entities that were not systemically-important, which was in line with domestic rules adopted or under discussion in the US and the EU. Similarly, the BCBS-IOSCO broadly supported the non-application of margin requirements to sovereigns and central banks (BCBS-IOSCO 2012).

The third issue in the negotiations of international standards concerned the use of initial margins for rehypothecation. While there was broad consensus that the rehypothecation (or re-use) of collaterals should be prohibited in order to ensure that the assets would be readily available, the SEC raised the issue of whether the rehypothecation of initial margins should be permissible in limited circumstances (interview, December 2018). The SEC also pointed out that the requirement would have a disproportionate impact on US broker-dealers in comparison to banks due to the differences in the regulatory capital treatment of initial margins deposited with third-party custodians (BCBS-IOSCO 2012). European regulators remained sceptical about rehypothecation because they worried that assets would ultimately be unavailable in case of necessity (interview, December 2018). The fourth issue was the initial margin threshold, that is, the amount under which a firm would have the option of not collecting initial margins. The use of thresholds could potentially mitigate the effects of the new rules on liquidity and the costs associated with the bilateral

[3] The Continuous Linked Settlement (CLS) was the result of the collaborative efforts of foreign exchange market participants and various central banks, including the Federal Reserve, the ECB, and the Bank of England in response to regulatory concerns regarding systemic risk arising from the arrangements used to settle foreign exchange transactions (*Euromoney*, 28 September 2012).

exchange of margins. However, there was no unanimous view concerning the design and calibration of the thresholds (BCBS-IOSCO 2012).

The fifth issue in the negotiations on margins was the calibration of the models and the use of internal models, or standardized schedules. In setting the rules to calculate initial margins for non-centrally cleared OTCDs, the BCBS-IOSCO adopted as a benchmark the approach used by CCPs—it was referred to as 'CCPs-like' (interview, December 2018)—which determined initial margins based on the market risk exposure of the position, defined as a 99% value-at-risk (VAR) over a fixed liquidation horizon that depended on the asset class. The BCBS-IOSCO recommended the use of a ten-day horizon for non-cleared derivatives, as opposed to three or five days for cleared OTCDs, based on a perceived higher risk of non-cleared transactions. The BCBS-IOSCO proposed two methods to calculate initial margin requirements for non-cleared derivatives. The first method, called the standard schedule approach, applied pre-calibrated weights. This approach was not risk-sensitive: it did not properly account for netting and hedging effects and led to an overestimation of margin requirements. Arguably, its main purpose was to act as a (costly) fallback option and motivate market participants to use the alternative internal model approach (ISDA 2018). The internal model approach required the use of a quantitative model for risk factors.

There was caution about the use of quantitative models (Gregory 2014). Thus, models could be internally developed, or could be provided by third parties, but should be subject to supervisory approval in each jurisdiction and by each institution seeking to use the model. If firms were unable or unwilling to develop reliable internal margin calculation models, the BCBS-IOSCO proposed a standardized schedule that set out the margin level for each broad category of derivatives (BCBS-IOSCO 2012). A related issue was the method for determining appropriate haircuts. These could include either internal or third-party quantitative model-based haircuts, to be approved by supervisors, or schedule-based haircuts, set by the BCBS-IOSCO.

The sixth issue discussed in setting international standards for margins was the choice of eligible collaterals. One approach would have been to limit eligible collaterals to only the most liquid, highest-quality assets, such as cash and high-quality sovereign debt. Another approach would have been to permit a broader set of eligible collaterals, including equity securities and corporate bonds, a position that was supported by EU regulators, who had adopted a similar stance in the negotiations of Basel III liquidity rules (Howarth and Quaglia 2013). There was agreement that the initial margins should be held in such a way as to ensure that the margins collected were immediately available in the event of the counterparty's default, and these margins should be fully protected in the event of bankruptcy (BCBS-IOSCO 2012).

In September 2013, the BCBS and the IOSCO issued the *Final Framework for Margin Requirements for Non-centrally Cleared Derivatives*. According to these globally agreed-upon standards, all financial firms and systemically important non-financial entities that traded non-centrally cleared derivatives had to exchange initial and variation margins. Compared with the near-final framework proposed in early 2013, the final requirements included the following modifications. First, foreign exchange forwards and swaps were exempted from initial margin requirements, but not from variation margins. Second, the one-time re-hypothecation of initial margin collaterals was permitted, subject to a number of conditions. There was the introduction of a universal initial margin threshold of €50 million,[4] below which a firm would have the option of not collecting initial margins. All margin transfers between parties would be subject to a de-minimis transfer amount not exceeding €100,000. A broad array of eligible collaterals was allowed. The requirement to collect and post initial margins on non-centrally cleared trades were to be phased in over a four-year period, beginning with the most systemically important derivatives market participants in December 2015, and would apply to all transactions that involved either financial firms, or systemically important non-financial entities. In 2015, the BCBS—IOSCO delayed the beginning of the phase-in period for collecting and posting initial and variation margins to September 2016 (for an overview of international standards for margins for uncleared derivatives see Table 8.1).

State-centric Explanation of International Standard Setting for Margins

The US was a pace-setter in promoting international margin requirements and was a first-mover at the domestic level. This jurisdiction had strong incentives to set relatively precise and stringent rules on non-centrally cleared OTCDs because of the vast amounts of uncleared OTCDs in the US (approximately, half of the global trade) and because the five largest dealer banks were based in the US. Furthermore, the potential risk for financial stability was posed, not only by the dealer banks, but also by other financial institutions, as highlighted

[4] This universal initial margin threshold was chosen because the results of the quantitative impact study conducted in 2012 indicated that application of this threshold could reduce the total liquidity costs by 56%.

Table 8.1 International standards for margins for uncleared derivatives

International standard-setting body	Date of issuance	Standards (framework, guidance, etc.)
BCBS-IOSCO	2013	Margins Requirements for Uncleared Derivatives
BCBS-IOSCO	2015	Revised Margins Requirements for Uncleared Derivatives
FSB-BCBS-CPMI-IOSCO	2018	Incentives to Centrally Clear OTCDs
FSB	2018	Review of OTC Derivatives Market Reforms

by the near failure of the insurer AIG (Tarullo 2011a). Through its London branch, AIG sold credit default swaps on more than $410 billion notional in mortgage-backed securities, but was not required to post initial margins to its counterparties. Consequently, after the crisis, the US authorities were keen to protect financial stability by introducing margin requirements for non-centrally cleared derivatives.

The Chairman of the Federal Reserve, Ben Bernanke (2009), considered margin as 'an appropriate cost of protecting against counterparty risk'. Yet, domestic rules on margin would not suffice to protect financial stability in the US because of the negative externalities related to uncleared derivatives traded outside the US, especially considering that more than half of the dealer banks were not based in the US. Furthermore, more stringent margin requirements in the US would have negative implications for the competitiveness of the financial industry and could encourage regulatory arbitrage outside the US. As Daniel Tarullo (2011a), a member of the Federal Reserve Board of Governors, explained in his testimony before the Congress, 'it is important that progress on reforming the OTCDs market continues at the international level.... There is a need for agreement on a topic not covered by the G-20 declaration – that of global minimum margin requirements for derivatives not cleared through a central counterparty. Such an agreement would increase the stability of the financial system by reducing the likelihood of a *race to the bottom* in jurisdictions that do not implement equivalent standards' (emphasis in *italics* added). Similarly, the Chair of the CFTC, Gary Gensler, called for an international agreement on margin requirements for uncleared derivatives (*Bloomberg*, 7 March 2012). For all of these reasons, the US was a first-mover domestically and a pace-setter internationally as far as margin requirements for uncleared derivatives are concerned.

Domestically, regulatory competences on derivatives were spread across several agencies: the CFTC (which had jurisdiction over most derivatives under the Dodd-Frank Act); the SEC; the prudential banking regulators, namely: the Federal Reserve, the OCC, the FDIC, the Farm Credit Administration, and the Federal Housing Finance Agency. However, the last two agencies were of marginal importance and indeed were not represented in the BCBS-IOSCO's *Working Group on Margin Requirements*. In April 2011, the CFTC and, separately, the Federal Reserve and the other prudential regulators, issued proposals requiring OTCDs dealers to collect initial and variation margins from counterparties that previously did not post them (*Risknet*, 13 April 2011). According to the draft texts, initial margins could be calculated using either an approved internal model, or a standardized table. The internal model should be at least as conservative as models used by CCPs ('CCPs like') and, at a minimum, should be based on potential future exposure at a 99% confidence level over a ten-day time period (most CCPs used a five-day holding period). A standardized table set a minimum amount of initial margins to be collected as a percentage of the swap's notional amount. Netting was not allowed and initial margins had to be segregated. In an attempt to prevent domestic banks from sidestepping the regulation by shifting their trades overseas, the proposed rules were to apply to US banks globally (*Risknet*, 2 June 2011).

Elected officials in the US worried about the effects of the proposed rules for the international level playing field. For example, Congressman Darrell Issa argued that 'there are going to be jurisdictions that will implement rules that are less stringent than the US in order to attract derivatives business' (*Risknet*, 20 October 2011). In August 2011, Congressman Spencer Bachus, Chair of the House Committee on Financial Services, sent a letter to Treasury Minister, Timothy Geithner, complaining there was no evidence that policymakers in other jurisdictions would adopt rules mirroring those proposed in the US (*Risknet*, 5 September 2011). The proposed rules also alarmed the financial industry because US dealers would suffer competitive disadvantages internationally, if their competitors did not face similar requirements. The large US dealer banks, in particular, stressed the negative impact resulting from the lack of international consistency—clients would trade with banks that did not require them to collateralize. Daniel Pinto, JP Morgan's Chief Operating Officer, argued that JP Morgan (one of the main US dealer banks) would 'obviously lose a portion or the totality of the business', if the EU did not adopt the US rules. Even if Europe did so, the rules would not be applied to European banks trading out of Asia (*Risknet*, 5 September 2011). Furthermore, the extraterritoriality of the proposed US rules would not help. JP Morgan's Chief Risk Officer, Barry Zubrow (2011), in his hearing before Congress, argued that if the proposals were implemented on an extraterritorial basis, it would 'kill our overseas swaps activities'.

The EU was keen to trade up margin requirements for uncleared OTCDs because, like the US, it faced a trade-off between domestic financial stability and international competitiveness. For example, a regulator of the French AMF noted that 'the US rules are a move in the right direction in that they create a cost differential between uncleared and cleared swaps. We agree with the substance and will be looking to implement similar requirements in Europe. While there may be some small differences, I think the rules will converge' (*Financial Times*, 20 December 2011). In the UK, a joint document of the FSA and Her Majesty's Treasury (2009) noted that 'bilateral collateralization arrangements [for derivatives] must be subject to robust risk management, which should include: regular (preferably, daily) valuation and margin call processes; strong legal and operational frameworks; and appropriate capital requirements'. Within the EU, the member states did not have domestic rules on margin and the EU was slow in developing domestic regulatory templates on this matter for a variety of reasons, some having to do with the cumbersome EU policy-process, others having to do with specific concerns about the interlinkages between margin and capital requirements.

Indeed, EU policymakers were concerned that the US approach would mean that banks could end up holding both margin and capital to cover the same risk. The US proposed minimum margin and capital standards. That meant that an OTCD dealer, which had fully collateralized its positions, was still required to hold minimum capital requirements (*Risknet*, 5 September 2011). For EU policymakers, the key issue was whether to use capital and/or margin and to consider the cumulative effects of these requirements (interview, November 2018). Following the introduction of capital and liquidity requirements set by the Basel III Accord, EU banks had to raise substantial amounts of capital and liquidity (Howarth and Quaglia 2016). EU policymakers worried that if margin requirements were added on top of capital and liquidity requirements, there would be a shortage of liquidity (i.e. collaterals) for banks and other financial institutions in the EU (interview, November 2018).

The EU was also concerned about the potential negative implications of margin requirements for the international competitiveness of its financial industry. In its proposal to improve the resilience of the OTCDs markets, the European Commission stressed the need to 'strengthen bilateral collateral management' as well as the 'importance of an internationally coordinated approach.... Given the global nature of the OTCDs market, the lack of internationally coordinated action would only lead to *regulatory arbitrage*' (emphasis in *italics* added). The ESMA Chair, Steven Maijoor (2013b) pointed out 'a golden opportunity for OTC derivatives regulators in the area of margin requirements for non-centrally cleared derivatives'. He noted that regulators in various jurisdictions had agreed to postpone the implementation of bilateral margin requirements until the BCBS-IOSCO group had finalized its standards. In light of this, 'OTC derivatives regulators should be able to achieve global consistency regarding bilateral margins' (Maijoor 2013a).

Overall, the 'great powers' had homogeneous preferences concerning the need to set post-crisis margin requirements for non-centrally cleared OTCDs and had aligned incentives to engage in international standard setting. They also had the market power to do so, given the size of their domestic financial sector. Prior to the crisis, the US and the EU accounted, respectively, for 24% and 58% of the global market in uncleared derivatives (Spagna 2019). Post-crisis, the US developed domestic regulatory capacity as well as a domestic regulatory template on margins, which were used to inform international standards. Thus, the requirements to use internal models or standardized ones, the segregation of assets, the exemption for foreign exchange derivatives and the rehypothecation of collaterals were 'uploaded' by the US into international standards. At the international level, the Federal Reserve co-chaired the BCBS-IOSCO *Working Group on Margin Requirements*, which included representatives of the Federal Reserve Board, the Federal Reserve of New York, the SEC, the CFTC, the FDIC, and the OCC. For the EU, besides representatives from seven member states, there were representatives from the European Commission, the ECB and the EBA. On the one hand, the large number of US and EU representatives increased the influence of these jurisdictions in international standard setting for margin and gave these jurisdictions a comprehensive view of the interlinked issues at stake. On the other hand, the fact that so many domestic regulatory authorities were involved in the US and the EU did not facilitate their process of internal and external coordination, and, at times, the different views of domestic regulators were reconciled in international standard-setting bodies, as elaborated in the penultimate section.

Other jurisdictions had no plans to impose margin requirements on uncleared derivatives, and some were sharply critical, arguing that the need to collect margins on uncleared trades was not obvious. One Asian regulator argued that the US was keen for other jurisdictions to adopt rules similar to those in the US, 'but it all depends on what is relevant for our market'. Another Asian regulator criticized the attempt to set a rigid set of standards, rather than allowing dealers to come up with their own solutions (*Financial Times*, 30 July 2012). Margin requirements had distributional implications across jurisdictions in that they were expected to be more burdensome for jurisdictions on the fringe, in particular in Asia, where the OTCDs market was flourishing, but where approximately 50 percent of the swaps were non-clearable. Thus, some dealers in the region would struggle to comply with the new requirements and would have to pay a considerable premium to margin their trades. The lack of margining and clearing infrastructures in Asia, even for standardized trades, was expected to generate additional costs for local firms. As one industry participant noted 'The cost of implementation and the cost of providing margins are what makes margin rules the most challenging part of OTCDs reforms. The coverage of instruments for margin rules for non-centrally cleared derivatives is much broader compared to the instruments that are required to be mandatorily cleared',[5] which highlights the interlinkages between the standards for mandatory centralized clearing (Chapter 4) and margins.

Transgovernmental Explanation of International Standard Setting for Margins

Two transgovernmental networks of domestic financial regulators were primarily involved in setting post-crisis international standards for margins for uncleared OTCDs: central bankers and banking regulators, gathered in the BCBS, and securities market regulators, gathered in the IOSCO. These networks had different compositions, competences, and regulatory outlooks. Pre-crisis, they had not engaged in joint standard setting, except for the *Principles for the Supervision of Financial Conglomerates*, issued in 1999 by the Joint Forum, composed by members of the BCBS, the IOSCO, and the IAIS. After the crisis, the BCBS-IOSCO had to start basically from scratch because there were no international or domestic rules on margins, even though these rules were in the process of being discussed in the US. Furthermore, at the domestic level, a variety of regulatory agencies were involved, especially in the US and the EU, which did not ease domestic and international coordination.

In setting international margins, different regulatory approaches had to be reconciled by international standard-setting fora. 'Banking regulators

[5] Cited in Hong Kong Lawyer 'Asia's OTC Derivatives Markets See Important Rule Implementations in 2017', available at http://www.hk-lawyer.org/content/asias-otc-derivatives-markets-see-important-rule-implementations-2017

preferred the use of capital requirements (for example, concerning OTCDs traded by banks), whereas securities markets regulators preferred the use of margins. Furthermore, banking regulators were used to focussing on entities [banks], whereas securities markets regulators generally focused on transactions. In addition, international cooperation among securities markets regulators was less advanced than among banking regulators' (interview, December 2018). As one participant recounts 'Banking regulators had set international capital requirements for banks already in 1989 with Basel I. With Basel II, the use of modelling, parameters and quantitative impact studies had been introduced—thus, the banking world was already more quantitative. By contrast, securities markets regulators had nothing comparable to the Basel accords, and indeed the IOSCO had failed to introduce international capital requirements for investment firms' (interview, November 2018). As a starting point, regulators in the BCBS-IOSCO 'decided to adopt initial margins, which were used by CCPs for cleared OTCDs, and apply them to uncleared OTCDs' (interview, December 2018).

In order to improve international coordination, the BCBS and the IOSCO set up a Working Group on Margin Requirements, which also involved members from the other two committees, namely, the CPSS and the CGFS. The Working Group was chaired by a central banker and banking regulator from the US Federal Reserve and a regulator from the Securities and Futures Commission of Hong Kong. It included an almost equal number of members from both parent committees as well as members from the secretariat of the BCBS, the IOSCO, the CPSS, and the FSB. 'The Working Group put together representatives of all these groups dealing with banks, securities markets and financial stability for a cross-cutting evaluation because margins for uncleared OTCDs were of interest to all these regulators, but they were not the specific competence of any of them .... The twenty people of the group did not participate as national representatives, if anything, as representative of their parent committees' (interview, November 2018). The Working Group was the key institutionalized mechanism for the coordination of transgovernmental networks of banking regulators and securities markets regulators on margins.

Furthermore, the mechanism of institutional deference or cross-referencing of rules was also used. Notably, the BCBS-IOSCO (2013) standards adopted the recommendation on variation margins issued by the BCBS-CPSS (2013) Working Group on Foreign Exchange Settlement, as part of the *Supervisory Guidance for Managing Risks Associated with the Settlement of Foreign Exchange Transactions*. Thus, the BCBS-IOSCO (2013, p. 6) stated that 'in developing variation margin standards for physically settled foreign exchange forwards and swaps, national supervisors should consider the recommendations in the BCBS supervisory guidance'. There were also informal mechanisms for coordination, such as frequent meetings, phone calls, etc. Yet, it was a process of learning by doing. With reference to the interlinkages between the elemental regimes on margins and capital, one regulator sitting in the BCBS-IOSCO Working Group noted that:

> In Basel III, we asked for capital requirements, that is to say, bank capital, for uncleared OTCDs as well as liquidity requirements (which was something that banks were used to); then, we asked for margins on uncleared OTCDs (which was something new for banks).... The problem was that, initially, the negative effects of the proposed new margin requirements on liquidity were underestimated because they were based on 'scholastic exercises' that used old data, in the absence of better data. To put it another way, whereas there were sophisticated internal models that tended to reduce capital requirements for banks, even if validated by the regulators, in the case of OTCDs, the internal models used by banks and other financial companies were inadequate. It became, therefore, clear that the initial proposal of the Working Group would have had a major impact on liquidity and was therefore revised twice. Eventually, there was also the need to spread the transition over several years (interview, December 2018).

Transgovernmental networks were instrumental in setting international margin standards by ironing out disagreements among jurisdictions. Initially, only the US and, to a lesser extent, the EU, supported margin requirements for non-centrally cleared OTCDs. However, after the establishment of the BCBS-IOSCO Working Group on Margin Requirements, it became clear that margin requirements would become part of the official regulatory agenda and, eventually, international standards would be set. The convening of the Working Group was also a way to 'co-opt' regulators from jurisdictions on the fringe, which were initially sceptical of margin requirements (interview, November 2018). Indeed, the co-chair of the Working Group was from the Hong Kong Supervisory Authority. The BCBS-IOSCO Working Group also facilitated the ironing out of disagreements among the main jurisdictions, for example, concerning margin requirements for foreign exchange derivatives. In the US, the Treasury had managed to exempt foreign exchange swaps and forwards from margin requirements. This domestic exemption was granted before the establishment of the BCBS-IOSCO Working Group, thus, the US needed to prevent the Working Group from recommending such a requirement (Spagna 2019). Moreover, the EU initially opposed the exemption of foreign exchanges from initial margins. As one participant recounted, 'US regulators thought that foreign exchange swaps and forwards were mostly short term and subject to risk mitigation, for example through CLS. Hence, they were to be warranted an exemption. By contrast, EU policymakers were against an exemption that could create loopholes' (interview, November 2018). This issue was controversial in the Working Group. In the end, however, EU policymakers agreed to an exemption from initial margins for foreign exchange derivatives. The exemption would also lessen the impact of the new rules on liquidity, which was a major concern for the EU (interview, December 2018).

This exemption was the main instance of direct political intervention in this international regulatory process, whereby the 'US Treasury sought technical cover for political decisions already taken by the Dodd-Frank Act' (interview, November 2018). And, in fact, the Federal Reserve and other central banks worried about the risks in the foreign exchange market. In order to introduce some level of oversight, while keeping the exemption formally intact, the Federal Reserve decided to take advantage of the work done by the BCBS-CPSS Working Group on Foreign Exchange Settlement Risk, which was chaired by Jean-Marie Davis of the New York Federal Reserve (Spagna 2019). The BCBC-CPSS (2013) Working Group on Foreign Exchange published some guidelines for banks to tackle foreign exchange risk. One of the guidelines recommended the use of variation margins. The BCBC-IOSCO Working Group on Margins subsequently 'imported' this guideline on the use of variation margin into its own framework. This decision was unproblematic because many European members of the Group supported margins for foreign exchange swaps and forwards (Spagna 2019).

Transgovernmental networks also facilitated the ironing out of disagreements within jurisdictions. Initially, EU regulators supported two-way margin, as did the CFTC, whereas the US prudential regulators supported one-way margin. Spagna (2019) explains:

> As a market regulator, the CFTC favoured a two-way arrangement protecting both counterparties, whereas the prudential regulators decided to focus primarily on the health of the individual banks, and thus one side of the transaction only. Unlike the CFTC, they preferred a one-way approach, arguing that it was unjustifiable to have assets flowing from the regulated banking sector to hedge funds, in particular, which were often domiciled in jurisdictions exercising light-touch regulation or no regulation at all. At first,

the prudential regulators prevailed, with the CFTC officially aligning its position, but the conflict kept brewing in the background.

During the discussion in the BCBS-IOSCO Working Group, EU regulators were able to persuade their US counterparts to adopt a two-way initial margin (interview, November 2018). The Group acted as an 'epistemic community, bound together by shared experiences, learning, and socialization' (Spagna 2019). The CFTC, which had initially lost this battle at the domestic level, was able to form a coalition with EU regulators, which, eventually, led to the adoption of two-way margin also in the US, highlighting the 'second-order effects' of international soft law, whereby transgovernmental fora can alter the balance of regulatory power at the domestic level (Newman and Posner 2018).

There were instances in which the Working Group remained deliberately ambiguous, or reached watered-down compromise solutions. For example, although all regulators in the Working Group supported segregation, this was a challenge for the EU, which did not have a common insolvency law. Hence, a flexible wording was adopted in international standards (Spagna 2019). Another instance of a compromise was the permission of one-time rehypothecation of collaterals. Initially, rehypothecation was proposed by the US, especially the SEC, but it was opposed by the EU. Eventually, one-time rehypothecation was allowed. The concern about potential liquidity shortage, which was particularly pressing for EU policymakers and was confirmed by the BCBS-IOSCO quantitative impact study, played a role in persuading them to agree to this (interview, December 2018).

Industry-Led Explanation of International Standard Setting for Margins

Margin requirements for non-centrally cleared derivatives had distributional implications for the financial industry: there were expected winners and losers in the financial sector. The most negatively affected were the dealer banks, the so-called Group of 14 (G14), which comprised the Bank of America, Barclays, BNP Paribas, Citigroup, Credit Suisse, Deutsche Bank, Goldman Sachs, HSBC, JPMorgan Chase, Morgan Stanley, Royal Bank of Scotland, Société Générale, UBS, and Wells Fargo. This became the G16, when Credit Agricole and Nomura joined in. The dealer banks were the main traders of OTCDs, including those non-centrally cleared, hence, margin requirements meant higher costs for these banks, decreasing the profitability of their business.

Prior to the crisis, the dealer banks derived approximately 40% of their profits from trading uncleared OTCDs for their own account or for third parties (Spagna 2019).

The mandatory use of margins would enhance transparency, reduce the profits of the dealer banks and/or increase costs for the buy-side and the end-users, which would, then, be incentivized to use standardized trades and clear through CCPs, where higher levels of transparency and lower costs prevailed (Spagna 2019). Yet, one interviewee (November 2018) noted that the dealer banks had complex portfolios, whereby various elements compensated each other in several ways (e.g. by asset class, or across countries). 'The impact of the new rules much depended on the business structure of individual companies, which had different internal models, some of which compensated for everything. We, regulators in the BCBS-IOSCO, did not make rules for our national system, but for companies, in particular, the twenty largest dealer banks. Of particular interest were the "big five" in the US, namely JP Morgan, Goldman Sachs, Bank of America Merril Lynch, City, Morgan Stanley.'

Initially, the dealer banks opposed the introduction of initial margin requirements, especially two-way margins, their preference was for one-way margins, whereby they would only collect them from their clients, rather than having to post initial margins. Having failed to kill off the proposed rules, the dealer banks mobilized in order to shape the content of the new rules so as to make them less precise and stringent (and thus, less costly to implement). This could be done, for example, by allowing the re-hypothecation of collaterals; allowing exemptions for certain types of OTCDs; setting minimum thresholds; devising internal models that would reduce margins and so on. When the phase-in of the new rules began in 2016, twenty large firms were initially required to collect and post initial margins for OTCDs. In 2018, the non-cleared margining regime required approximately fifty financial groups to do so. A cumulative \$131 billion of initial margins for non-centrally cleared OTCDs were posted at end of 2017. In the case of cleared OTCDs, client initial margins reached a cumulative total of \$196 billion at the end of 2017 (ISDA-SIFMA 2018).

Other parts of the financial industry, notably, the buy-side, such as pension funds and investment funds and non-financial end-users, would also incur costs and benefits, following the introduction of margin requirements. However, the distributional implications of the new rules depended on their specific content, in particular, exemptions and thresholds. On the buy-side, financial companies were keen on the new rules to set (high) thresholds below which the margins would not be applied. On other issues, such as the prohibition of rehypothecation of collaterals and the use of two-way margins, the preferences of the buy-siders were not aligned. Some participants supported two-way margins, stressing the benefit of risk-reduction by receiving collaterals from the dealer banks. Others opposed it, arguing that the dealer banks would price-in the costs of posting collaterals to their clients (Spagna 2019). End-users, mostly non-financial companies, were keen for the new rules not to apply to them. At the same time, the introduction of margins provided new business opportunities to the financial industry. For example, Tri-optima (which is part of the Chicago Mercantile Exchange—CME) entered the market in order to provide collaterals for margins on uncleared OTCDs (interview, December 2018). Finally, CCPs were indirectly affected by margin requirements because the higher the margins for uncleared OTCDs, the higher the costs of not clearing via CCPs, which, in turn, could encourage counterparties to make greater use of central clearing.

The financial industry articulated three main arguments to influence the making of the new international rules (see Spagna 2019). First, it rebutted the claims that OTCDs had substantially contributed to the building up of the crisis. Second, it argued that after the crisis, high capital requirements on non-centrally cleared OTCDs already offered extra protection with a view to safeguarding financial stability. Finally, the financial industry warned against the shortage of liquidity as well as the macroeconomic costs of margin requirements. In terms of strategy, the financial industry mobilized in several regulatory venues and sought to build coalitions, including non-financial end-users (see also Pagliari and Young 2014). Even so, the financial industry failed to prevent international standards for margins.

The dealer banks were the most negatively affected by the new rules and, therefore, were the most engaged in the international regulatory debate. They also had considerable human and financial resources to deploy. The amendments suggested by the ISDA were designed to make the proposed rules less costly for the dealer banks. At the outset, the ISDA (2012) strongly opposed the two-way exchange of initial margins, arguing that they would cause a significant liquidity drain on the market, ranging from \$15.7 trillion to \$29.9 trillion. It strategically drew attention to the overlap between margin requirements and capital requirements set by Basel III, arguing that the latter were more appropriate than the former in order to safeguard the resilience of the financial system. The Basel III Accord imposed capital requirements on exposures specifically arising from OTCDs. The revisions of Basel III, especially the credit valuation adjustment (CVA) capital charges (which are discussed in Chapter 6), added considerably to the existing capital requirements. The ISDA drastically concluded that the BCB-IOSCO margin proposal would 'cause irreparable damage to the OTCDs business because of the dramatic increase in the cost of providing such products'. It (over)estimated that the cost of borrowing the required collaterals was likely to lead to a twenty-fold increase in the cost of providing plain vanilla interest rate OTCDs.

In order to reduce these negative effects and the compliance costs for the dealer banks, the ISDA (2013b) asked to exclude some entities—such as non-financial end-users, sovereigns, and central banks—and some products—such as foreign exchange OTCDs and special purpose vehicles—from the scope of the proposed rules, to set thresholds and to use internal models for initial margin calculations (see also AFME, ASIFMA, GFMA, SIFMA 2013). Furthermore, eligible collaterals and appropriate haircuts for the collaterals used should be determined by the parties involved. Finally, segregation and third-party custody should not be required; rehypothecation should not be prohibited; and a longer transition period was needed. Similarly, the Securities Industry and Financial Markets Association (SIFMA) (2013) proposed amendments designed to make the new requirement less expensive for industry. It opposed the two-way initial margin requirements for all financial counterparties (see also IIF 2013). It argued that 'undue emphasis had been placed on replicating for non-centrally cleared derivatives the margin framework that applied to centrally cleared derivatives'. In contrast to the pre-crisis period, bilateral counterparties were subject to enhanced capital requirements on their OTCDs portfolio, so initial margins were unnecessary.

Various banking associations in Europe expressed homogeneous preferences with a view to making the content of the proposed rules less stringent. The European Banking Federation (EBF) (2012) criticized the two-way initial margin requirement, which should be reconsidered, opting, instead, for the exchange of variation margins and capital requirements. The European Banking Federation (2013b) also supported exemptions for foreign exchange derivatives and special purpose vehicles; the re-hypothecation for both variation and initial margins; and a longer transition period (2020, instead of 2015). The French Banking Federation (FBF) (2012, 2013b) recognized the need for the bilateral exchange of variation margins, but felt that posting two-way initial margins for banks was 'totally disproportionate'. It argued that banks were already subject to Basel III, hence the posting of initial margins was redundant, given the capital requirements for counterparty risk. Similarly, the German Banking Industry Committee (2013) stressed that the combined effects of different sets of international rules adopted post-crisis—namely,

Basel III, the requirements for central clearing, and the margins for uncleared OTCDs—would put a strain on liquidity and the availability of collaterals.

Individual banks expressed preferences similar to those of the banking associations, but also made some specific requests related to their business model. For example, State Street Bank (2013), a large custodian bank, argued that third-party custody remained the 'most robust form of collateral protection'. However, Deutsche Bank (2012) opposed the segregation of collaterals with third-party custodians, pointing out that there are 'concentration risks in the financial system via the reliance on a small number of third-party custodians'. It also stressed that banks were already subject to prudential regulation, which was 'particularly intense' for systemically important banks, like the Deutsche Bank. Strategically, seeking to broaden the support for its position by building a coalition with non-financial users, the Deutsche Bank (2013) noted that 'Users of non-centrally cleared derivatives are generally those with a genuine need for a product that cannot be centrally cleared. These proposals thus risk penalizing those many genuine users.'

Barclays (2013) highlighted the interlinkage of the elemental regime on margins and that on bank capital, postulating a choice between a strict margin regime, proposed by the BCBS-IOSCO, coupled with lower capital requirements for banks; or a minimum initial margins regime, relying on bank capital to support credit risk. According to Barclays, Basel III struck the right balance between these two factors, so it was unnecessary to mandate an initial margins regime. Furthermore, this UK-based bank questioned whether margins were the best way to promote central clearing, given that the differentiated risk weight of Basel III for cleared and uncleared OTCD, respectively, 2% vs 100%, already did so (see Chapter 7). Barclays supported variation margins, mitigated by rehypothecation, but opposed two-way initial margins, which were seen as particularly costly for industry.

The European Fund and Asset Management Association (EFAMA) (2012, 2013), which represented European fund managers, articulated the distinctive interests of these buy-siders. It disagreed that that asset managers should post and collect initial margins, arguing that funds (especially the Undertakings for the Collective Investment in Transferable Securities) were subject to stricter rules than other financial institutions. According to this association, regulated funds should be exempted from posting initial margins because of their very low risk of default. It also argued that the collateralization of cleared and non-cleared OTCDs was different for investment funds in comparison to banks. Therefore, funds would face a liquidity shortage. Like other market players, the

EFAMA pointed out the cumulative effects of different regulatory initiatives for both cleared and uncleared derivatives, and more generally, it stressed the interlinkages between several post-crisis elemental regimes on derivatives. For example, collateral requirements for both cleared and uncleared derivatives would have significant effects on liquidity because the same assets would be required to cover the same instruments. In order to reduce compliance costs, the EFAMA supported the application of minimum thresholds, the use of two-way margins for variation margins and the phase-in of the requirements. The Managed Funds Association (MFA) (2013, 2012), a US association of hedge funds, supported two-way initial margins and segregation, but was concerned that buy-side participants would bear the sell-side counterparties' costs associated with the establishment of segregated custodian accounts. The Alternative Investment Management Association (AIMA) (2013), the association of alternative investment fund managers in Europe, believed that initial margins should be segregated and not rehypothecated. In order to reduce compliance costs, the Investment Management Association (IMA) (2013b), which represents managed funds in Europe, supported the application of minimum thresholds, the use of two-way margins, and the exemption of foreign exchange contracts and the phase-in period.

The competition between CCPs and dealer banks also entered the international regulatory debate. The European Association of Clearing Houses (EACH) (2012), the only association of CCPs that responded to the consultation of the BCBS-IOSCO (2012), argued that the proposals for margin requirements for uncleared derivatives were 'less prescriptive' and 'onerous' than equivalent requirements for centrally cleared derivatives. In many cases, the proposals put forward by the BCBS-IOSCO would lead to 'more flexible' and 'less onerous' margins for non-centrally cleared derivatives than for centrally-cleared derivatives. Consequently, the promotion of central clearing would not be encouraged unless the capital requirements for uncleared OTCDs were sufficiently penalizing, compared with the requirements for cleared derivatives. The EACH (2012) teased out several inconsistencies in the regulation of cleared and uncleared OTCDs. For example, the BCBS-IOSCO consultative document proposed a more 'liberal approach' to the quality of collaterals than the one proposed for CCPs. The prescribed haircut levels for collaterals of uncleared OTCDs were substantially lower than those for OTCDs cleared through CCPs. Furthermore, the threshold for the initial margin exemption was not available for CCPs. Basically, seeking to bring grist to its mill, the EACH called for more stringent rules for uncleared derivatives.

The main transnational associations of dealer banks and buy-siders (e.g. tthe AIMA, the MFA, the IIF) favoured greater international harmonization and consistency. The Alternative Investment Management Association (AIMA) (2013) regarded the BCBS-IOSCO's work on margin requirements as crucial for a 'workable and consistent inter-jurisdictional framework'. The Alternative Investment Management Association (AIMA) (2013) and the Managed Funds Association (MFA) (2013) called for the harmonization of margin requirements across jurisdictions, otherwise, market participants would have to monitor and comply with multiple margin regimes, which would be costly and burdensome. Furthermore, different margin requirements across jurisdictions would encourage regulatory arbitrage and favour market participants established in jurisdictions with lower margins. The Institute of International Finance (IIF 2013) noted that the BCBS-IOSCO proposal envisaged a 'unilateral decision' by a jurisdiction concerning the consistency of another jurisdiction's margin rules with the BCBS-IOSCO rules. Instead, an 'international solution' was needed in order to determine which jurisdictions were compliant with international rules, for example, by asking the FSB, the BCBS or the IOSCO to issue a list of compliant jurisdictions.

In the meantime, the dealer banks mobilized to promote private sector governance on margin models. In 2013, the ISDA sought an understanding from the BCBS-IOSCO Working Group on Margin Requirements to develop a standard initial margin model for margining non-centrally cleared derivatives. The proposal for the model followed the guidelines on margin requirements for non-centrally cleared derivatives issued by the BCBS-IOSCO in September 2013. The ISDA model would give market participants a common methodology to calculate margins (*Global Capital Euroweek*, 10 December 2013). The Standard Initial Margin Model Committee of ISDA, which was composed of dealer banks and buy-side participants, identified key criteria that the standard initial margin model should satisfy. The ISDA decided to base the Standard Initial Margin Model on the sensitivity-based approach used in the Basel Committee's Fundamental Review of the Trading Book (BCBS 2014c) (*Global Capital Euroweek*, 9 January 2015).

Conclusions

The elemental regimes for cleared and uncleared derivatives function in different ways, but they are interlinked. Margin requirements entered the international post-crisis regulatory agenda once it became clear that a substantial amount of OTCDs would remain non-centrally cleared and higher capital requirements for uncleared OTCDs would not suffice to safeguard financial stability and promote central clearing. Unlike other elemental regimes concerning various aspects of derivatives markets, such as mandatory centralized trading and clearing (see Chapter 4), margin requirements were quite precise, stringent and consistent, similar to derivatives-related capital rules (Chapter 7). Rules on trade reporting, including entity, product, and transaction identifiers (Chapter 5), were also rather precise, and consistent, but their competitive implications were much more limited, as compared to margin and capital requirements.

The US was a pace-setter internationally and a first-mover domestically. This jurisdiction introduced national rules on margins before international standards were set, but it advocated international standards in order to avoid negative externalities and prevent regulatory arbitrage. The EU faced similar concerns and, therefore, its regulatory preferences were by and large aligned to those of the US. Other jurisdictions, especially in Asia, reluctantly agreed to international rules on margins. On the one hand, this confirms a state-centric explanation, whereby the agreement of the 'great powers' was necessary and sufficient to set international standards, despite the reluctance of other jurisdictions. On the other hand, the foot-dragging of the reluctant jurisdictions manifested itself at the national level, during the process of protracted and patchy domestic implementation.

Transgovernmental networks in international standard-setting bodies were instrumental in setting international standards, also, at times, by reconciling heterogenous preferences among jurisdictions and within jurisdictions. In the international standard-setting process, there were some contentious issues, such as the exemptions for certain OTCDs, the threshold and methodology to calculate margins and the types of collaterals. Different preferences of various jurisdictions had to be taken into consideration in order to set international standards and this was facilitated by the dialogue taking place through transgovernmental networks, notably, the BCBS-IOSCO Working Group on Margins. Transgovernmental networks also fostered rules consistency, for example, between centrally cleared and non-centrally-cleared derivatives, or between capital and margin, and helped to manage the regime complexity resulting from several interlinked elemental regimes concerning derivatives.

Despite the strong opposition of the financial industry, especially the powerful dealer banks, new international margin requirements were adopted. To be fair, the financial industry was aware of the risks related to uncleared OTCDs and the inadequacy of the pre-crisis risk assessment methods. Yet, the industry worried about the expected costs of the new rules. Therefore, although it was unable to prevent the new rules, it mobilized in a variety of regulatory venues in order to shape their content by making them less precise and stringent. Private actors, which on certain issues had homogenous preferences, were successful in watering down some of the proposed rules, although that can partly be ascribed to regulators' concern about liquidity (i.e. the availability of collaterals). The financial industry also drew attention to the need for consistency among various elemental regimes concerning derivatives as well as their cumulative effects.

9
Conclusions

This concluding chapter, first, carries out an overall assessment of the post-crisis international regulation of derivatives and teases out some open issues. It compares the regulatory dynamics of various elemental regimes concerning derivatives markets, by underscoring similarities and differences, and by explaining how regime complexity has been managed with a view towards promoting rule precision, stringency, and consistency. The second section summarizes the main theoretical and empirical findings of the research. The last section details the book's broader empirical and theoretical contributions to the field as well as providing recommendations for future research.

Overall Assessment of Post-Crisis International Derivatives Regulation

After the financial crisis of 2008, the regulation of derivatives markets underwent a major overhaul with a view to mitigating systemic risk, improving transparency and protecting against market abuse. Internationally, post-crisis derivatives regulation resulted in a regime complex composed of nested, overlapping, parallel, and interlinking elemental regimes. Overall, there was a relatively good degree of international cooperation in promoting precise, stringent, and consistent standards for derivatives, even though there was considerable variation across elemental regimes and cooperation improved over time. This positive assessment is particularly true if one compares derivatives to other financial services—such as shadow banking—where post-crisis international regulatory reforms were limited, and if one considers the scope, complexity and interlinkages of the regulatory reforms on derivatives, the number of standard-setting bodies involved and the absence of a centralized coordination authority. Furthermore, international standards have to be negotiated among and, eventually, agreed upon by a multitude of jurisdictions, which have dissimilar domestic economic, political and legal contexts. It is a challenging multi-dimensional chess game.

The Politics of Regime Complexity In International Derivatives Regulation. Lucia Quaglia, Oxford University Press (2020).
 DOI: 10.1093/oso/9780198866077.003.0001

Post-crisis elemental regimes on derivatives had different degrees of precision, stringency, and consistency (for an overview see Figure 9.1, the arrows indicates regulatory interlinkages). The *international standards* adopted by the IOSCO concerning the *centralized trading* and *clearing* of derivatives were very general. Precise and stringent international rules were not sponsored by the main jurisdictions, which adopted domestic rules with considerable extra-territorial reach. Regulators and the financial industry were internally divided concerning the need for centralized trading. In contrast, they supported derivatives clearing through CCPs (hence the elemental regime on derivatives clearing was interlinked with the elemental regime on CCPs), but not 'one size fits all' mandatory rules.

International standards for the reporting of derivatives trades were not set initially, and the main jurisdictions adopted domestic regulation that made subsequent international harmonization more difficult. Once the US and, later, the EU, came to realize the negative effects of dissimilar domestic regulation for cross-border data aggregation, they acted as delayed pace-setters in the international harmonization of trade reporting, which was also supported by large transnational financial firms. Transgovernmental networks of regulators sprang into action, and eventually, relatively precise and consistent rules were issued on trade reporting, albeit some gaps remained concerning the harmonization of other critical data and cross-border data sharing.

International standards for the resilience, recovery, and resolution of CCPs became relatively more precise, stringent and consistent over time. After the introduction of mandatory centralized clearing for certain types of derivatives as well as capital and margin requirements to incentive clearing through CCPs, the main jurisdictions were keen to tighten up the regulation of CCPs. This was intended to protect financial stability and preserve the competitiveness of the domestic financial industry. By and large, the financial industry supported the reforms concerning the regulation of CCPs, although it sought to water down some of the rules proposed. A variety of transgovernmental networks gathered in the FSB, the CPSS/CPMI, and the IOSCO were involved in regulating the 3 Rs of CCPs.

The post-crisis *elemental regime on bank capital* was interlinked with elemental regimes on derivatives trading and clearing. That was specifically the case of bank capital for CVA, the inclusion of cleared derivatives in the leverage ratio and capital for bank exposures to CCPs. For these aspects, as for other parts of Basel III, the US and the UK were pace-setters internationally. The EU, in principle, agreed to the need to tighten up capital requirements for banks. In practice, however, the EU faced a 'trilemma' concerning financial stability, financial industry competitiveness, and the impact of capital rules on economic growth (Howarth and Quaglia 2016). Transgovernmental networks were instrumental in ironing out disagreements among and within

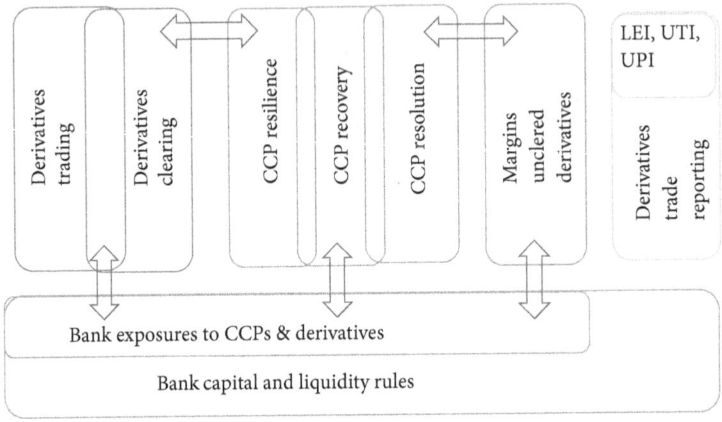

Figure 9.1 Elemental regimes of the international derivatives complex

jurisdictions. Despite the pushback from the financial industry, precise, stringent, and consistent capital rules were adopted by the BCBS.

The post-crisis *elemental regime on margins* for non-centrally cleared derivatives was interlinked with the elemental regime on derivatives clearing via CCPs. The US, followed by the EU, promoted precise, stringent, and consistent international rules in order to protect financial stability and avoid negative externalities from jurisdictions that did not want to introduce rules on margins. International margin requirements were also needed to protect the international competitiveness of the financial industry in the US and the EU because margins implied extra costs for industry. Transgovernmental networks were instrumental in ironing out disagreements among and within jurisdictions and, despite the opposition of the financial industry, margins requirements were adopted by the BCBS-IOSCO.

It is true that several derivatives standards, at least initially, had limited precision, stringency, and consistency (Knaack 2015, 2018; Gravelle and Pagliari 2018; Posner 2018). Indeed, this was sometimes the price to be paid in order to reach compromise solutions that would be acceptable to the political authorities, regulators and private financial actors in various jurisdictions. As one regulator acknowledged, 'there is a trade-off: granular and strict international rules are then difficult to implement domestically and vice versa' (interview, January 2019). Moreover, there was a 'genuine lack of knowledge' on certain topics (interview, March 2019), which was acquired over time. For instance, as far as recovery and resolution of CCPs were concerned, the Secretary-General of the FSB noted, that 'these are topics where—fortunately—we do not have much recent experience to draw on. On the one hand, this is a measure of the success of CCPs. But on the other hand... stress events can have unexpected outcomes and there is no room for complacency' (Domanski 2019). Some international standards that initially had limited precision, stringency, and consistency, notably rules on CCPs and trade reporting, developed over time. Some examples were the: CPMI-IOSCO (2017c) *Guidance on the Resilience and Recovery of CCPs* and the FSB (2017a) *Guidance on the Resolution of CCPs*, as well as the CPMI-IOSCO (2018a) *Guidance on the Harmonisation of Critical OTCDs Data Elements*, the CPMI-IOSCO (2017a) *Guidance Harmonisation of the Unique Product Identifier*, the CPMI-IOSCO (2017b) *Guidance Harmonisation of the Unique Transaction Identifier* and the FSB (2017b) *Governance Arrangements for the Unique Transaction Identifier*.

As time went by, international standards tackled controversial issues that had previously been side-stepped. For example, capital requirements for CCPs and the amount of their skin in the game were not agreed to internationally in the aftermath of the crisis. Subsequently, the FSB held public consultations with a view to setting international rules on the treatment of CCPs equity in resolution (FSB 2018b). Indeed, it is important to bear in mind that international regulation on derivatives evolved by trial and error, as pointed out by several interviewees. Several international standards were repeatedly revised, also in light of their cumulative and interlinked effects. For instance, *Margin Requirements for Non-centrally Cleared Derivatives* were revised by the BCBS-IOSCO in 2015 and 2019. The leverage ratio was revised by the BCBS several times.

The overall evaluation of post-crisis international regulatory reforms of derivatives markets is positive. Mandatory clearing requirements, together with capital and margin requirements, increased the total number of firms clearing derivatives via CCPs and the notional amounts cleared. That was true for products subject to mandatory clearing and for those centrally cleared on a voluntary basis.[1] Besides regulatory incentives, there were other incentives, such as market liquidity, counterparty credit risk management, and netting efficiencies, for large firms to clear. However, the incentives to clear were fewer for small firms, given the relatively high fixed costs of accessing central clearing and the practical difficulties in doing so (FSB, BCBS, CPMI, IOSCO 2018a). On the one hand, higher levels of collateralization for uncleared derivatives and more financial resources available to CCPs contributed to the resilience of the financial system and so did higher bank capital levels.

[1] For instance, clearing levels increased from 24% in 2009 to 62% in 2017 for interest rate derivatives worldwide (FSB, BCBS, CPMI, IOSCO 2018a).

On the other hand, the global clearing networks became more concentrated and the financial interdependence between CCPs and clearing members highlighted the 'CCP-bank nexus', especially in periods of financial stress (FSB, BCBS, CPMI, IOSCO 2018b).[2]

Although domestic compliance with international derivatives standards is beyond the scope of this book, a bird's eye view of the annual FSB's monitoring exercises suggests a good implementation record worldwide, which was quicker in the jurisdictions with the largest derivatives markets and for the less controversial standards. The FSB (2018c) *Review of OTC Derivatives Market Reforms* noted that central clearing obligations had been broadly implemented, leading to a significant increase in the central clearing of some OTCDs asset classes, notably, interest rates derivatives. Trade reporting requirements covering the vast majority of OTCDs were in place in most FSB jurisdictions. Interim capital requirements for non-centrally cleared derivatives were in force in almost all FSB jurisdictions, although many jurisdictions delayed the implementation of the final capital standards, specifically, capital requirements for counterparty credit risk and for bank exposures to CCPs. The areas of reform that were the least advanced in terms of domestic implementation were margin requirements for non-centrally cleared derivatives because several jurisdictions missed the internationally agreed upon deadlines, and platform trading, given that domestic rules were in place in only half the FSB jurisdictions (FSB 2018c).

There are several open issues concerning the regulation of global derivatives markets. To begin with, despite the considerable level of post-crisis international cooperation, full regulatory consistency across jurisdictions is elusive for a variety of reasons. First, domestic financial regulation, even when based on international standards, is set through national political processes that take the local characteristics of financial markets into account (Mosley 2010; Howarth and Quaglia 2013; Young 2014), for example, exempting certain entities or products. This, however, can create inconsistency across jurisdictions. Second, small regulatory differences matter very much in derivatives markets. Third, several international standards for derivatives were issued after domestic legislation in core jurisdictions had been adopted, notably, the Dodd-Frank Act (2010) in the US and EMIR (2012) in the EU.

[2] Approximately 88% of financial resources, including initial margin and default funds, were held by 10 CCPs and more than 80% of CCPs were exposed to at least 10 global systemically important banks. Furthermore, five firms, all bank-affiliated, accounted for over 80% of total client margin for cleared interest rate swaps in the US, the UK, and Japan (FSB, BCBS, CPMI, IOSCO 2018b).

In general, the *domestic implementation* of international standards remains the Achille's heel of international financial regulation (Zurn and Joerges 2005). In fact, international standards are sometimes general, and, therefore, can be implemented through different domestic rules. Consequently, although most jurisdictions base their domestic rules on international standards, when these standards are transposed into detailed domestic rules, these might differ (Verdier 2012; Zaring 2013). Other times, domestic non-compliance or partial compliance is a deliberate strategy designed to tailor international rules to the specificities of the domestic context due to pressure from elected officials and lobbying by the financial industry (Mosley 2010; Walter 2008; Quaglia 2019; Young 2014).[3] In order to deal with the problem of domestic compliance and foster the consistent implementation of derivatives regulation across jurisdictions, international standard-setters provided additional guidance over time. Furthermore, the FSB annually monitored state compliance with derivatives standards[4] (e.g. FSB 2017c, 2018c) so as to exert peer pressure on jurisdictions to implement domestically the regulatory reforms agreed upon internationally.

The second open issue in the regulation of global derivatives markets is *extraterritoriality*, meaning that domestic rules are applied to foreign entities and products (Barr and Miller 2006; Brummer 2010a; Coffee 2014; Scott 2014). Jurisdictions do not only need to regulate domestic entities and transactions, but also foreign entities active in the domestic market and transactions with foreign counterparts. Given the globalization of finance and the high degree of financial interdependence, not regulating foreign entities and transactions relevant to the domestic market could encourage regulatory arbitrage and could endanger investor protection and financial stability. However, foreign entities and transactions are already subject to the regulation and supervision of other jurisdictions. As a result, financial entities and transactions may become subject to multiple regulatory and supervisory regimes, which can be overlapping, inconsistent, and conflicting. This partly explains the transatlantic disputes that emerged concerning the regulation and supervision of CCPs, trade repositories and trading platforms (see Buxbaum 2016; Coffee 2014; Lehmann 2017; Scott 2014; Pagliari 2013b; Quaglia 2017b).

[3] There are also cases of 'mock compliance' (Chey 2014, 2007, 2006; Walter 2008), which occurs when a jurisdiction formally adopts a certain international standard, but behaves inconsistently. This 'cosmetic compliance' is more common in jurisdictions on the fringe than in the main jurisdictions, which can more openly defy international rules.

[4] Furthermore, the FSB conducts thematic and country-specific peer reviews and the IMF conducts Article IV consultations and the Financial Sector Assessment Programme (FSAP).

International standard-setters have paid increasing attention to this problem. For example, a recent report by the IOSCO (2019) examined the regulatory tools associated with the concept of deference[5] (e.g. passporting, substituted compliance, and equivalence) as well as bilateral arrangements in the form of MoUs that could contribute to deal with extraterritoriality in cross-border regulatory issues.

The more recent issue that has emerged in the regulation of global derivatives markets and that largely ensues from the open issues discussed above is *market fragmentation* (FSB 2019a; IOSCO 2019; Giancarlo 2019; IIF 2019; ISDA 2019), also in the context of Brexit (James and Quaglia 2020a,b). Fragmentation can occur for several reasons, including market-led practices, investor preferences and domestic legislation that is not related to financial services (e.g. taxation). However, it can also be an unintended consequence of regulation (FSB 2019a). In fact, the authorities often seek to balance potential trade-offs between the benefits of cross-border financial activity, the need to tailor domestic regulatory frameworks in the local context and, the fulfilment of the domestic mandate to safeguard investor protection and financial stability (IOSCO 2019). Thus, financial regulation and supervision may induce market fragmentation if domestic rules diverge, have an extraterritorial reach and include the so-called 'location policies', for example, on trade execution and clearing. Trading location policies result from the requirements that certain trades must be executed on designated platforms within a particular jurisdiction. Clearing location policies result from the requirements in some jurisdictions that certain trades (e.g. yen-denominated swaps in Japan) be cleared through CCPs within their borders.

The G20 Leaders at the Buenos Aires Summit in 2018 stressed the importance of 'an open and resilient financial system, grounded in agreed international standards' and of 'continued regulatory and supervisory cooperation to address fragmentation'. The FSB (2019a)[6] and the IOSCO (2019) published two reports on market fragmentation, coordinating their work so as to mitigate overlaps. Of particular concern were differences in the scope of products and entities covered by central trading and clearing mandates. These were exactly the areas in which international standards were 'thinner' and regulatory inconsistency across jurisdictions was greater. As the Governor of the

[5] Deference means that a regulator refrains from imposing its own rules where the rules of another regulator apply. The basis of deference is the idea that foreign rules are comparable to domestic rules because they fulfil similar objectives (Lehmann 2017).

[6] The FSB report also included a stocktaking from the work of other international standard-setting bodies, such the BCBS, the CPMI, the IOSCO, the IAIS, the IMF, the World Bank, and the OECD.

Bank of England, Mark Carney (2017a), noted, 'the global financial system is at a fork in the road', and therefore, the combination of 'robust international standards', 'consistent domestic implementation', and 'intensive supervisory cooperation' were the 'high road to a responsible, open financial system' (see also Carney 2017b, 2019).

Main Findings of the Research

This book began with a puzzle concerning the international regulation of derivatives, which, prior to the 2008 crisis, were not subject to public regulation, despite the risk they posed. Moreover, whereas pre-crisis international standard setting in finance took place in a silos-like structure, after the crisis, a vast array of new international standards concerning different aspects of derivatives markets were issued jointly, or separately, by a variety of international bodies, without a clear hierarchical structure. All this resulted in regime complexity, which needed to be managed. The regulation of derivatives was a particularly 'hard case' for international cooperation because public regulation was new, without a focal standard-setter. This book addresses three interconnected questions. What factors drove international standard setting concerning derivatives markets post-crisis? Why did international regime complexity emerge? How was it managed and with what outcome?

The research deployed an analytical framework that combined three mainstream theoretical approaches that have been used to explain international standard setting. To begin with, the *state-centric* account (Donnelly 2014; Drezner 2007; Fioretos 2011, 2010; Goldbach 2015a,b; Helleiner 2014; Henning 2017; Knaack 2015; Posner 2010; Rixen 2013, 2010; Simmons 2001; Singer 2004, 2007; Thiemann 2014, 2018), which emphasizes the preferences and power of the main jurisdictions, explains whether international rules were set (or not) as well as the broad content of these rules. Jurisdictions faced a dilemma between financial stability and the competitiveness of their financial industry (Kapstein 1992, 1989; Singer 2007, 2004; James and Quaglia 2020a).

The US and the UK were the main markets for derivatives. However, other large jurisdictions in continental Europe, such as France and Germany as well as some financial centres in Asia (notably, Singapore), developed a growing interest in this flourishing business. In a nutshell, unless the main jurisdictions, first and foremost, the US, acted as pace-setters at the international level, international rules were not set. Other jurisdictions were mostly fence-sitters.

The main exceptions were the UK and the EU on certain issues, such as CCPs regulation and margin requirements for uncleared derivatives. Sometimes, the jurisdictions on the fringe (notably, those in Asia) acted as foot-draggers, either at the international level or at the domestic level, resisting regulation that would dampen the development of their derivatives business (Li 2018).

The preferences of the main jurisdictions were influenced by existing domestic regulatory templates, domestic adjustment costs to international rules and negative cross-border externalities that these rules were designed to address. Daniel Tarullo (2011b), member of the Board of Governors of the Federal Reserve, explained that 'in recognition of the fact that financial distress can quickly and dramatically cross national borders', the goals that informed US involvement in international financial regulatory efforts were 'to protect our own financial system by promoting the adoption of strong, common regulatory standards and effective supervisory practices for large financial firms and important financial market infrastructures around the world. Such standards and practices can also help prevent major competitive disadvantage for US firms.' To a large extent, these considerations also apply to other jurisdictions with large financial sectors, first and foremost, the UK and the EU.

Although the (financial) 'great powers' sought to promote relatively precise, stringent, and consistent elemental regimes on several aspects of derivatives markets, they encountered several hindrances in doing so. At the domestic level, regulatory competences on derivatives were fragmented and in-flux, given the outpouring of post-crisis regulation. Both the US and the EU, which are compounded multi-level jurisdictions, had a multitude of domestic regulators with different compositions, competences, and regulatory outlooks. At times, domestic regulatory agencies engaged in bureaucratic politics and turf fighting. A notable instance was the tug of war between the SEC and CFTC in regulating and supervising swaps (Woolley and Ziegler 2011). In the banking sector, the main prudential regulators (the Federal Reserve, the OCC and the FDIC, which was also the resolution authority) often did not sing from the same script (Lavelle 2019). In the EU, the revision of EMIR in the context of Brexit triggered a power struggle among the ESMA, the ECB, and the national regulators in the member states (James and Quaglia 2020b). Within the SSM, the ECB and national central banks did not always see eye to eye concerning prudential banking regulation and supervision (Gren et al. 2015; Moschella and Quaglia 2020).

Transgovernmental networks of domestic regulators, such as central bankers, banking regulators, and securities markets regulators (Ahdieh 2015;

Brummer 2015; Coen and Thatcher 2008; Jordana 2017; Turk 2014; Verdier 2009) played a crucial role in managing regime complexity on derivatives—they were at the forefront of the quest for 'the holy grail of international cooperation and consistency', as stated by the Chair of the ESMA, Steven Maijoor (2013b). The work of transgovernmental networks facilitated the ironing out disagreements among jurisdictions. In the case of the Basel III Accord, which was the cornerstone of the elemental regime on bank capital, the BCBS successfully reconciled (at times, papering over) the different preferences of the US and the UK, which wanted stringent capital rules, and the rest of the EU and Japan, which worried about the effects of these rules on the real economy (Howarth and Quaglia 2016). In the case of margins for non-centrally cleared derivatives, initially, only the US and, to a lesser extent, the EU, supported the establishment of international rules. However, the convening of the BCBS-IOSCO Working Group on Margin Requirements was instrumental in co-opting regulators from jurisdictions on the fringe, which were sceptical of margin requirements. Not only standards for margins were eventually issued, but they were also relatively granular. Furthermore, the BCBS-IOSCO Working Group on Margins reconciled the (at times, different) preferences of the US and the EU, for example, with reference to initial margin exemptions for foreign exchanges derivatives and the adoption of two-way margins (Spagna 2019).

International standard-setting bodies also brought together the priorities of various networks of regulators and domestic regulatory agencies. Central bankers generally have an economics background, whereas securities regulators are usually lawyers. Furthermore, central bankers tend to be more autonomous from elected officials and the financial industry than securities markets regulators. Central bankers do oversight, which is system-wide, informal, often based on 'moral suasion'. Securities regulators do supervision, which is a formal process based on rules and litigation. Also, the tools to promote the resilience of banks and CCPs are different: capital is used for banks, whereas capital has a limited role in promoting the resilience of CCPs. For CCPs, margins are more important than capital. Thus, banking regulators are keen on capital, whereas securities markets regulators favour margins. These views needed to be brought together with reference to the elemental regimes on bank capital and margins. Furthermore, banking regulators mainly worry about the resilience of banks and the banking sector. Securities markets regulators prioritize central clearing via CCPs by not penalizing clearing members and their customers. These views needed to reconciled in regulating CCPs and bank exposures to CCPs.

That said, there were bureaucratic and political limitations to the activity of transgovernmental networks and their ability to deal with regime complexity (Brummer 2015; Turk 2014; Verdier 2009). On certain issues that were controversial, either from a bureaucratic or a political point of view, no agreement was reached and/or the standards issued remained rather general. To begin with, aspects that were sensitive for regulators and played into bureaucratic politics concerned the extra-territoriality of domestic rules and the use of regulatory deference. As mentioned above, international standards did not substantially tackle these matters, even though doing so could have contributed to preventing jurisdictional conflicts and market fragmentation (Posner 2018).

At other times, the standards issued were deliberately ambiguous, as in the case of CCPs' access to central bank liquidity, on which various central banks had differing views. Certain issues were politically controversial and, therefore, granular international standards were not issued, or remained rather general. For instance, for a variety of reasons mentioned above, international standards for derivatives trading were not set, even though one international standard-setter, the IOSCO, would have been the focal standard-setter. In the negotiation of the so-called Basel IV, regulators in the BCBS had to postpone the reaching of an agreement because of the opposition from their respective domestic political authorities. However, despite delays and revisions, an agreement was eventually reached in Basel in 2017.

Transgovernmental networks played a particularly important role in fostering regulatory consistency across elemental regimes and sets of standards. In fact, the activities of international standard-setters were coordinated through a variety of formal tools. First, there was *institutional deference* and *cross-referencing* across standards. For instance, the BCBS deferred to the CPSS-IOSCO rules on the resilience of CCPs in order to determine which CCPs were 'qualifying CCPs' for regulatory capital purposes. Likewise, the FSB and the CPSS-IOSCO deferred to the ISO, which set the data code for international trade reporting. The tool of cross-referencing was used by the CPSS-IOSCO *Recovery of Financial Market Infrastructures* (2014), which referred to the *FSB's Key Attributes of Effective Resolution Regimes for Financial Institutions* (2014) and to the CPSS-IOSCO (2012a) *Principles on Financial Market Infrastructures.* The FSB (2014b) *Key Attributes of Effective Resolution Regimes for Financial Institutions* made clear that their scope was aligned with that of the CPSS-IOSCO *Principles* (2012a), taking into account the CPSS-IOSCO *Report on Recovery of Financial Market Infrastructures* (2012c).

Joint working groups were set up. Thus, the CPSS-IOSCO set up working groups on trade reporting, CCPs resilience and recovery. There was a BCBS-CPSS-IOSCO working group on capital for bank exposures to CCPs and a BCBC-IOSCO working group on margins. The FSB also set up working groups with a mixed membership, such as the Aggregation Feasibility Study Group, co-chaired by a central bank and a securities market regulator. There were also *joint studies*. For instance, the FSB-BCBS-CPMI-IOSCO formed a joint Derivatives Assessment Team that produced two reports (2014, 2018a) to evaluate the combined effects of several post-crisis regulatory standards that were intended to incentivize central clearing. Of particular importance for the regulation of CCPs was the work plan agreed upon in 2015, which clarified the allocation of work between the various standard-setters involved (the FSB, the BCBS, and the CPMI-IOSCO). Subsequently, the Joint Chairs' Report in 2017 confirmed that the initial work plan had on the whole been completed. Furthermore, *informal tools*, such as the sharing of best practices, personal interactions and the involvement of the same officials in several meetings in different capacities were also used.

The *business-led* explanation (e.g. Baker 2010; Lall 2012; Pagliari and Young 2014; Tsingou 2008; Underhill and Zhang 2008; Young 2012), which stresses the preferences and power of the financial industry, partly accounts for the limited precision and stringency of some post-crisis rules. On the one hand, the financial industry was unable to prevent certain new rules, even when it strongly opposed them, as in the cases of margins and capital requirements (notably, the leverage ratio). The partial exception was the regulation of derivatives trading, which, for a variety of reasons not only related to the pushback from the financial industry, remained very 'thin' at the international level. On the other hand, the financial industry was successful in watering-down bank capital and margins requirements, which were particularly costly for private actors. However, this trend, which was often referred to as regulatory 'recalibration', was also the result of the cumulative effects of post-crisis rules, and their interlinkages. These effects were analyzed and acknowledged by domestic regulators and international standard-setting bodies, as elaborated above.

The financial industry was often internally divided concerning the regulation of various aspects of derivatives markets because the specific preferences of private actors depended on the expected costs and benefits of the rules under discussion. Thus, international standards designed to promote the trading of derivatives on exchanges or multilateral platforms were welcome by these private actors because this meant more business for them. In contrast, these measures were resisted by the dealer banks, which were heavily engaged in and profited from OTCDs trading. Similarly, the obligation to centrally clear standardized OTCDs via CCPs was welcome by CCPs. For the dealer banks and the end-users, central clearing implied higher costs related to the compensation for the clearing services they received. However, central clearing also involved the benefit of netting transactions and reduced the risk related to bilateral dealing (e.g. the risk that the counterpart of the transaction would not complete it).

The competition between CCPs, dealer banks, buy-siders, and end-users was paramount when rules on the recovery and resolution of CCPs were discussed. In a nutshell, CCPs were keen to pass the costs of recovery and resolution of ailing CCPs on to direct participants (dealer banks) and indirect participants (buy-siders and end-users). In contrast, direct and indirect participants wanted CCPs resources to be the first line of defence in recovery and resolution. In the case of trade reporting, initially, there was no pushback from the financial industry. However, this matter became contested once domestic rules proliferated and diverged, increasing the reporting costs for private actors engaged in cross-border business, who would have preferred harmonized rules, whereas domestic firms worried about the switchover costs ensuing from harmonization. On the one hand, lobbying from the transnational financial industry was instrumental in keeping the international harmonization of trade reporting on the agenda. On the other hand, the main drive came from regulators, especially those in large jurisdictions, who were unable to aggregate and analyze data due to their different formats.

Among players in the same 'category', notably, CCPs and dealer banks, there was cooperation and competition. CCPs competed with each other to attract business, but also cooperated in order to promote central clearing. Global CCPs had interests that were often different from those of small CCPs, which primarily carried out clearing for the domestic market. The dealer banks competed with each other to attract business, but also cooperated on issues, such as recovery and resolution, which juxtaposed their interests to those of CCPs. Furthermore, the large dealer banks had interests that were different from those of small domestic banks, which often accessed CCPs via clearing members (i.e. the dealer banks). The groups of the buy-siders and end-users were the most variegated. The buy-side included hedge funds, mutual funds, pension funds, private equity funds, and insurance companies. Non-financial end-users utilized derivatives to hedge on interest rates, foreign currencies, and commodity prices. Around 65% of OTCD trades turnover involved non-financial firms, which were active in various market segments, especially commodity derivatives.

At times, private actors engaged in international venue shopping, augmenting regime complexity, when it was in their interest to do so. For example, when capital rules for bank exposures to CCPs were discussed, the banks regarded the BCBS as their preferred interlocutor, partly because they were used to interact with this committee, partly because they hoped to find a sympathetic hearing with banking regulators. And, in fact, the formula for calculating the hypothetical capital needs of CCPs—and, on the basis of this, bank exposures to CCPs—put forward by the BCBS was less penalizing for banks than the formula elaborated by the CPSS-IOSCO. Not surprisingly, banks supported the BCBS's formula and opposed the CPSS-IOSCO's formula. With reference to bank capital and margins requirements on derivatives, the financial industry complained in several international fora about the cumulative and interlinked effects of these sets of rules. Hence, the financial industry pointed out the necessity to recalibrate (i.e. to lower) capital requirements to banking regulators in the BCBS, as well as the necessity to recalibrate (i.e. to lower) margin requirements to securities markets regulators in the IOSCO.

At other times, when imprecise or inconsistent rules were costly for the financial industry, especially for transnational firms, they contributed to international regulatory cooperation by mobilizing in a variety of venues. This was very important with reference to the regulation of the resilience, recovery, and resolution of CCPs, and the harmonization of trade reporting. In the case of capital and margins requirements, as pointed out above, there was some strategic lobbying by the financial industry, which deliberately overestimated the costs of the reforms and sought to play regulators against each other. However, there were also legitimate concerns about the cumulative (and, at times, unintended) effects of international rules, as pointed out by the financial industry to several international standard-setting bodies. Finally, the financial industry stressed the need for an overall assessment of the regulatory interlinkages among the elemental regimes on derivatives and the consistency of post-crisis financial rules.

Contributions to the Literature and Proposals for Further Research

This book contributes to two bodies of scholarly works in international relations and international political economy. To begin with, it speaks to the literature on regime complexity in international relations. Globalization and policy interdependence have led to the proliferation of formal organizations and less formal transgovernmental bodies (Colgan et al 2012) augmenting regime complexity in world politics and the global economy. This trend is relatively new in finance, and is partly the result of the sheer number of regulatory reforms undertaken after the crisis. Partly, it has to do with regulatory interlinkages between various sets of rules issued by a multitude of standard-setting bodies. The early works on regime complexity set out to explain why international complexity emerged (e.g. Alter and Meunier 2006; Raustiala and Victor 2004). Subsequent works explored what effects regime complexity produced (e.g. Alter and Meunier 2009). A third, more recent body of literature set out to explain how regime complexity was managed (e.g. Breen, Hodson and Moschella 2020; Heldt and Schmidtke 2019; Pratt 2018, 2019; Johnson and Urpelainen 2012). This book contributes to all of these three perspectives on regime complexity, but, especially to the second and third themes.

It is argued that the (financial) 'great powers' can play an important role in managing regime complexity and promoting international regulatory consistency if their preferences are similar and there are no major foot-dragging jurisdictions. The US, the UK, and the EU have technical expertise deriving from overseeing leading international financial centres as well as financial and human resources to deploy in international standard setting. These jurisdictions also have considerable bargaining power due to their market size and regulatory capacity. In the case of derivatives, the US, the UK, and the EU value the collective goods produced by elemental regimes within the complex and therefore have an incentive to avoid inconsistencies across regimes. Yet, the effectiveness of the US and the EU in advancing international cooperation is often weakened by the fact that several domestic regulatory agencies are involved in a variety of international bodies, sometimes with limited domestic coordination.

Consequently, transgovernmental networks are particularly important in managing regime complexity through a variety of formal and informal coordination tools, which are identified in this book. As for the financial industry, private actors engage in international venue shopping, augmenting regime complexity, when it is in their interest to do so. At other times, they contribute to managing regime complexity by stressing the need for rule consistency in a variety of regulatory venues. Although regime complexity is often seen as a 'pathology' that undermines governance effectiveness, the effects of regime complexity in derivatives are positive overall. There is a sensible division of work among international standard-setting bodies, which allows the efficient use of their respective expertise.

This book also speaks to the literature on the political economy of financial regulation and to the field of international political economy more broadly. It puts forward an explanation that combines mainstream theoretical approaches in order to provide a comprehensive analysis of post-crisis international standard setting concerning derivatives. This composite approach has considerable added value because it offers a more well-rounded understanding of the regulatory dynamics than 'monothematic' explanations. Furthermore, it can be applied to other areas of financial regulation and, potentially, to international standard setting in other policy areas.

This research adds to our understanding of state-centric, transgovernmental, and industry-led explanations. Although the era of US hegemony in finance (Simmons 2001) has ended, the US is still 'the' pace-setter in the regulation of global finance (Helleiner 2014). The US often forges an alliance with the UK, given their shared financial interests (James and Quaglia 2020a). This 'Anglo-Saxon alliance' will become more important after Brexit, when the UK's positions will be less constrained by EU regulatory templates and by the quest for EU cohesiveness on the international stage (Moschella and Quaglia 2016; Quaglia 2014c). After the crisis, the EU has increased its international regulatory clout in finance (Posner 2009; Mügge 2014; Quaglia 2014a), but not as much as the US. Furthermore, a 'euro area dimension' within the EU has come to the fore (Epstein 2019; James and Quaglia 2020b).

This research takes a mid-way position concerning the importance of transgovernmental networks. On one hand, regulators gathered in international standard-setting bodies are instrumental in facilitating agreement on precise, stringent and consistent rules. In particular, they deploy a variety of formal and informal tools in order to coordinate their activities and manage regulatory interlinkages. On the other hand, networks of regulators tend to be less effective when dealing with distributional conflicts, which might elicit intensive industry lobbying, or issues that are politically salient, which might trigger political intervention. Furthermore, the soft law issued by international standard-setters is often rather general and needs to be implemented at the domestic level. That said, the domestic implementation of international derivatives standards worldwide is rather good, as explained above. Furthermore, international soft law also produces important second-order effects at the domestic level (Newman and Posner 2018).

As for the business-led explanation, this research confirms that the power of the financial industry tends to be greater if the regulatory issues under discussion are not politically salient (Culpepper 2011; Pagliari 2013a). Thus, the international regulation of certain aspects of derivatives markets was relaxed once the memories of the crisis faded away. Furthermore, if the industry is not internally divided and is able to form broader coalitions (Pagliari and Young 2014; Young and Pagliari 2015), for example, with non-financial derivatives end-users, it is more influential in the regulatory process (for instance, concerning the treatment of client cleared derivatives derivatives in the leverage ratio). Yet, various parts of the financial industry often have different (at times, competing) preferences, for example, exchanges versus other trading venues; CCPs against direct participants (dealer banks) and indirect participants (buy-siders and end-users). Private actors engage in international venue shopping (Beyers and Kerremans 2012; Eckhardt and De Bievre 2015) in order to further their particularistic interests. Yet, by lobbying in several venues, the financial industry can also contribute to promoting regulatory consistency and precision, if private actors are negatively affected by imprecise and inconsistent rules.

Finally, this book contributes to the literature on post-crisis reforms in finance (Botzem 2014; Ban and Gabor 2016; Fioretos 2010; Gabor 2016a; Goldbach 2015a,b; Helleiner 2014; Knaack 2015; Lall 2012, 2014; Maynz 2012, 2015; Moschella and Tsingou 2013a,b; Mügge and Stellinga 2015; Mügge and Perry 2014; Newman and Posner 2018; Pagliari 2012; Porter 2014a,b; Posner 2015; Rixen 2013, 2010; Simmons 2001; Singer 2004, 2007; Thiemann 2014, 2018; Tsingou 2010a, 2015a,b; Young 2012, 2014). Several works that have examined the international regulatory response to the financial crisis have pointed out the limited scope and stringency of the reforms adopted, despite the devastating effects of the crisis (Baker and Underhill 2015; Helleiner 2014; Macartney 2019; Moschella and Tsingou 2013a,b; Moschella 2015; Tsingou 2015b; Underhill 2015). For example, post-crisis bank capital requirements were traded up, but some academics (e.g. Admati and Hellwig 2014) and policymakers (e.g. Haldane 2012) argued that this capital increase was insufficient to ensure the resilience of the banking sector. Stringent international rules on hedge funds and credit rating agencies were not adopted (Quaglia 2014a). The international regulation of shadow banking also remained rather 'thin' (see Ban and Gabor 2016; Ban, Seabrooke, and Freitas 2016; Nesvetailova 2015). In other words, the status quo prevailed (Helleiner 2014), or, at the very least, regulatory changes were incremental (Moschella and Tsingou 2013a,b; Maynz 2012, 2015).

With specific reference to derivatives, previous studies underplayed the extent of international cooperation and stressed, instead, the regulatory disputes that emerged among jurisdictions (Knaack 2018, 2015; Gravelle and Pagliari 2018, Posner 2018). In contrast, this research highlights the broad scope and considerable consistency of post-crisis reforms of international derivatives regulation and explains the remarkable level of international cooperation that underpinned these regulatory efforts, contributing to make the global derivative markets more resilient. As noted by the FSB (2020: 1), the covid pandemic represents 'the biggest test of the post-crisis financial system to date.... This exogenous shock has placed the financial system under strain'. Despite the unprecedented challenges posed by the pandemic, including extreme volatility in financial markets and massive volumes of trading and clearing, derivatives markets and market infrastructures, in particular CCPs, 'have functioned well'—'CCPs and their large clearing members have shown resilience' (FSB 2020: 6).

Three areas for further research can be identified. First, this book deliberately focuses its analysis at an international level, that is to say, international standard setting, investigating the domestic level only in so far as this is necessary in order to shed light on the main dynamics at an international level. Further research could examine the interactions between regulatory dynamics at the two levels in a more systematic way, and how they mutually affect each other. It would also be interesting to investigate rule consistency vertically, that is, between international and domestic rules, as well as horizontally, that is, rule convergence and diverge across jurisdictions. Second, this analysis focused on post-crisis regulatory reforms during the last ten years or so, because there was little international public regulation of derivatives markets prior to the crisis. By its very nature, the last decade was an 'untypical' regulatory period, in the wake of the largest financial crisis in a generation. Future research might analyze regulatory developments and the evolution of regime complexes over a longer period of time. Finally, further research could investigate and compare regime complexity in a variety of policy areas, inside and outside of the field of finance. It would be interesting to assess which explanations 'travel' better across policy areas, and which dynamics, instead, are more distinctive of a specific policy area.

References

Abbott, K.W., Genschel, P., Snidal, D., and Zangl, B. (2015) *International Organizations as Orchestrators*, Cambridge: Cambridge University Press.

Abbott, K.W., Genschel, P., Snidal, D., and Zangl, B. (2016) 'Two logics of indirect governance: Delegation and orchestration', *British Journal of Political Science* 46 (4): 719–29.

Abbott, K.W., Keohane, R., Moravcsik, A., Slaughter, A.-M., and Snidal, D. (2000) 'The concept of legalization', *International Organization* 54 (3): 401–19.

Admati, A. and Hellwig, M. (2014) *The Bankers' New Clothes: What's Wrong with Banking and What to Do about It*, Princeton: Princeton University Press.

Adolph, C. (2013) *Bankers, Bureaucrats and Central Bank Politics: The Myth of Neutrality*, Cambridge: Cambridge University Press.

Ahdieh, R. (2015) 'Coordination and conflict: The persistent relevance of networks in international financial regulation', *Law and Contemporary Problems* 78 (4): 75–101.

Alessandri, P. and Haldane, A. (2009) 'Banking on the state', Speech, Bank of England, 6 November, London, https://www.bankofengland.co.uk/-/media/boe/files/paper/2009/banking-on-the-state

Alter, K.J. and Meunier, S. (2006) 'Nested and overlapping regimes in the transatlantic banana trade dispute', *Journal of European Public Policy* 13 (3): 362–82.

Alter, K.J. and Meunier, S. (2009) 'The politics of international regime complexity', *Perspectives on Politics* 7 (1): 13–24.

Alter, K.J. and Raustiala, K. (2018) 'The rise of international regime complexity', *Annual Review of Law and Social Sciences* 14: 329–49.

Alternative Investment Management Association (AIMA) (2011) 'Response to review of the Markets in Financial Instruments Directive, 1 February, London, available at https://circabc.europa.eu/webdav/CircaBC/FISMA/markt_consultations/Library/financial_services/MIFID%20-%20Review%20of%20the%20Markets%20in%20Financial%20Instruments%20Directive%20(2011)/registered_organisation

Alternative Investment Management Association (AIMA) (2013) 'Response to second consultative document on margin requirements for non-centrally-cleared derivatives', 15 March, London, available at https://www.bis.org/publ/bcbs242/aima.pdf

Alternative Investment Management Association (AIMA) (2016) 'Response to consultation on resilience and recovery of CCPs', 18 October, London, available at https://www.bis.org/cpmi/publ/comments/d149/aima.pdf

Alternative Investment Management Association (AIMA) and Managed Fund Association (MFA) (2013) 'Response to consultation on recovery of financial market infrastructures', 11 October, London, available at https://www.bis.org/cpmi/publ/comments/d109/aimaandmfa.pdf

Arner, D.W. and Taylor, M.V. (2009) 'The global financial crisis and the financial stability board: Hardening the soft law of international financial regulation', *University of New South Wales Law Journal* 32 (2): 488–513.

Association for Financial Markets in Europe (AFME) (2011) 'Response to review of the Markets in Financial Instruments Directive', 1 February, London, available at https://circabc.europa.eu/webdav/CircaBC/FISMA/markt_consultations/Library/financial_services/MIFID%20-%20Review%20of%20the%20Markets%20in%20Financial%20Instruments%20Directive%20(2011)/registered_organisation/AFME%20-%20Association%20for%20Financial%20Markets%20in%20Europe.pdf

Association for Financial Markets in Europe (AFME), Asia Securities Industry & Financial Markets Association (ASIFMA), Global Financial Markets Association (GFMA), Securities Industry and Financial Markets Association (SIFMA) (2013) 'Response to second consultative document on margin requirements for non-centrally-cleared derivatives', 15 March, London, available at https://www.bis.org/publ/bcbs242/gfma.pdf

Bach, D. and Newman, A.L. (2007) 'The European regulatory state and global public policy: micro-institutions, macro-influence', *Journal of European Public Policy* 14 (6): 1–20.

Bach, D. and Newman, A.L. (2010) 'Transgovernmental networks and domestic policy convergence: evidence from insider trading regulation', *International Organization* 64: 505–28.

Bach, D. and Newman, A.L. (2014) 'Domestic drivers of transgovernmental regulatory co-operation', *Regulation & Governance* 8 (4): 395–417.

Bach, T., De Francesco, F., Maggetti, M., and Ruffing, E. (2016a) 'Special Issue: Symposium: Transnational regulatory networks as means of EU governance: the administrative dimension of multilevel coordination', *Public Administration* 94 (1).

Bach, T., De Francesco, F., Maggetti M., and Ruffing, E. (2016b) 'Transnational bureaucratic politics: An institutional rivalry perspective on EU network governance', *Public Administration* 94 (1): 9–24.

Bailey, A. (2014) 'The Bank of England's perspective on CCP risk management, recovery and resolution arrangement', Speech, Bank of England, 24 November, London, available at https://www.bankofengland.co.uk/-/media/boe/files/speech/2014/the-boes-perspective-on-ccp-risk-management-recovery-and-resolution-arrangements

Baker, A. (2010) 'Restraining regulatory capture? Anglo-America, crisis politics and trajectories of change in global financial governance', *International Affairs* 86: 647–63.

Baker, A. (2013a) 'The new political economy of the macroprudential ideational shift', *New Political Economy* 18 (1): 112–39.

Baker, A. (2013b) 'The gradual transformation? The incremental dynamics of macroprudential regulation', *Regulation & Governance* 7: 417–34.

Baker, A. and Underhill, G.R. (2015) 'Economic ideas and the political construction of the financial crash of 2008', *British Journal of Politics and International Relations* 17(3): 381–90.

Ban, C. and Gabor D. (2016) 'The political economy of shadow banking', *Review of International Political Economy* 23 (6): 901–14.

Ban, C., Seabrooke, L., and Freitas, S. (2016) 'Grey matter in shadow banking: international organizations and expert strategies in global financial governance', *Review of International Political Economy* 23 (6): 1001–33.

Bank of England (2012) *Financial Stability Report*, June, London, available at https://www.bankofengland.co.uk/financial-stability-report/2012/june-2012.

Banque de France (2017) *Financial Stability Review*, April, Paris, available at https://publications.banque-france.fr/sites/default/files/medias/documents/fsr21_web.pdf

Banque de France and the Autorité de Contrôle Prudentiel et de Résolution (2018) 'Leverage ratio and client clearing', *Discussion Paper*, April, Paris, available at https://acpr.banque-france.fr/sites/default/files/medias/documents/acpr_discussion_paper_-_lr_and_client_clearing.pdf

Barclays (2013) 'Response to second consultation on margin requirements for non centrally cleared derivatives', 15 March, London, available at https://www.bis.org/publ/bcbs242/barclays.pdf

Barr, M. and Miller, G. (2006) 'Global administrative law: The view from Basel', *European Journal of International Law* 17 (1): 15–46.

Basel Committee on Banking Supervision (BCBS) (2010a) *Basel III: A Global Regulatory Framework for More Resilient Banks and Banking Systems*, December, Basel, available at https://www.bis.org/publ/bcbs189_dec2010.pdf

Basel Committee on Banking Supervision (BCBS) (2010b) *Consultative Document Capitalisation of bank exposures to central counterparties*, December, Basel, available at https://www.bis.org/publ/bcbs190.pdf

Basel Committee on Banking Supervision (BCBS) (2011) *Revisions to the Basel II Market Risk Framework*, February, Basel, available at https://www.bis.org/publ/bcbs193.pdf.

Basel Committee on Banking Supervision (BCBS) (2012) *Interim Capital Requirements for Bank Exposure to CCP*, July, Basel, available at https://www.bis.org/publ/bcbs227.htm.

Basel Committee on Banking Supervision (BCBS) (2013a) *Consultative Document Capital Treatment of Bank Exposures to Central Counterparties*, June, Basel, available at https://www.bis.org/publ/bcbs253.htm

Basel Committee on Banking Supervision (BCBS) (2013b) *Non-internal Model Method for Capitalising Counterparty Credit Risk Exposures* (NIMM), June, Basel, available at https://www.bis.org/publ/bcbs254.htm

Basel Committee on Banking Supervision (BCBS) (2013c) *Revised Basel III Leverage Ratio Framework and Disclosure Requirements*, June, Basel, available at https://www.bis.org/publ/bcbs251.pdf

Basel Committee on Banking Supervision (BCBS) (2014a) *Regulatory Consistency Assessment Programme Assessment of Basel III regulations European Union*, December, Basel, available at https://www.bis.org/bcbs/publ/d300.pdf

Basel Committee on Banking Supervision (BCBS) (2014b) *Basel III Leverage Ratio Framework and Disclosure Requirements*, January, Basel, available at https://www.bis.org/publ/bcbs270.htm

Basel Committee on Banking Supervision (BCBS) (2014c) *Fundamental Review of the Trading Book: A Revised Market Risk Framework*, January, Basel, available at https://www.bis.org/publ/bcbs265.pdf

Basel Committee on Banking Supervision (BCBS) (2014d) *Capital Treatment of Bank Exposures to Central Counterparties*, April, Basel, available at https://www.bis.org/publ/bcbs282.htm

Basel Committee on Banking Supervision (BCBS) (2015) *Review of the Credit Valuation Adjustment Risk Framework*, July, Basel, available at https://www.bis.org/bcbs/publ/d325.pdf

Basel Committee on Banking Supervision (BCBS) (2016a) *Minimum Capital Requirements for Market Risk in the Trading Book*, January, Basel, available at https://www.bis.org/bcbs/publ/d352.pdf

Basel Committee on Banking Supervision (BCBS) (2016b) *Consultative Document Revisions to the Basel III Leverage Ratio Framework*, April, Basel, available at https://www.bis.org/bcbs/publ/d365.htm

Basel Committee on Banking Supervision (BCBS) (2017) *Basel III: Finalising Post-crisis Reforms*, December, Basel, available at https://www.bis.org/bcbs/publ/d424.pdf

Basel Committee on Banking Supervision (BCBS) (2019) *Revisions to Leverage Ratio*, June, Basel, available at https://www.bis.org/bcbs/publ/d468.htm

Basel Committee on Banking Supervision (BCBS) and Committee on Payment and Settlement Systems (2013) *Supervisory Guidance for Managing Risks Associated with the Settlement of Foreign Exchange Transactions*, February, Basel, available at https://www.bis.org/publ/bcbs241.pdf

Basel Committee on Banking Supervision (BCBS)—International Organization of Securities Commissions (IOSCO) (1995) *Framework for Supervisory Information about the Derivatives Activities of Banks and Securities Firms*, May, Basel, available at https://www.bis.org/publ/bcbs19.pdf

Basel Committee on Banking Supervision (BCBS)—International Organization of Securities Commissions (IOSCO) (2005) *Amendment on Application of Basel II to Trading activities*, July, Basel, available at https://www.bis.org/publ/bcbs116.htm

Basel Committee on Banking Supervision (BCBS)—International Organization of Securities Commissions (IOSCO) (2012) *Consultative Document Margin Requirements for Non-Centrally-Cleared Derivatives*, July, Basel, available at https://www.bis.org/publ/bcbs226.htm

Basel Committee on Banking Supervision (BCBS)—International Organization of Securities Commissions (IOSCO) (2013) *Margin Requirements for Uncleared Derivatives*, September, Basel, available at https://www.bis.org/publ/bcbs261.pdf.

Basel Committee on Banking Supervision (BCBS)—International Organization of Securities Commissions (IOSCO) (2015) *Revision Margin Requirements for Non-centrally Cleared Derivatives*, March, Basel, available at https://www.bis.org/bcbs/publ/d317.htm

Bell, D. and Hindmoor, A. (2015) *Masters of the Universe, Slaves of the Market*, Cambridge, MA: Harvard University Press.

Bell, S. and Hindmoor, A. (2016) 'Structural power and the politics of bank capital regulation in the United Kingdom', *Political Studies* 65 (1): 103–21.

Bell, S. and Hindmoor, A. (2018) 'Are the major global banks now safer? Structural continuities and change in banking and finance since the 2008 crisis', *Review of International Political Economy* 25 (1): 1–27.

Bernanke, B. (2009) *Testimony before the Committee on Banking, Housing, and Urban Affairs, US Senate*, 3 December, Washington, available at https://www.federalreserve.gov/newsevents/testimony/bernanke20091203a.htm.

Bernanke, B. (2011) 'Clearing houses, financial stability, and financial reform', Speech, Federal Reserve, 4 April, Washington, available at https://www.federalreserve.gov/newsevents/speech/bernanke20110404a.htm

Beyers, J. and Kerremans, B. (2012) 'Domestic embeddedness and the dynamics of multi-level Venue Shopping in Four EU Member States', *Governance* 25 (2): 263–90.

Biggins, J. and Scott, C. (2013) 'Private governance, public implications and the tightrope of regulatory reform: The ISDA credit derivatives determinations committees', *Osgoode CLPE Research Paper* N. 57, Toronto.

Black, J. (2008) 'Constructing and contesting legitimacy and accountability in polycentric regulatory regimes', *Regulation & Governance* 2 (2): 137–64.

Blackrock (2014) 'Central clearing counterparties: too big to fail?', April, London, available at https://www.blackrock.com/corporate/literature/whitepaper/viewpoint-ccp-tbtf-april-2014.pdf

Blackrock (2016a) 'Response to resilience and recovery of CCPs: Further guidance', 18 October, London, available at https://www.bis.org/cpmi/publ/comments/d149/overview.htm

Blackrock (2016b) 'Revisiting the 3 R's for Central Clearing Counterparties', October, London, available at https://www.blackrock.com/corporate/literature/whitepaper/viewpoint-ccps-resiliency-recovery-resolution-october-2016.pdf

Blackrock (2018) 'An end-investor perspective on central clearing looking back to look forward', September, London, available at https://www.blackrock.com/corporate/literature/whitepaper/viewpoint-end-investor-perspective-central-clearing-looking-back-to-look-forward.pdf

Botzem, S. (2013) 'Continuity of expert rule: global accountancy regulation after the crisis' in M. Manuela and E. Tsingou (eds), *Great Expectations, Slow Transformations*, Colchester: ECPR Press.

Botzem, S. (2014) *The Politics of Accounting Regulation: Organizing Transnational Standard Setting in Financial Reporting*, Cheltenham: Edward Elgar.

Botzem, S. and Quack, S. (2009) '(No) limits to Anglo-American accounting? Reconstructing the history of the International Accounting Standards Committee: A review article', *Accounting, Organizations and Society* 34 (8): 988–99.

Breen, M., Hodson, D., and Moschella, M. (2020) 'Incoherence in regime complexes: A sentiment analysis of EU–IMF surveillance', *Journal of Common Market Studies* 58 (2): 419–37.

Brummer, C. (2010a) 'How international financial law works (and how it doesn't)', *Georgetown Law Journal* 99: 257–327.

Brummer, C. (2010b) 'Why soft law dominates international finance—and not trade', *Journal of International Economic Law* 13 (3): 623–43.

Brummer, C. (2015) *Soft Law and the Global Financial System*, Cambridge: Cambridge University Press.

Brunnermeier, M., Crockett, A., Goodhart, C., Persaud, A.D., and Shin, H.S. (2009) 'The fundamental principles of financial regulation', *Geneva Reports on the World Economy*, 11.

Buckley, J., Howarth, D., and Quaglia, L. (2012) 'Internal market: The ongoing struggle to "protect" Europe from its money men', *Journal of Common Market Studies, Annual Review* 48 (s1): 119–41.

Busch, M.L. (2007) 'Overlapping institutions, forum shopping, and dispute settlement in international trade, *International Organization* 61: 735–61.

Büthe, T. and Mattli, W. (2011) *The New Global Rulers: The Privatization of Regulation in the World Economy*, Princeton: Princeton University Press.

Buxbaum, H.L. (2016) 'Transnational legal ordering and regulatory conflict: Lessons from the regulation of cross-border derivatives', *Mauer School of Law, Legal Studies Research Paper Series*, 365.

Cafferman, K. and Zeff, S.A. (2006) *Financial reporting and global capital markets: A history of the International Accounting Standards Committee, 1973–2000*, Oxford: Oxford University Press.

Carney, M. (2013) 'The UK at the heart of a renewed globalisation', Speech, Bank of England, 23 October, London, available at https://www.bis.org/review/r131025g.pdf

Carney, M. (2014) 'The future of financial reform', Speech, Bank of England, 17 November, London, available at https://www.fsb.org/wp-content/uploads/The-future-of-financial-reform.pdf

Carney, M. (2017a) 'What a difference a decade makes', Speech, Bank of England, 20 April, London, available at https://www.fsb.org/wp-content/uploads/What-a-Difference-a-Decade-Makes.pdf

Carney, M. (2017b) 'A fine balance', Speech, Bank of England, 20 June, London, available at https://www.bankofengland.co.uk/speech/2017/a-fine-balance.

Carney, M. (2019) 'The global outlook', Speech, Bank of England, 12 February, London, available at https://www.bankofengland.co.uk/-/media/boe/files/speech/2019/the-global-outlook-speech-by-mark-carney

CCP12 (2013) 'Response to consultation on capital treatment of bank exposures to central counterparties', 27 September, Shanghai, available at https://www.bis.org/publ/bcbs253/ccp12.pdf

CCP12 (2016) 'Response to consultation on resilience and recovery of CCPs', 17 October, Shanghai, available at https://www.bis.org/cpmi/publ/comments/d149/ccp12.pdf

Cerny, P. (2010) *Rethinking World Politics: A Theory of Transnational Pluralism*, Oxford: Oxford University Press.

Chalmers, A.W. (2015) 'Financial industry mobilisation and securities markets regulation in Europe', *European Journal of Political Research* 54 (3): 482–501.

Chen, C.H. (2017) 'Extraterritoriality of the regulations and interconnections of the derivatives market: Legal implications for East and Southeast Asia', *Masaryk University Journal of Law and Technology* 11 (2): 323–49.

Chey, H-K. (2006) 'Explaining cosmetic compliance with international regulatory regimes: The implementation of the Basle Accord in Japan, 1998–2003', *New Political Economy* 11 (2): 271–89.

Chey, H-K. (2007) 'Do markets enhance convergence on international standards? The case of financial regulation', *Regulation & Governance* 1 (4): 295–311.

Chey, H-K. (2014) *International Harmonization of Financial Regulation? The Politics of Global Diffusion of the Basel Capital Accord*, London: Routledge.

Chicago Mercantile Exchange (CME) (2011a) 'Response to consultation on the review of Markets in Financial Instruments Directive', 2 February, New York.

Chicago Mercantile Exchange (CME) (2011b) 'Response to consultation on bank exposures to CCPs', 4 February, New York, available at https://www.bis.org/publ/bcbs190/cmegroup.pdf

Chicago Mercantile Exchange (CME) (2013) 'Response to consultation on authorities' access to trade repository data', 10 May, New York, available at https://www.bis.org/cpmi/publ/comments/d108/cmeg.pdf

Chicago Mercantile Exchange (CME) (2017) 'Response to consultation on resolution of CCPs', 13 March, New York, available at https://www.fsb.org/wp-content/uploads/CME-Group-1.pdf

Chong Tee, O. (2017) 'Opening address at ISDA Regulators and Industry Forum', Speech, Monetary Authority of Singapore, 13 November, Singapore, available at https://www.mas.gov.sg/news/speeches/2017/opening-address-at-isda-regulators-and-industry-forum

Chow, J., Tan, J., and Won, J. (2016) 'Liquidity and policy analyses for platform trading of OTC derivatives: A perspective of smaller markets', *Staff Paper*, N. 54, Monetary Authority of Singapore, Singapore, available at https://www.mas.gov.sg/-/media/MAS/resource/news_room/Staff-Papers/MAS-Staff-Paper-No54–Liquidity-and-Policy-Analyses-for-Platform-Trading-of-OTC-Derivatives.pdf

Chuan Teck, L. (2012) 'Making the trading of derivatives safer', Speech, Monetary Authority of Singapore, 29 November, Singapore, available at https://www.mas.gov.sg/news/speeches/2012/making-the-trading-of-derivatives-safer.

Chwieroth, J. (2009) *Capital Ideas: The IMF and the Rise of Financial Liberalization*, Princeton: Princeton University Press.

Chwieroth, J.M. (2015) 'Professional ties that bind: how normative orientations shape IMF conditionality', *Review of International Political Economy* 22 (4): 757–87.

Clapp, J. and Helleiner, E. (2012) 'Troubled futures? The global food crisis and the politics of agricultural derivatives regulation', *Review of International Political Economy* 19 (2): 181–207.

Coen, D. and Thatcher, M. (2008) 'Network governance and multi-level delegation: European networks of regulatory agencies', *Journal of Public Policy* 28 (1): 49–71.

Cœuré, B. (2012) 'The reform of financial regulation: priorities from an ECB perspective', Speech, ECB, 6 March, Frankfurt, available at https://www.ecb.europa.eu/press/key/date/2012/html/sp120306.en.html

Cœuré, B. (2014) 'The known unknowns of central clearing', Speech, ECB, 29 March, Frankfurt, available at https://www.ecb.europa.eu/press/key/date/2014/html/sp140331.en.html

Cœuré, B. (2015) 'Addressing global data availability challenges', Speech, ECB, 10 September, ECB, Frankfurt, available at https://www.ecb.europa.eu/press/key/date/2015/html/sp150910.en.html

Coeure, B. (2017) 'Setting standards for granular data', Speech, ECB, 28 March, Frankfurt, available at https://www.ecb.europa.eu/press/key/date/2017/html/sp170328.en.html

Cœuré, B. (2018) 'A cooperative approach to CCP recovery and resolution', Speech, 4 May, Frankfurt, available at https://www.bis.org/review/r180504a.htm

Coffee, J.C. Jr. (2014) 'Extraterritorial financial regulation: Why ET Can't come home', *Cornell Law Review* 99(6): 1259–302.

Colgan, J.D., Keohane, R.O. and Van de Graaf, T. (2012) 'Punctuated equilibrium in the energy regime complex', *Review of International Organizations* 7 (2): 117–43.

Committee on Payments and Market Infrastructures (CPMI)—International Organization of Securities Commissions (IOSCO) (2014) *Recovery of Financial Market Infrastructures*, October, Basel, available at https://www.bis.org/cpmi/publ/d121.htm

Committee on Payments and Market Infrastructures (CPMI)—International Organization of Securities Commissions (IOSCO) (2015) *Consultative paper on Harmonisation of the Unique Product Identifier*, December, Basel, available at https://www.iosco.org/library/pubdocs/pdf/IOSCOPD519.pdf

Committee on Payments and Market Infrastructures (CPMI)—International Organization of Securities Commissions (IOSCO) (2017a) *Guidance Harmonisation of the Unique Product Identifier*, September, Basel, available at https://www.bis.org/cpmi/publ/d169.htm.

Committee on Payments and Market Infrastructures (CPMI)—International Organization of Securities Commissions (IOSCO) (2017b) *Guidance Harmonisation of the Unique Transaction Identifier*, February, Basel, available at https://www.bis.org/cpmi/publ/d158.htm

Committee on Payments and Market Infrastructures (CPMI)—International Organization of Securities Commissions (IOSCO) (2017c) *Resilience and Recovery of Central Counterparties (CCPs): Further Guidance on the Principle for Financial Market Infrastructures*, July, Basel, available at https://www.bis.org/cpmi/publ/d163.htm

Committee on Payments and Market Infrastructures (CPMI)—International Organization of Securities Commissions (IOSCO) (2018a) *Guidance on the Harmonisation of Critical OTCDs Data Elements (other than UTI and UPI*, April, Basel, available at https://www.bis.org/cpmi/publ/d175.htm

Committee on Payments and Market Infrastructures (CPMI)—International Organization of Securities Commissions (IOSCO) (2018b) *Framework for Supervisory Stress Testing of*

Central Counterparties (CCPs), April, Basel, available at https://www.iosco.org/library/pubdocs/pdf/IOSCOPD599.pdf

Committee on Payment and Settlement Systems (CPSS) (1998) *OTC Derivatives: Settlement Procedures and Counterparty Risk Management*, September, Basel, available at https://www.bis.org/publ/ecsc08.htm

Committee on Payment and Settlement Systems (CPSS)—International Organization of Securities Commissions (IOSCO) (2001) *Recommendations for Securities Settlement Systems*, November, Basel, available at https://www.bis.org/cpmi/publ/d46.pdf

Committee on Payment and Settlement Systems (CPSS)—International Organization of Securities Commissions (IOSCO) (2004) *Recommendations for Central Counterparties*, November, Basel, available at https://www.bis.org/cpmi/publ/d64.pdf

Committee on Payment and Settlement Systems (CPSS)—International Organization of Securities Commissions (IOSCO) (2012a) *Principles on Financial Market Infrastructures*, April, Basel, available at https://wwa.bis.org/cpmi/publ/d101a.pdf

Committee on Payment and Settlement Systems (CPSS)—International Organization of Securities Commissions (IOSCO) (2012b) *Data Reporting and Aggregation*, January, Basel, available at https://www.bis.org/cpmi/publ/d100.htm

Committee on Payment and Settlement Systems (CPSS)—International Organization of Securities Commissions (IOSCO) (2012c) *Report on Recovery and Resolution of Financial Market Infrastructures*, July, Basel, available at https://www.bis.org/press/p120731.htm

Committee on Payment and Settlement Systems (CPSS)—International Organization of Securities Commissions (IOSCO) (2013) *Authorities' Access to Trade Repository Data*, August, Basel, available at https://www.bis.org/cpmi/publ/d110.pdf

Cooper, A. F. and Thakur, R. (2013) *The Group of Twenty (G20)*, London: Routledge.

Cosimano, T.F. and Hakura, D.S. (2011) 'Bank behavior in response to Basel III: A cross-country analysis', *IMF Working Paper*, No 119, Washington.

Council of Ministers (2016) *Outcome of the Council meeting*, 12 July, Brussels.

Culpepper, P.D. (2011) *Quiet Politics and Business Power*, Cambridge: Cambridge University Press.

Cunliffe, J. (2018) 'Central clearing and resolution: Learning some of the lessons of Lehman', Speech, Bank of England, 5 June, London, available at https://www.bis.org/review/r180606c.pdf

De Bièvre, D., and Poletti, A., and Thomann, L. (2014) 'To enforce or not to enforce? WTO judicialization, forum shopping and global regulatory harmonization', *Regulation & Governance* 8 (3): 269–86.

De Burca, G., Keohane R.O., and Sabel, C.F. (2013) 'New modes of pluralist global governance', *New York University Journal of International Law& Politics* 45: 723–86.

De Burca, G., Keohane R.O., and Sabel, C.F. (2014) 'Global experimentalist governance', *British Journal of Political Science* 44 (3): 477–86.

De Larosière, J., L. Balcerowicz, O. Issing, R. Masera, C. Mc Carthy, L. Nyberg, J. Pérez, and O. Ruding (2009) *Report of the High-level Group on Financial Supervision in the EU*, February, Brussels.

Depository Trust & Clearing Corporation (DTCC) (2011a) 'Response to consultation on OTC Derivatives Data Reporting and Aggregation Requirement', 23 September, New York, available at https://www.bis.org/cpmi/publ/comments/d96/dtcc.pdf

Depository Trust & Clearing Corporation (DTCC) (2011b) 'Response to consultation on bank exposure to CCPs', 4 February, New York, available at https://www.bis.org/publ/bcbs190/dtacc.pdf

Depository Trust & Clearing Corporation (DTCC) (2013a) 'Response to consultation on recovery of financial market infrastructures', 11 October, New York, available at https://www.bis.org/cpmi/publ/comments/d109/dtcc.pdf

Depository Trust & Clearing Corporation (DTCC) (2013b) 'Response to consultation on Authorities' Access to Trade Repository Data', 10 May, New York, available at https://www.bis.org/cpmi/publ/comments/d108/dtcc.pdf

Depository Trust & Clearing Corporation (DTCC) (2016) 'Response to consultation on resilience of recovery of CCPs', 18 October, New York, available at https://www.bis.org/cpmi/publ/comments/d149/dtcc.pdf

Depository Trust & Clearing Corporation (DTCC) (2018) *A Progress Report on OTCD Trade Repositories*, April, New York, available at https://ioandc.com/wp-content/uploads/2018/04/9-DTCC-WHITE-PAPER_4.24.18.pdf

Deutsche Bank (2011) 'Response to the consultation on OTC derivatives data reporting and aggregation requirements', September, Frankfurt.

Deutsche Bank (2012) 'Response to first consultation on margin requirements for non centrally cleared derivatives', 28 September, Frankfurt, available at https://www.bis.org/publ/bcbs226/deutschebank.pdf

Deutsche Bank (2013) 'Response to second consultation on margin requirements for non centrally cleared derivatives', 15 March, Frankfurt, available at https://www.bis.org/publ/bcbs242/deutschebankag.pdf

Djelic, M.-L. and Quack, S. (eds) (2010) *Transnational Communities: Shaping Global Economic Governance*, Cambridge: Cambridge University Press.

Dodd, M. (2018) 'Markets: Exchange or Over-the-Counter', IMF, 18 December, Washington, available at https://www.imf.org/external/pubs/ft/fandd/basics/markets.htm

Dodd-Frank Wall Street Reform and Consumer Protection (Dodd-Frank) Act (2010) US Congress, Washington.

Domanski, D. (2019) 'CCP resilience, recovery and resolution: Completing the journey towards resilient derivatives markets', Speech, FSB, 27 February, available at https://www.fsb.org/wp-content/uploads/S270219.pdf

Domanski, D., Gambacorta, L. and Piccillo, C. (2015) 'Central clearing: Trends and current issues', *BIS Quarterly Review* 59–76, available at https://www.bis.org/publ/qtrpdf/r_qt1512g.pdf

Donnelly, S. (2012) 'Institutional change at the top: From the Financial Stability Forum to the Financial Stability Board' in Maynz, R. (ed.), *Crisis and Control: Institutional Change in Financial Market Regulation*, Frankfurt: Campus.

Donnelly, S. (2014) 'Power politics and the undersupply of financial stability in Europe', *Review of International Political Economy* 21 (4): 980–1005.

Draghi, M. (2008) 'A vision of a more resilient global economy', *Financial Times*, 13 November, London.

Drezner, D.W. (2007) *All Politics is Global: Explaining International Regulatory Regimes*, Princeton: Princeton University Press.

Drezner, D.W. (2009) 'The power and peril of international regime complexity', *Perspectives on Politics* 7 (1): 65–70.

Duff, A. W. and Zaring, D. (2013) 'New paradigms and familiar tools in the new derivatives regulation', *George Washington Law Review* 81 (3): 677–706.

Eckhardt, J. and De Bievre, D. (2015) 'Boomerangs over lac Léman: Transnational lobbying and foreign venue shopping in WTO dispute settlement', *World Trade Review* 13 (2): 507–30.

Epstein, R.A. (2019) *Banking on Markets—The Transformation of Bank-State Ties in Europe and Beyond*, Oxford: Oxford University Press.

Eurex (2011) 'Response to consultation on bank exposures to CCPs', 3 February, Frankfurt, available at https://www.bis.org/publ/bcbs190/eurexclearingag.pdf

Eurex (2013) 'Response to consultation on recovery of financial market infrastructures', 11 October, Frankfurt, available at https://www.bis.org/cpmi/publ/comments/d109/eurexclearing.pdf

Eurex (2017) 'Response to consultation on resolution of CCPs', 13 March, Frankfurt, available at https://www.fsb.org/wp-content/uploads/Eurex-Clearing-1.pdf

European Association of Clearing Houses (EACH) (2012) (EACH) 'Response to consultation on margin requirements for non centrally-cleared derivatives', 28 September, Brussels, available at https://www.bis.org/publ/bcbs226/eaocche.pdf

European Association of Clearing Houses (EACH) (2013) 'Response to consultation on recovery of financial market infrastructures', 11 October, Brussels, available at https://www.bis.org/cpmi/publ/comments/d109/eaoccch.pdf

European Association of Clearing Houses (EACH) (2016) 'Response to consultation on resilience and recovery of CCPs', 15 October, Brussels, available at https://www.bis.org/cpmi/publ/comments/d149/each.pdf

European Association of Clearing Houses (EACH) (2017) 'Response to consultation on resolution of CCPs', March, Brussels, available at https://www.fsb.org/wp-content/uploads/European-Association-of-Clearing-Houses.pdf

European Banking Federation (EBF) (2010) 'Response to consultation on derivatives and market infrastructures', 9 July, Brussels, available at https://www.abbl.lu/content/uploads/2017/06/ebf-response-to-the-european-commission-s-public-consultation-on-derivatives-and-market-infrastructures.pdf

European Banking Federation (EBF) (2011) 'Response to the consultation on OTC derivatives data reporting and aggregation requirements', 27 September, Brussels, available at http://www.ebf-fbe.eu/uploads/0331-2011-EBF_letter_on_CPSS-IOSCO_Report_on_requirements_for_OTC_derivatives_data_reporting_and_aggregation.pdf

European Banking Federation (EBF) (2012) Response to consultation on margin requirements for non-centrally cleared derivative', 12 October, Brussels, available at https://www.bis.org/publ/bcbs226/ebf.pdf

European Banking Federation (EBF) (2013a) 'Response to consultation on recovery of financial market infrastructure', 15 October, Brussels, available at https://www.bis.org/cpmi/publ/comments/d109/europeanbanking.pdf

European Banking Federation (EBF) (2013b) 'Response to consultation on margin requirements for non-centrally cleared derivative', 15 March, Brussels, available at https://www.bis.org/publ/bcbs242/europeanbanking.pdf

European Central Bank (ECB) (2009) 'OTC derivatives and post trading infrastructures', *Working Paper*, ECB, September, Frankfurt, available at https://www.ecb.europa.eu/pub/pdf/other/overthecounterderivatives200909en.pdf

European Central Bank (ECB) (2011) *Eurosystem Oversight Policy Framework*, 11 September, Frankfurt, available at https://www.ecb.europa.eu/pub/pdf/other/eurosystem oversightpolicyframework2011en.pdf

European Commission (2009) *Commission Communication—Driving European Recovery*, 4 March Brussels, available at https://eur-lex.europa.eu/legal-content/EN/TXT/?uri=celex:52009DC0114

European Fund and Asset Management Association (EFAMA) (2011) 'Response to consultation on derivatives and market infrastructures', 1 September, Brussels, available at https://circabc.europa.eu/webdav/CircaBC/FISMA/markt_consultations/Library/financial_ser vices/MIFID%20-%20Review%20of%20the%20Markets%20in%20Financial%20Instruments %20Directive%20(2011)/registered_organisation

European Fund and Asset Management Association (EFAMA) (2012) 'Response to first consultation on margins requirements, 28 September, Brussels, available at https://www.bis.org/publ/bcbs226/efaamae.pdf

European Fund and Asset Management Association (EFAMA) (2013) 'Response to second consultation on margins requirements', 13 March, Brussels, available at https://www.bis.org/publ/bcbs242/efama.pdf

European Market Infrastructure Regulation (EMIR) (2012) *Regulation of the European Parliament and of the Council*, 2 June, Brussels.

European Savings Banks Group (ESBG)—World Savings Banks Institute (2010) 'Response to bank exposures to CCPs', 2 February, Brussels, available at https://www.bis.org/publ/bcbs190/wsbiesbg.pdf

Farrell, H. and Newman, A.L. (2010) 'Making global markets: Historical Institutionalism in International Political Economy', *Review of International Political Economy* 17 (4): 609–38.

Farrell, H. and Newman, A.L. (2014a) 'Domestic institutions beyond the nation state: Charting the new interdependence approach', *World Politics* 66 (2): 331–66.

Farrell, H. and Newman, A.L. (2014b) 'The new politics of interdependence: Cross-national layering in Trans-Atlantic regulatory disputes', *Comparative Political Studies* 48 (4): 497–526.

Farrell, H. and Newman, A.L. (2016) 'The new interdependence approach: Theoretical development and empirical demonstration', *Review of International Political Economy* 23 (5): 713–36.

Faruqui, U., Huang, W., and Takáts E. (2018) 'Clearing risks in OTC derivatives markets: The CCP-bank nexus', *BIS Quarterly Review*, 16 December, Basel, available at ttps://www.bis.org/publ/qtrpdf/r_qt1812h.htm

Federation of European Stock Exchanges (FESE) (2011) 'Response to consultation on the review of Markets in Financial Instruments Directive', 2 February, Brussels, available at https://circabc.europa.eu/webdav/CircaBC/FISMA/markt_consultations/Library/financial_services/MIFID%20-%20Review%20of%20the%20Markets%20in%20Financial%20Instruments%20Directive%20(2011)/registered_organisation/FESE.pdf

Ferran, E., Moloney, N., Hill, G.J., and Coffee, J.C. Jr. (2012) *The Regulatory Aftermath of the Global Financial Crisis*, Cambridge: Cambridge University Press.

Financial Services Authority (FSA) (2009) *The Turner Review: A Regulatory Response to the Global Banking Crisis*, March, London, available at http://www.actuaries.org/CTTEES_TFRISKCRISIS/Documents/turner_review.pdf

Financial Services Authority (FSA) and Her Majesty's Treasury (2009) *Reforming OTC Derivatives Markets: A UK Perspective*, December London, available at http://www.fsa.gov.uk/pubs/other/reform_otc_derivatives.pdf

Financial Stability Board (FSB) (2010) *Implementing OTC Derivatives Market Reform*, October, Basel, available at http://www.financialstabilityboard.org/publications/r_101025.pdf

Financial Stability Board (FSB) (2011) *Key Attributes of Effective Resolution Regimes for Financial Institutions*. November, Basel, available at https://www.fsb.org/work-of-the-fsb/policy-development/effective-resolution-regimes-and-policies/key-attributes-of-effective-resolution-regimes-for-financial-institutions/#footnote-1

Financial Stability Board (FSB) (2012) *Governance of the LEI system*, June, Basel, available at https://www.fsb.org/2012/06/fsb-report-global-legal-entity-identifier-for-financial-markets/

Financial Stability Board (FSB) (2014a) *Feasibility Study on Aggregation of OTC Derivatives Trade Repository Data*, September, Basel, available at http://www.fsb.org/2014/09/pr_140919/

Financial Stability Board (FSB) (2014b) *Key Attributes of Effective Resolution Regimes for Financial Institutions* (revised), October, Basel, available at https://www.fsb.org/wp-content/uploads/r_141015.pdf

Financial Stability Board (FSB) (2017a) *Guidance on Resolution and Resolution Planning for Central Counterparties (CCPs)*, July, Basel, available at https://www.fsb.org/2017/07/guidance-on-central-counterparty-resolution-and-resolution-planning-2/

Financial Stability Board (FSB) (2017b) *Governance Arrangements for the Unique Transaction Identifier (UTI): Conclusions and Implementation Plan*, December, Basel, available at https://www.fsb.org/2017/12/governance-arrangements-for-the-unique-transaction-identifier-uti-conclusions-and-implementation-plan/

Financial Stability Board (FSB) (2017c) *Review of OTC Derivatives Market Reforms*, June, Basel, available at http://www.fsb.org/wp-content/uploads/P290617-1.pdf

Financial Stability Board (FSB) (2018a) *Compendium of Standards*, Basel, available at https://www.fsb.org/work-of-the-fsb/about-the-compendium-of-standards/

Financial Stability Board (FSB) (2018b) *Financial Resources to Support CCP Resolution and the Treatment of CCP Equity in Resolution*, November, Basel, available at https://www.fsb.org/2018/11/financial-resources-to-support-ccp-resolution-and-the-treatment-of-ccp-equity-in-resolution/

Financial Stability Board (FSB) (2018c) *OTC Derivatives Market Reforms: Thirteenth Progress Report on Implementation*, November, Basel, available at https://www.fsb.org/2018/11/otc-derivatives-market-reforms-thirteenth-progress-report-on-implementation/

Financial Stability Board (FSB) (2019a) *Report on Market Fragmentation*, June, Basel, available at https://www.fsb.org/wp-content/uploads/P040619-2.pdf

Financial Stability Board (FSB) (2019b) *Governance Arrangements for the Unique Product Identifier*, October, Basel, available at https://www.fsb.org/wp-content/uploads/P091019.pdf

Financial Stability Board (FSB) (2020) COVID-19 Pandemic: Financial Stability Implications and Policy Measures Taken, July, Basel, available at https://www.fsb.org/wp-content/uploads/P150720-2.pdf

Financial Stability Board (FSB), Basel Committee on Banking Supervision (BCBS), Committee on Payments and Market Infrastructures (CPMI), International Organization of Securities Commissions (IOSCO) (2015) *CCPs Workplan*, April, Basel, available at https://www.bis.org/cpmi/publ/d134b.pdf

Financial Stability Board (FSB), Basel Committee on Banking Supervision (BCBS), Committee on Payments and Market Infrastructures (CPMI), International Organization of Securities Commissions (IOSCO) (2018a) *Incentives to Centrally Clear Over-the-Counter (OTC) Derivatives*, November, Basel, available at https://www.fsb.org/2018/11/incentives-to-centrally-clear-over-the-counter-otc-derivatives-2/

Financial Stability Board (FSB), Basel Committee on Banking Supervision (BCBS), Committee on Payments and Market Infrastructures (CPMI), International Organization of Securities Commissions (IOSCO) (2018b) *Analysis of Central Clearing Interdependencies*, August, Basel, available at https://www.fsb.org/wp-content/uploads/P090818.pdf

Fioretos, O. (2010) 'Capitalist diversity and the international regulation of hedge funds', *Review of International Political Economy* 17 (4): 696–723.

Fioretos, O. (2011) *Creative Reconstructions: Multilateralism and European Varieties of Capitalism after 1950*, Ithaca: Cornell University Press.

French Banking Federation (FBF) (2012) 'Response to first consultation on margins for non-centrally cleared OTCD', 28 September, Paris, available at https://www.bis.org/publ/bcbs226/frenchbankingfe.pdf

French Banking Federation (EBF) (2013a) 'Response to consultation on recovery of financial market infrastructure', 13 October, Paris, available at https://www.bis.org/cpmi/publ/comments/d109/aftiandfbf.pdf

French Banking Federation (FBF) (2013b) 'Response to second consultation on margins for non-centrally cleared OTCD', 15 March, Paris, available at https://www.bis.org/publ/bcbs242/frenchbankingfe.pdf

Futures Industry Association (FIA) (2013) 'Response to consultation on bank exposures to CCPs', 27 September, Washington, available at https://www.bis.org/publ/bcbs253/fia.pdf

G20 (2009a) 'Communiqué G20 Leaders Summit London', 2–3 April.

G20 (2009b) 'Communiqué G20 Leaders Summit Pittsburgh', 24–25 September.

G20 (2011) 'Communiqué G20 Leaders Summit Cannes', 3–4 November.

G20 (2012) 'Communiqué G20 Leaders Summit Los Cabos', 18–19 June.

G20 (2016) 'Communiqué G20 Leaders Summit Hangzhou', 4–5 September.

G30 (2009) *Financial Reform: A Framework for Financial Stability*, Washington, DC.

Gabor, D. (2016a) 'The (impossible) repo trinity: the political economy of repo markets', *Review of International Political Economy* 23 (6): 967–1000.

Gabor, D. (2016b) 'A step too far? The European financial transactions tax on shadow banking', *Journal of European Public Policy* 23 (6): 925–45.

Gadinis, S. (2014) 'The Financial Stability Board: The new politics of international financial regulation', *Texas International Law Journal* 48 (2):157–76.

Gadinis, S. (2015) 'Three pathways to global standards: Private, regulator, and ministry networks', *American Journal of International Law* 109 (1): 1–57.

Gehring, T. and Faude, B. (2014) 'A theory of emerging order within institutional complexes: How competition among regulatory international institutions leads to institutional adaptation and division of labor', *Review of International Organizations* 9 (4): 471–98.

Geithner, T. (2009) *Testimony before the House Financial Services Committee*, 26 March, Washington, available at https://www.treasury.gov/press-center/press-releases/Pages/tg71.aspx

Genito, L. (2019) 'Mandatory clearing: The infrastructural authority of central counterparty clearing houses in the OTC derivatives market', *Review of International Political Economy*, DOI: 10.1080/09692290.2019.1616596

George, A.L. and Bennett, A. (2005) *Case Studies and Theory Development in Social Sciences*, Harvard: Harvard University Press.

German Banking Industry Committee (2013) 'Response to second, consultation on margins for non-centrally cleared derivatives', 15 March, Berlin, available at https://www.bis.org/publ/bcbs242/gbic.pdf

Giancarlo, C. (2017) 'Changing swaps trading liquidity, market fragmentation and regulatory comity in post-reform global swaps markets', Speech, CFTC, 10 May, Washington, available at www.cftc.gov/PressRoom/SpeechesTestimony/opagiancarlo-22

Giancarlo, C. (2019) 'Opening statement before the Global Markets Advisory Committee meeting', CFTC, 15 April, Washington, https://www.cftc.gov/PressRoom/SpeechesTestimony/giancarlostatement041519

Global Legal Entity Identifier Foundation (GLEIF) (2017) 'Response to consultation on proposed framework for post-implementation evaluation of the effects of the G20 financial regulatory reforms', 8 May, Basel, available at https://www.fsb.org/wp-content/uploads/GLEIF.pdf

Goldbach, R. (2015a) *Global Governance and Regulatory Failures*, Basingstoke: Palgrave.

Goldbach, R. (2015b) 'Asymmetric influence in global banking regulation, transnational harmonization, the competition State, and the roots of regulatory failure', *Review of International Political Economy* 22 (6): 1087–1127.

Goodhart, C. (2011) *The Basel Committee on Banking Supervision: A History of the Early Years 1974–1997*, Cambridge: Cambridge University Press.

Gracie, A. (2015) 'CCP resolution and the ending Too Big to Fail agenda', Speech, Bank of England, 22 October, London, available at https://www.bis.org/review/r151229b.pdf

Gravelle, M. and Pagliari, S. (2018) 'Global markets, national toolkits', in Helleiner, E., Pagliari, S., and Spagna, I. (eds), *Governing the World's Biggest Market: The Politics of Derivatives Regulation After the 2008 Crisis*, Oxford: Oxford University Press.

Graz, C. and Noelke, A. (eds) (2008) *Transnational Private Governance and its Limits*, London: Routledge.

Greenwood, J. and Roederer-Rynning, C. (2015) 'The 'Europeanization' of the Basel Process'. *Regulation & Governance* 9 (4): 325–38.

Gregory, J. (2014) *Central Counterparties: Mandatory Clearing and Bilateral Margin Requirements for OTC Derivatives*, London: Wiley and Sons.

Gren, J., Howarth D., and Quaglia L. (2015), 'Supranational banking supervision in Europe: The construction of a credible watchdog', *Journal of Common Market Studies Annual Review*, 53 (s1): 181–99.

Griffith, S.J. (2014) 'Substituted compliance and systemic risk: How to make a global market in derivatives regulation', *Minnesota Law Review* 98: 1292–1373.

Gruenberg, M.J. (2018) 'Statement on notice of proposed rulemaking on supplementary leverage ratio issued by the Federal Reserve and OCC', FDIC, 11 April, Washington, available at https://www.fdic.gov/news/news/speeches/spapr1218.pdf

Hakelberg, L. (2016) 'Coercion in international tax cooperation: Identifying the prerequisites for sanction threats by a great power', *Review of International Political Economy* 23 (3): 511–41.

Hakelberg, L. and Rixen, T. (2020) 'Is neoliberalism still spreading? The impact of international cooperation on capital taxation', Review of International Political Economy, https://doi.org/10.1080/09692290.2020.1752769

Haldane, A.G. (2012) 'The dog and the frisbee', Speech, Bank of England, 31 August, London, available at https://www.bis.org/review/r120905a.pdf

Heldt, E.C. and Schmidtke, H. (2019) 'Explaining coherence in international regime complexes: How the World Bank shapes the field of multilateral development finance', *Review of International Political Economy*, DOI: 10.1080/09692290.2019.1631205

Helfer, L. (2009) 'Regime shifting in the international intellectual property system', *Perspectives on Politics* 7 (1): 39–44.

Helleiner, E. (2010) 'The Financial Stability Board and International Standards', *IGI G20 Papers* No. 1, available at https://www.cigionline.org/sites/default/files/g20_no_1_1.pdf

Helleiner, E. (2011) 'Reining in the market: Global governance and the regulation of OTC derivatives', in Claes, D.H. and Knutsen, C-H. (eds), *Governing the Global Economy: Politics, Institutions, and Economic Development*, London: Routledge.

Helleiner, E. (2013) 'Did the financial crisis generate a fourth pillar of global economic architecture?', *Swiss Political Science Review* 19 (4): 558–63.

Helleiner, E. (2014) *The Status Quo Crisis: Global Financial Governance after the 2008 Financial Meltdown*, Oxford: Oxford University Press.

Helleiner, E. and Pagliari, S. (2010) 'The end of self-regulation? Hedge funds and derivatives in global financial governance', in E. Helleiner, S. Pagliari, and H. Zimmerman (eds), *Global Finance in Crisis: The Politics of International Regulatory Change*, London: Routledge.

Helleiner, E. and Pagliari, S. (2011) 'The end of an era in international financial regulation? A postcrisis research agenda', *International Organization* 65: 169–200.

Helleiner, E., Pagliari, S., and Spagna, I. (eds) (2018) *Governing the World's Biggest Market: The Politics of Derivatives Regulation after the 2008 Crisis*, Oxford: Oxford University Press.

Henning, C. R. (2017) *Tangled Governance*, Oxford: Oxford University Press.

Her Majesty's Treasury (2009) *Reforming Financial Markets*, July, London, available at https://webarchive.nationalarchives.gov.uk/20090805000034/http://www.hm-treasury.gov.uk/d/reforming_financial_markets080709.pdf

Herring, R.J. (2007) 'The rocky road to implementation of Basel II in the United States', *Atlantic Economic Journal* 35: 411–29.

Hoenig, T. (2015) 'The leverage ratio and derivatives', Speech, FDIC, 16 September, Washington, available at https://www.fdic.gov/news/news/speeches/spsep1615.html

Hoenig, T. (2018) 'Finding the right balance', Speech, FDIC, 28 March, Washington, available at https://www.fdic.gov/news/news/speeches/spmar2818.html

Hong Kong Monetary Authority (2015) 'A first analysis of derivatives data in the Hong Kong Trade Repository', June, Hong Kong, available at https://www.hkma.gov.hk/media/eng/publication-and-research/quarterly-bulletin/qb201506/fa.pdf

Howarth, D. and Quaglia, L. (2013) 'Banking on stability: The political economy of new capital requirements in the European Union', *Journal of European Integration* 35 (3): 333–46.

Howarth, D. and Quaglia, L. (2016) 'The comparative political economy of Basel III in Europe', *Policy and Society* 35 (3): 205–14.

Huhtaniemi, H. and Peters, M. (2017) 'Central counterparty recovery and resolution: The European Perspective', *Journal of Financial Market Infrastructures* 6 (1): 79–106.

Institute of International Finance (IIF) (2010) 'Global financial industry support constructive dialogue to secure financial stability', 10 June, Washington, available at https://www.iif.com/Advocacy/Regulatory-Reports/lapg-931/6

Institute of International Finance (IIF) (2013) 'Response to second consultation on margin requirements for non-centrally cleared derivative', 15 March, Washington, available at https://www.bis.org/publ/bcbs242/iif.pdf

Institute of International Finance (IIF) (2019) *Addressing Market Fragmentation: The Need for Enhanced Global Regulatory Cooperation*, January, Washington, available at https://www.iif.com/Portals/0/Files/IIF%20FSB%20Fragmentation%20Report.pdf

International Banking Federation (2011) 'Response to consultation on bank exposure to CCPs', 10 February, London, available at https://www.bis.org/publ/bcbs190/internationalba.pdf

International Capital Market Association (ICMA) (2013) 'Response to consultation on authorities' access to trade repository data', 10 May, London, available at https://www.icmagroup.org/assets/documents/Regulatory/ERC-Contributions/CPSS-IOSCO-response-re-TR-data-10-May-2013.pdf

International Monetary Fund (IMF) (2019) *People's Republic of China-Hong Kong Special Administrative Region: 2018 Article IV Consultation*, January, Washington, available at https://www.imf.org/en/Publications/CR/Issues/2019/01/25/People-s-Republic-of-China-Hong-Kong-Special-Administrative-Region-2018-Article-IV-46539

International Organization of Securities Commissions (IOSCO) (2010) 'IOSCO forms Task Force on OTC Derivatives Regulation', 15 October, Madrid, available at https://www.iosco.org/news/pdf/IOSCONEWS191.pdf

International Organization of Securities Commissions (IOSCO) (2011) *Report on Trading of OTC Derivatives*, February, Madrid, available at https://www.iosco.org/library/pubdocs/pdf/IOSCOPD345.pdf

International Organization of Securities Commissions (IOSCO) (2012a) *Requirements for Mandatory Clearing of OTC Derivatives via CCPs*, February, Madrid, available at https://www.iosco.org/library/pubdocs/pdf/IOSCOPD374.pdf

International Organization of Securities Commissions (IOSCO) (2012b) *Follow-On Analysis to the Report on Trading of OTC Derivatives*, January, Madrid, available at https://www.iosco.org/library/pubdocs/pdf/IOSCOPD368.pdf

International Organization of Securities Commissions (IOSCO) (2012c) *International Standards for Derivatives Markets Intermediary Regulation*, June, Madrid, available at https://www.iosco.org/library/pubdocs/pdf/IOSCOPD381.pdf

International Organization of Securities Commissions (IOSCO) (2019) *Market Fragmentation and Cross-border Regulation*, June, Madrid, available at https://www.iosco.org/library/pubdocs/pdf/IOSCOPD629.pdf

Investment Association (2016) 'Response to consultation on resilience and recovery of CCPs', 18 October, London, available at https://www.bis.org/cpmi/publ/comments/d149/ia.pdf

Investment Management Association (IMA) (2011) 'Response to review of the Markets in Financial Instruments Directive', 2 February, London, available at https://circabc.europa.eu/webdav/CircaBC/FISMA/markt_consultations/Library/financial_services/MIFID%20-%20Review%20of%20the%20Markets%20in%20Financial%20Instruments%20Directive%20(2011)/registered_organisation

Investment Management Association (IMA) (2013a) 'Response to consultation on recovery of financial market infrastructure', 10 October, London, available at https://www.bis.org/cpmi/publ/comments/d109/investmentmanag.pdf

Investment Management Association (IMA) (2013b) 'Response to second consultation on margin requirements for non-centrally cleared derivative', 15 March, London, available at https://www.bis.org/publ/bcbs242/investmentmanag.pdf

International Swaps and Derivatives Association (ISDA) (2010) 'Comments on consultation on the regulation of the over-the-counter (OTC) derivatives markets', 14 June, New York, available at https://www.isda.org/a/sQDDE/press061410.html

International Swaps and Derivatives Association (ISDA) (2011a) *Counterparty Credit Risk Management in the US Over-the-Counter (OTC) Derivatives Markets, Part II*, November, New York, available at https://www.isda.org/a/feiDE/counterparty-credit-risk-ii-monolines.pdf

International Swaps and Derivatives Association (ISDA) (2011b) 'Response to consultation on principles for financial market infrastructure', 22 June, New York, available at https://www.bis.org/cpmi/publ/comments/d94/isda.pdf

International Swaps and Derivatives Association (ISDA) (2011c) 'Response to consultation on OTC derivatives data reporting and aggregation requirements', 23 September, New York, available at https://www.bis.org/cpmi/publ/comments/d96/isda.pdf

International Swaps and Derivatives Association (ISDA) (2012) 'Response to consultation on margin requirements for non-centrally-cleared derivatives', 28 September, New York, available at https://www.isda.org/a/NMDDE/isda-response-to-bcbs-iosco-study-on-margin.pdf

International Swaps and Derivatives Association (ISDA) (2013a) *Non-Cleared OTC Derivatives: Their Importance to the Global Economy*, March, New York, available at https://www.isda.org/a/gPDDE/non-cleared-otc-derivatives-paper.pdf

International Swaps and Derivatives Association (ISDA) (2013b) 'Response to second consultation on margin requirements for non-centrally-cleared derivatives', 15 March, New York.

International Swaps and Derivatives Association (ISDA) (2013c) *CCP Loss Allocation at the End of the Waterfall*, August, London, available at https://www.isda.org/a/jTDDE/ccp-loss-allocation-waterfall-0807.pdf

International Swaps and Derivatives Association (ISDA) (2015a) *Unique Trade Identifier (UTI): Generation, Communication and Matching*, 20 July, New York.

International Swaps and Derivatives Association (ISDA) (2015b) 'CCP default management, recovery and continuity: A proposed recovery framework', 26 January, New York, available at https://www.isda.org/a/KiDDE/ccp-default-management-recovery-and-continuity-26-01-2015.pdf

International Swaps and Derivatives Association (ISDA) (2015c) 'Response to consultation on cross-border regulation', 23 February, New York, available at https://www.isda.org/a/4niDE/iosco-cross-border-consultation-response-for-submission.pdf

International Swaps and Derivatives Association (ISDA) (2018) *Margin Requirements for Non-cleared Derivatives*, April, London, available at https://www.isda.org/a/cpmEE/Margin-Requirements-for-Noncleared-Derivatives-April-2018.pdf

International Swaps and Derivatives Association (ISDA) (2019) *Regulatory Driven Market Fragmentation*, January, available at https://www.isda.org/a/wpgME/Regulatory-Driven-Market-Fragmentation-January-2019-1.pdf

International Swaps and Derivatives Association (ISDA), Asia Securities Industry & Financial Markets Association (ASIFMA), Association for Financial Markets in Europe (AFME), Futures Industry Association (FIA), Global Financial Markets Association (GFMA), Institute of International Finance (IIF), Securities Industry and Financial Markets Association (SIFMA) (2016a) 'Response to consultation on resolution of CCPs', 13 March, London, available at https://www.fsb.org/wp-content/uploads/FIA-GFMA-IIF-ISDA.pdf

International Swaps and Derivatives Association (ISDA), Asia Securities Industry & Financial Markets Association (ASIFMA), Association for Financial Markets in Europe (AFME), Clearing House, Futures Industry Association (FIA), Global Financial Markets Association (GFMA), Institute of International Finance (IIF), Securities Industry and Financial Markets Association (SIFMA) (2016b) 'Response to consultation on resilience and recovery of CCPs', 18 October, London, available at https://www.bis.org/cpmi/publ/comments/d149/fiaetal.pdf

International Swaps and Derivatives Association (ISDA), Asia Securities Industry & Financial Markets Association (ASIFMA), Association for Financial Markets in Europe (AFME), British Bankers Association (BBA), Global Financial Markets Association (GFMA), Institute of International Finance (IIF), Securities Industry and Financial Markets Association (SIFMA) (2011) 'Response to Consultation on bank exposures to CCPs, 4 February, available at https://www.bis.org/publ/bcbs190/abgii.pdf

International Swaps and Derivatives Association (ISDA), Association for Financial Markets in Europe (AFME), Associazione Italiana Intermediari dei Mercati Finanziari (ASSOSIM), British Bankers Association (BBA), and the Nordic Securities Association (2010) 'Response to consultation on standardisation and exchange trading of OTC derivatives', August, New York, available at https://www.google.com/url?sa=t&rct=j&q=&esrc=s&source=web&cd=1&ved=2ahUKEwj16vuGgJbkAhVG16QKHYejDugQFjAAegQIAhAC&url=https%3A%2F%2Fwww.esma.europa.eu%2Ffile%2F9317%2Fdownload%3Ftoken%3D1YcklaCM&usg=AOvVaw3JEZlAj2ICQumZ8SGkUTEV

International Swaps and Derivatives Association (ISDA), Clearing House, Global Financial Markets Association (GFMA), Institute of International Finance (IIF), and Japan Financial Markets Council (2016) 'Response to consultation on revisions to the Basel III leverage ratio framework', New York, available at https://www.isda.org/a/xTiDE/final-joint-trade-response-bcbs-lr2016.pdf

International Swaps and Derivatives Association (ISDA), Global Financial Markets Association (GFMA), Institute of International Finance (IIF) (2013a) 'Response to consultation on capital treatment of bank exposures to central counterparties', 27 September, New York, available at https://www.bis.org/publ/bcbs253/ja.pdf

International Swaps and Derivatives Association (ISDA), the Clearing House and the Institute for International Finance (IIF) (2013b) 'Response to consultation on recovery of financial market infrastructures', 11 October, London, available at https://www.bis.org/cpmi/publ/comments/d109/iiatch.pdf

International Swaps and Derivatives Association (ISDA), Securities Industry and Financial Markets Association (SIFMA) (2018) 'Initial margin for non-centrally cleared derivatives: issues for 2019 and 2020', July, New York, available at https://www.sifma.org/wp-content/uploads/2018/07/Initial-Margin-for-Non-Centrally-Cleared-Derivatives-Issues-for-2019-and-2020.pdf

Joint Forum (1999) *Principles for the Supervision of Financial Conglomerates*, February, Basel, available at https://www.bis.org/publ/bcbs47.pdf

Joint Forum (2001) *Compendium of Standards*, July, Basel, available at https://www.bis.org/publ/joint02.pdf

JP Morgan (2010) 'Response to consultation on standardisation and exchange trading of OTC derivatives', 8 August, New York, available at https://www.google.com/url?sa=t&rct=j&q=&esrc=s&source=web&cd=1&ved=2ahUKEwj40PuGgpbkAhVJaVAKHUmxDUoQFjAAegQIAxAC&url=https%3A%2F%2Fwww.esma.europa.eu%2Ffile%2F9376%2Fdownload%3Ftoken%3D7vxJ6Fc0&usg=AOvVaw1_FSEny9M0jH62eHLV4CoP

JP Morgan (2011) 'Response to consultation on MiFID', 2 February, New York, available at https://circabc.europa.eu/webdav/CircaBC/FISMA/markt_consultations/Library/financial_services/MIFID%20-%20Review%20of%20the%20Markets%20in%20Financial%20Instruments%20Directive%20(2011)/registered_organisation/JP%20Morgan%20(1).pdf

JP Morgan (2014) 'Leveraging the Leverage Ratio', New York, available at https://www.jpmorgan.com/jpmpdf/1320634324649.pdf

James, S. and Quaglia, L. (2020a) *The UK and Multi-level Financial Regulation: From the Crisis to Brexit*, Oxford: Oxford University Press.

James, S. and Quaglia, L. (2020b) 'The political economy of Euro clearing', *Review of International Political Economy*, https://doi.org/10.1080/09692290.2019.1699148.

Johnson, T. and Urpelainen, J. (2012) 'A strategic theory of regime integration and separation', *International Organization* 66 (4): 645–77.

Jordana, J. (2017) 'Trans-governmental networks as regulatory intermediaries: Horizontal collaboration and the realities of soft power', *Annals of the American Academy of Political and Social Science* 670: 245–61.

Jouyet, J-P. (2009) 'The future of financial regulation', *Financial Stability Review*, Banque de France, September, Paris, available at https://publications.banque-france.fr/sites/default/files/medias/documents/financial-stability-review-13_2009-09.pdf

Kalyanpur, N. and Newman, A.L. (2017) 'Form over function in finance: international institutional design by bricolage, *Review of International Political Economy* 24 (3): 363–92.

Kapstein, E.B. (1989) 'Resolving the regulator's dilemma: International coordination of banking regulations', *International Organisation* 43 (2): 323–47.

Kapstein, E.B. (1992) 'Between power and purpose: Central bankers and the politics of regulatory convergence', *International Organization* 46 (1): 265–87.

Karmel, R. and Kelly, C. (2009) 'The hardening of international soft law in finance', *Brooklyn Journal of International Law* 34: 884–950.

Kastner, L. (2014) '"Much ado about nothing?" Transnational civil society, consumer protection and financial regulatory reform', *Review of International Political Economy* 21 (6): 1313–45.

Kempthorne, D. (2013) *Governing International Securities Markets: IOSCO and the Politics of International Securities Market Standards*, Doctoral Thesis, University of Waterloo, available at http://hdl.handle.net/10012/7661

Keohane, R.O. and Nye, J.S. (1974) 'Transgovernmental relations and international organizations', *World Politics* 27: 39–62.

Keohane, R.O. and Victor, D.G. (2011) 'The regime complex for climate change', *Perspectives on Politics* 9 (1): 7–23.

Kirton, J. (2016) *G20 Governance for a Globalized World*, Aldershot: Ashgate.

Knaack, P. (2015) 'Innovation and deadlock in global financial governance: Transatlantic coordination failure in OTC derivatives regulation', *Review of International Political Economy* 22 (6): 1–32.

Knaack, P. (2017) 'An unlikely champion of global finance: Why is China exceeding international banking standards?', *Journal of Current Chinese Affairs* 46 (2): 41–79.

Knaack, P. (2018) 'A web without a center: Fragmentation in the OTC derivatives trade reporting system', in E. Helleiner, S. Pagliari, and I. Spagna (eds), *Governing the World's Biggest Market*, Oxford: Oxford University Press.

Koremenos, B., Lipson, C., and Snidal, D. (2001) 'The rational design of international institutions', *International Organization* 55 (4): 761–99.

KPGM (2018) 'Basel 4: CVA Risk', 23 March, available at https://home.kpmg.com/xx/en/home/insights/2018/03/basel-4-cva-risk-fs.html

Lall, R. (2012) 'From failure to failure: The politics of international banking regulation', *Review of International Political Economy* 19 (4): 609–38.

Lall, R. (2014) 'Timing as a source of regulatory influence: A technical elite network analysis of global finance', *Regulation & Governance* 9 (2): 125–43.

Lavelle, K.C. (2013) *Money and Banks in the American Political System*, Cambridge: Cambridge University Press.

Lavelle, K.C. (2019) 'US foreign policy and the governance of finance', *Business and Politics* 21 (1): 1–26.

Leblond, P. (2011) 'EU, US and international accounting standards: A delicate balancing act in governing global finance', *Journal of European Public Policy* 18 (3): 443–61.

Lehmann, M. (2017) 'Legal fragmentation, extraterritoriality and uncertainty in global financial regulation', *Oxford Journal of Legal Studies* 37 (2): 406–34.

Li, Y-W. V. (2018) 'Power plays from the fringe', in E. Helleiner, S. Pagliari, and I. Spagna (eds), *Governing the World's Biggest Market*, Oxford: Oxford University Press.

Litan, R. (2010) *The Derivatives Dealer's Club and Derivates Markets Reform*, Washington: Brookings.

Lockwood, E. (2018) 'The politics and practices of central clearing in OTC derivatives markets', in E. Helleiner, S. Pagliari, and I. Spagna (eds), *Governing the World's Biggest Market: The Politics of Derivatives Regulation after the 2008 Crisis*, Oxford: Oxford University Press.

London Clearing House (LCH) (2013) 'Response to consultation on recovery of financial market infrastructures', 11 October, London, available at https://www.bis.org/cpmi/publ/comments/d109/lchclearnet.pdf

London Stock Exchange (LSE) (2010) 'Response to consultation on standardisation and exchange trading of OTC Derivatives', 16 August, London, available at https://www.lseg.com/sites/default/files/content/documents/otc-16-08-10.pdf

Macartney, H. (2010) *Variegated Neoliberalism: EU varieties of capitalism and International Political Economy*, London: Routledge.

Macartney, H. (2019) *The Bank Culture Debate: Ethics, Values, and Financialization in Anglo-America*, Oxford: Oxford University Press.

Macey, J. (2003) 'Regulatory globalization as a response to regulatory competition', *Faculty Scholarship Series Paper* N. 1418, available at https://digitalcommons.law.yale.edu/cgi/viewcontent.cgi?article=2420&context=fss_papers

Maijoor, S. (2013a) 'EMIR: A fair price for safety and transparency', Speech, ESMA, 27 March, Paris, available at https://www.esma.europa.eu/sites/default/files/library/2015/11/2013-428.pdf

Maijoor, S. (2013b) 'International coordination of the regulation and supervision of OTC derivatives market', Speech, ESMA, 17 October, Paris, available at https://www.esma.europa.eu/document/international-coordination-regulation-and-supervision-otc-derivatives-markets-american-bar

Managed Fund Association (MFA) (2012) 'Response to first consultation margin on margins for non-centrally cleared derivatives', 28 September, Washington, available at https://www.bis.org/publ/bcbs226/mfam.pdf

Managed Fund Association (MFA) (2013) 'Response to second consultation on margins for non-centrally cleared derivatives', 15 March, Washington available at https://www.bis.org/publ/bcbs242/managedfundsass.pdf

Marcacci, A. (2012) 'IOSCO: The world standard setter for globalized financial markets', *Richmond Journal of Global Law and Business* 12: 23–44.

Marcacci, A. (2014) 'IOSCO and the spreading of a US-Like regulatory philosophy around the world', *European Business Law Review* 25 (6): 759–809.

Mattli, W. and Woods, N. (eds) (2009) *The Politics of Global Regulation*, Princeton: Princeton University Press.

Maynz, R. (ed.) (2012) *Crisis and Control: Institutional Change in Financial Market Regulation*, Cologne: Max Planck Institute for the Study of Societies.

Maynz, R. (ed.) (2015) *Negotiated Reform: The Multilevel Governance of Financial Regulation*, Frankfurt: Campus Verlag.

McDonald, P. and Paulson, A. (2015) 'AIG hindsight', *Journal of Economic Perspectives* 29 (2): 81–106.

McDonald, R. and Paulson, A. (2017) 'What went wrong at the AIG', available at https://insight.kellogg.northwestern.edu/article/what-went-wrong-at-aig

McDowell, D. (2012) 'The US as "sovereign international last-resort lender": The Fed's currency swap programme during the Great Panic of 2007–09', *New Political Economy* 17 (2): 157–78.

McKeen-Edwards, H. and Porter, T. (2013) *Transnational Financial Associations and the Governance of Global Finance*, London: Routledge.

Mersch, E. (2017) 'Evolving regulatory environment for CCPs – the perspective of a central bank', Speech, ECB, 10 November, Frankfurt, available at http://www.ecb.europa.eu/press/key/date/2017/html/ecb.sp171110.en.html

Mersch, E. (2018) 'Euro Clearing – the open race', Speech, ECB, 29 May, Frankfurt, available at https://www.ecb.europa.eu/press/key/date/2018/html/ecb.sp180529.en.html

Miller, M. (2014) 'Congressional Hearing', 2 February, Committee on Banking, Housing, and Urban Affair, Senate, Washington.

Moloney, N. (2014) *EU Securities and Financial Markets Regulation*, Oxford: Oxford University Press.

Morin, J-F. and Orsini, A. (2014) 'Policy coherency and regime complexes: The case of genetic resources', *Review of International Studies* 40 (2): 303–24.

Morse, J.C. and Keohane, R.O. (2014) 'Contested multilateralism', *Review of International Organisation* 9 (4): 385–412.

Moschella, M. (2015) 'The institutional roots of incremental ideational change: The IMF and capital controls after the global financial crisis', *British Journal of Politics and International Relations* 17 (3): 442–460.

Moschella, M. and Quaglia, L. (2013) 'Speaking with one voice in international finance? The EU and the institutional features of global financial regulatory bodies', *Rivista Italiana di Scienza Politica* 43 (2): 179–200.

Moschella, M. and Quaglia, L. (2016) 'To agree or not to agree: the EU in the G 20', *Journal of European Public Policy* 23 (6): 906–24.

Moschella, M. and Quaglia, L. (2020) 'Banking Union to the rescue? How supranational institutions influenced crisis management in Italy', *South European Society and Politics.*

Moschella, M. and Tsingou, E. (2013a) 'Regulating finance after the crisis: Unveiling the different dynamics of the regulatory process' *Regulation & Governance* 7 (4): 407–16.

Moschella, M. and Tsingou, E. (eds) (2013b) *Great Expectations, Slow Transformations: Incremental Change in Financial Governance*, Colchester: ECPR Press.

Mosley, L. (2003). 'Attempting global standards: national governments, international finance, and the IMF's data regime', *Review of International Political Economy* 10 (2): 331–62.

Mosley, L. (2010) 'Regulating globally, implementing locally: The financial codes and standards effort', *Review of International Political Economy* 17 (4): 724–61.

Mügge, D. (2010) *Widen the Market, Narrow the Competition: Banker Interests and the Making of a European Capital Market*, Colchester: ECPR.

Mügge, D. (2011a) 'The European presence in global financial governance: A principal-agent perspective', *Journal of European Public Policy* 18 (3): 383–402

Mügge, D. (2011b) 'The limits of legitimacy and the primacy of politics in financial governance', *Review of International Political Economy* 18 (1): 52–74.

Mügge, D. (ed.) (2014) *Europe and the Governance of Global Finance*, Oxford: Oxford University Press.

Mügge D. and Perry, J. (2014) 'The flaws of fragmented financial standard setting: Why substantive economic debates matter for the architecture of global governance', *Politics & Society* 42 (2): 194–222.

Mügge, D. and Stellinga, B. (2015) 'The unstable core of global finance: Contingent valuation and governance of international accounting standards', *Regulation & Governance* 9 (1): 47–62.

Murphy, E. and Senior, S. (2013) 'Changes to the Bank of England', *Bank of England Quarterly Bulletin*, 53 (1): 20–28, available at https://www.bankofengland.co.uk/-/media/boe/files/quarterly-bulletin/2013/changes-to-the-boe.pdf?la=en&hash=14AD9B3A7E860A2180F0F064DE54795B06A24856

Nesvetailova, A. (2015) 'A crisis of the overcrowded future: Shadow banking and the political economy of financial innovation', *New Political Economy* 20 (3): 431–53.

Newman, A.L and Bach, D. (2014) 'The European Union as hardening agent: Soft law and the diffusion of global financial regulation', *Journal of European Public Policy* 21 (3): 430–52.

Newman, A.L. and Posner, E. (2016a) 'Transnational feedback, soft law, and preferences in global financial regulation', *Review of International Political Economy* 23 (1): 123–52.

Newman, A.L. and Posner, E. (2016b) 'Structuring transnational interests: The second-order effects of soft law in the politics of global finance', *Review of International Political Economy* 23 (5): 768–98.

Newman, A.L. and Posner, E. (2018) *Voluntary Disruptions. International Soft Law, Finance, and Power*, Oxford, UK: Oxford University Press.

New York Stock Exchange (NYSE)—Euronext (2011) 'Response to consultation on the review of Markets in Financial Instruments Directive', 2 February, New York, available at https://circabc.europa.eu/webdav/CircaBC/FISMA/markt_consultations/Library/financial_services/MIFID%20-%20Review%20of%20the%20Markets%20in%20Financial%20Instruments%20Directive%20(2011)/registered_organisation/NYSE%20EURONEXT.pdf

Norman, P. (2008) *Plumbers and Visionaries: Securities Settlement and Europe's Financial Market*, Chichester: John Wiley & Sons.

Oatley, T. and Nabors, R. (1998) 'Redistributive cooperation: Market failures, wealth transfer and the Basle Accord', *International Organization* 52 (1): 35–54.

O'Malia, S. (2013) 'Keynote Address', Speech, CFTC, 24 April, Washington, available at http://www.mondovisione.com/media-and-resources/news/speech-by-cftc-commissioner-scott-d-omalia-federal-reserve-bank-of-new-york

O'Malia, S. (2014) 'The future of financial standards', Speech, 25 March, CFTC, Washington, available at https://www.cftc.gov/PressRoom/SpeechesTestimony/opaomalia-34

Orsini, A., Morin, J-F., and Young, O. (2013) 'Regime complexes: A buzz, a boom, or a bust for global governance?', *Global Governance* 19 (1): 27–39.

Pagliari, S. (2012) 'Who governs finance? The shifting public-private divide in the regulation of derivatives, rating agencies and hedge funds', *European Law Journal* 18 (1): 44–61.

Pagliari, S. (2013a) *Public Salience and International Financial Regulation. Explaining the International Regulation of OTC Derivatives, Rating Agencies, and Hedge Funds*, Doctoral dissertation, University of Waterloo.

Pagliari, S. (2013b) 'A wall around Europe? The European regulatory response to the global financial crisis and the turn in Transatlantic relations', *Journal of European Integration* 35 (4): 391–408.

Pagliari, S. (2013c) 'Governing financial stability: The Financial Stability Board as the emerging pillar in global economic governance', in M. Moschella and K. Weaver (eds), *Handbook of Global Economic Governance*, London: Routledge.

Pagliari, S. (2018) 'The second half: Interest group conflicts and coalitions in the implementation of the Dodd-Frank Act derivatives rules', in E. Helleiner, S. Pagliari, and I. Spagna (eds), *Governing the World's Biggest Market: The Politics of Derivatives Regulation after the 2008 Crisis*, Oxford: Oxford University Press.

Pagliari S. and Young K.L. (2014) 'Leveraged interests: Financial industry power and the role of private sector coalitions', *Review of International Political Economy* 21 (3): 575–610.

Palan, R. (2003) *The Offshore World: Sovereign Markets, Virtual Places, and Nomad Millionaires*, Ithaca: Cornell University Press.

Palan, R., Murphy, R., and Chavagneux, C. (2013) *Tax Havens*, Ithaca: Cornell University Press.

Perry, J. and Nölke, A. (2006) 'The political economy of international accounting standards', *Review of International Political Economy* 13 (4): 559–86.

Peters, G.B. (2002) *The Politics of Bureaucracy*, London: Routledge.

Peters, G.B. (2006) 'Concepts and theories of horizontal policy management', in Peters, G., and Pierre, J. (eds), *Handbook of Public Policy*, London: Sage.

Peters, M. (2019) 'CCP resolution, loss allocation and shareholders' rights', *Journal of Financial Regulation and Compliance* 27 (2): 141–59.

Porter, T. (2014a) (ed.) *Transnational Financial Regulation after the Crisis*, London: Routledge.

Porter, T. (2014b) 'Technical systems and the architecture of transnational business governance interactions', *Regulation & Governance* 8 (1): 110–25.

Posner, E (2009) 'Making rules for global finance: Transatlantic regulatory cooperation at the turn of the Millennium', *International Organization* 63 (4): 665–99.

Posner, E. (2010) 'Sequence as explanation: The international politics of accounting standards', *Review of International Political Economy* 14 (4): 639–64.

Posner, E. (2015) 'International financial regulatory cooperation', in Zeitlin, J. (ed.), *Extending Experimentalist Governance? The European Union and Transnational Regulation*, Oxford: Oxford University Press.

Posner, E. (2018) 'Financial regulatory cooperation: Coordination of derivatives markets', in E. Helleiner, S. Pagliari, and I. Spagna (eds), *Governing the World's Biggest Market*, Oxford: Oxford University Press.

Powell. J. (2014) 'A financial system perspective on central clearing of derivatives', Speech, Federal Reserve, 6 November, Washington, available at https://www.federalreserve.gov/newsevents/speech/powell20141106a.htm

Powell, J. (2015) 'Central clearing in an interdependent world', Speech, Federal Reserve, 17 November, Washington, available at https://www.federalreserve.gov/newsevents/speech/powell20151117a.htm

Powell, J. (2017) 'Central clearing and liquidity', Speech, Federal Reserve, 23 June, Washington, available at https://www.federalreserve.gov/newsevents/speech/files/powell20170623a.pdf

Pratt, T. (2018) 'Deference and hierarchy in international regime complexes', *International Organization* 72: 561–90.

Pratt, T. (2019) 'Vertically differentiated cooperation: Explaining policy change in international regime complexes', available at https://static1.squarespace.com/static/5c54747ad7819e06b909fb1f/t/5cb1e0ffee6eb001467d9c3c/1555161343948/Vertical_April2019.pdf

Quaglia, L. (2014a) *The European Union and Global Financial Regulation*, Oxford: Oxford University Press.

Quaglia L (2014b) 'The European Union, the USA and international standard-setting in finance', *New Political Economy* 19 (3): 427–44.

Quaglia, L. (2014c) 'The sources of European Union influence in international financial regulatory fora', *Journal of European Public Policy* 21 (3): 327–45.

Quaglia, L. (2015) 'The politics of "third country equivalence" in post-crisis financial services regulation in the European Union', *West European Politics* 38 (1): 167–84.

Quaglia, L. (2017a) 'The political economy of post-crisis international standards for resolving financial institution', *New Political Economy* 22 (5): 595–609.

Quaglia, L. (2017b) 'Regulatory power, post-crisis transatlantic disputes and the network structure of the financial industry', *Business & Politics* 19 (2): 241–66.

Quaglia, L. (2019) 'The politics of state compliance with international financial standards', *Governance* 32 (1): 45–62.

Quaglia, L. and Spendzharova, A. (2017) 'Post-crisis reforms in banking: Regulators at the interface between domestic and international governance', *Regulation & Governance* 11 (4): 323–450.

Quaglia, L. and Spendzharova, A. (2019) 'Regulators and the quest for coherence in finance: the case of los absorbing capacity for banks', *Public Administration* 97 (3): 499–512.

Quaglia, L. and Spendzharova, A. (2020a) 'Disentangling derivatives: International Policy Reforms Concerning Central Counterparties', mimeo.

Quaglia, L. and Spendzharova, A. (2020b) 'Regime complexity and managing financial data streams: The orchestration of trade reporting for derivatives', mimeo.

Quarles, R. (2018) 'Early observations on improving the effectiveness of post-crisis regulation', Speech, Federal Reserve, 19 January, Washington, available at https://www.federalreserve.gov/newsevents/speech/quarles20180119a.htm

Quillin, B. (2008) *International Financial Co-operation: Political Economics of Compliance with the 1988 Basel Accord*, London: Routledge.

Raustiala, K. and Victor, D.G (2004) 'The regime complex for plant genetic resources', *International Organization* 58 (2): 277–309.

REGIS TR (2011) 'Response to the consultation on OTC derivatives data reporting and aggregation requirements', 13 September, Frankfurt.

Rehlon, A. and Nixon, D. (2015) 'Central counterparties: What are they, why do they matter and how does the Bank supervise them?', *Bank of England Quarterly Bulletin*, N. 3: 1–10, available at http://www.eachccp.eu/wp-content/uploads/2015/12/qb1302ccpsbs.pdf

Rixen, T. (2010) 'Bilateralism or multilateralism? The political economy of avoiding international double taxation', *European Journal of International Relation* 16 (4): 589–614.

Rixen, T. (2013) 'Why reregulation after the crisis is feeble: Shadow banking, offshore financial centers, and jurisdictional competition', *Regulation & Governance* 7 (4): 435–59.

Ross, V. (2014) 'Keynote address to ICI Global Trading and Market Structure Conference', Speech, ESMA, 14 December, Paris, available at https://www.esma.europa.eu/sites/default/files/library/2015/11/2014-1575_verena_ross_-_keynote_address_to_ici_global_trading_u_market_structure_conference_london_9_december_2014.pdf

Ross, V. (2017) 'Keynote speech at the ASIFMA annual conference', Speech, ESMA, 30 November Paris, available at https://www.esma.europa.eu/press-news/esma-news/verena-ross-keynote-address-asifma-annual-conference-2017

Royal Bank of Scotland (RBS) (2010) 'Response to consultation on standardisation and exchange trading of OTC Derivatives', Edinburgh, August.

Ruffini, I. and Steigerwald, R. (2014) 'OTC derivatives: A primer on market infrastructure and regulatory policy', *Economic Perspectives*, Federal Reserve Bank of Chicago, N.3: 80–99.

Russo, D. (2013) 'CPSS-IOSCO principles for financial market infrastructures: Vectors of international convergence', *Banque of France Financial Stability Review*, April, Paris, available at https://www.banque-france.fr/sites/default/files/medias/documents/financial-stability-review-17_2013-04.pdf

Ryan, P.J. and Ziegler, N.J. (2015) 'Patchwork pacesetter: The United States in the multilevel process of financial market regulation', in R. Maynz (ed.), *Multilevel Governance of Financial Market Reform*, Cologne: Max Planck Institute.

Schoenmaker D. (2013) *Governance of International Banking: The Financial Trilemma*, Oxford: Oxford University Press.

Scott, J. (2014) 'Extraterritoriality and territorial extension in EU Law', *American Journal of Comparative Law* 62 (1): 87–126.

Seabrooke, L. and Henriksen, L.F. (eds) (2017) *Professional Networks in Transnational Governance*, Cambridge: Cambridge University Press.

Seabrooke, L. and Tsingou, E. (2014) 'Distinctions, affiliations, and professional knowledge in financial reform expert groups', *Journal of European Public Policy* 21 (3): 389–407.
Seabrooke, L. and Wigan, D. (2016) 'Powering ideas through expertise: professionals in global tax battles', *Journal of European Public Policy* 23 (3): 357–74.
Seabrooke, L. and Wigan, D. (2017) 'The governance of global wealth chains', *Review of International Political Economy* 24 (1): 1–29.
Securities Industry and Financial Markets Association (SIFMA) (2011) 'Response to consultation on OTC derivatives data reporting and aggregation requirements', 23 September, New York, available at https://www.bis.org/cpmi/publ/comments/d96/sifma.pdf
Securities Industry and Financial Markets Association (SIFMA) (2013) 'Second consultation on margin requirements for non-centrally cleared derivatives', 15 March, New York, available at https://www.iosco.org/library/pubdocs/403/pdf/SIFMA%20Securities%20Industry%20and%20Financial%20Markets%20Association.pdf
Sharman, J.C. (2006) *Havens in a Storm: The Struggle for Global Tax Regulation*, Ithaca: Cornell University Press.
Sharman, J.C. (2011) *The Money Laundry: Regulating Criminal Finance in the Global Economy*, Ithaca: Cornell University Press.
Simmons, B.A. (2001) 'The international politics of harmonization: The case of capital market regulation', *International Organization* 55 (3): 589–620.
Singer, D.A. (2004) 'Capital rules: The domestic politics of international regulatory harmonization', *International Organization* 58 (3): 531–65.
Singer, D. A. (2007) *Regulating Capital: Setting Standards for the International Financial System*. Ithaca: Cornell University Press.
Singh, M. and Turing, D. (2018) 'Central counterparties resolution: An unresolved problem', *IMF Working Paper*, N. 1865, available at https://www.imf.org/~/media/Files/Publications/WP/2018/wp1865.ashx.
Slaughter, A-M. (2004) *A New World Order*, Princeton: Princeton University Press.
Slaughter, A-M., and Zaring, D. (2006) 'Networking goes international: an update', *Annual Review of Law and Social Science* 2: 211–29.
Sommers, J.E. (2010) 'Clearinghouses as mitigators of systemic risk', Speech, CFTC, 30 September, Washington, available at https://www.cftc.gov/PressRoom/SpeechesTestimony/opasommers-10
Spagna, I. (2019) *Dealer Bank Influence and the International Political Economy of Over-the-Counter Derivatives Regulation: The Introduction of Mandatory Margin Requirements for Non-Centrally Cleared Derivatives after the Global Financial Crisis of 2008*, Doctoral Thesis, University of Waterloo.
State Street Bank (2013) 'Response to second consultation on margin requirements for non-centrally cleared derivatives', 15 March, Boston, available at https://www.bis.org/publ/bcbs242/statestreet.pdf
Tarullo, D.K. (2011a) *Testimony before the Committee on Financial Services*, House of Representatives, 16 June, Washington, available at https://www.bis.org/review/r110617e.pdf
Tarullo, D.K. (2011b) 'The international agenda for financial regulation', Speech, Federal Reserve, 4 November, Washington, available at https://www.bis.org/review/r111107b.pdf
Thatcher, M. and Coen, D. (2008) 'Reshaping European regulatory space: An evolutionary analysis', *West European Politics* 31 (4): 806–36.
Thiemann, M. (2014) 'In the shadow of Basel: How competitive politics bred the crisis', *Review of International Political Economy* 21 (6): 1203–39.

Thiemann, M. (2018) *The Growth of Shadow Banking: A Comparative Institutional Analysis*, Cambridge: Cambridge University Press.

Tradeweb (2010) 'Response to consultation on standardisation and exchange trading of OTC Derivatives', 8 August, London.

Trondal, J., Marcussen, M., Larsson, T., and Veggeland, F. (2013) *Unpacking International Organisations: The Dynamics of Compound Bureaucracies*, Manchester: Manchester University Press.

Tsingou, E. (2006) 'The Governance of OTC Derivatives Markets', in P. Mooslechner, H. Schubert, and B. Weber (eds), *The Political Economy of Financial Market Regulation: The Dynamics of Inclusion and Exclusion*, Cheltenham: Edward Elgar.

Tsingou, E. (2008) 'Transnational private governance and the Basel process: Banking regulation, private interests and Basel II', in J.C. Graz and A. Nölke (eds), *Transnational Private Governance and Its Limits*, London: Routledge.

Tsingou, E. (2010a) 'Regulatory reactions to the global credit crisis: Analyzing a policy community under stress', in E. Helleiner, S. Pagliari, and H. Zimmerman (eds), *Global Finance in Crisis: The Politics of International Regulatory Change*, London: Routledge.

Tsingou, E. (2010b) 'Global financial governance and the developing anti-money laundering regime: What lessons for international political economy?', *International Politics* 47 (6): 617–37.

Tsingou, E. (2015a) 'Club governance and the making of global financial rules', *Review of International Political Economy* 22 (2): 225–56.

Tsingou, E. (2015b) 'Transnational veto players and the practice of financial reform', *British Journal of Politics & International Relations* 17 (2): 318–34.

Tucker, P. (2011) 'Clearing houses as system risk managers', Speech, Bank of England, 1 June, London, available at https://www.bis.org/review/r110608g.pdf

Tucker, P. (2013) 'Central counterparties in evolving capital markets: Safety, recovery and resolution', *Banque de France Financial Stability Review*, No. 17, April, Paris, available at http://www.eachccp.eu/wp-content/uploads/2015/12/speech650.pdf

Turk, M. (2014) 'Reframing international financial regulation after the global financial crisis: Rational states and interdependence, not regulatory networks and soft law', *Michigan Journal of International Law* 36 (1): 60–128.

Underhill, G.R.D. (ed.) (1997) 'The making of the European financial area: Global market integration and the EU Single Market for financial services', in G.R.D. Underhill (ed.), *The New World Order in International Finance*, London: Macmillan.

Underhill, G.R.D. (2015) 'The emerging post-crisis financial architecture: The path-dependency of ideational adverse selection', *British Journal of Politics and International Relations* 17(3): 461–93.

Underhill, G.R.D. and Zhang, X, (2008) 'Setting the rules: Private power, political underpinnings, and legitimacy in global monetary and financial governance', *International Affairs* 84 (3): 535–54.

Urpelainen, J. and Van de Graaf, T. (2015) 'Your place or mine? Institutional capture and the creation of overlapping international institutions', *British Journal of Political Science* 45 (4): 799–827.

US Treasury (2009) *Financial Regulatory Reform: A New Foundation*, August, Washington, available at https://www.treasury.gov/initiatives/wsr/Documents/FinalReport_web.pdf

US Treasury (2017) *A Financial System that Creates Economic Opportunities*, October, Washington, available at https://www.treasury.gov/press-center/press-releases/documents/a-financial-system-capital-markets-final-final.pdf

Verdier, P-H. (2009) 'Transnational regulatory networks and their limits', *Yale Journal of International Law* 34 (1): 113–72.

Verdier, P.-H. (2012) 'US implementation of Basel II: Lessons for informal international lawmaking', in J. Pauwelyn, R. Wessel, and J. Wouters (eds), *Informal International Lawmaking*, Oxford: Oxford University Press.

Viljanen, M. (2015) 'CVA: the first sign of BCBS strategic change?', *Journal of Financial Regulation and Compliance* 23 (3): 230–51.

Walter, A. (2008) *Governing Finance: East Asia's Adoption of International Standards*, Ithaca: Cornell University Press.

White, M. (2013) 'Capitalization of Bank Exposures to Central Counterparties', Speech, 12 April, Banque of Montreal, Montreal.

White, P. (2009) 'Over-the-counter derivatives', Speech, Federal Reserve, 22 June, Washington, available at https://www.federalreserve.gov/newsevents/testimony/white20090622a.htm

Woll, C. (2013) 'Lobbying under pressure: The effect of salience on European hedge fund regulation', *Journal of Common Market Studies* 51 (3): 555–72.

Wood, D. (2005) *Governing Global Banking: The Basel Committee and the Politics of Financial Globalisation*, Aldershot: Ashgate.

Woolley, J.T. and Ziegler, J.N. (2011) 'The two-tiered politics of financial reform in the United States', *IRLE Working Paper*, No. 111-11.

Young, K.L. (2012) 'Transnational regulatory capture? An empirical examination of the transnational lobbying of the Basel Committee on Banking Supervision', *Review of International Political Economy* 19 (4): 663–88.

Young, K.L. (2014) 'Losing abroad but winning at home: European financial industry groups in global financial governance since the crisis', *Journal of European Public Policy* 21 (3): 367–88.

Young, K.L. and Pagliari, S. (2015) 'Capital united? Business unity in regulatory politics and the special place of finance', *Regulation & Governance* 11 (1): 3–23.

Zaring, D. (2013) 'Sovereignty mismatch and the new administrative law', *Washington University Law Review* 91 (1): 59–112.

Zeitlin, J. (ed.) (2015) *Extending Experimentalist Governance? The European Union and Transnational Regulation*, Oxford: Oxford University Press.

Zhou, T. (2016) 'Overview on derivatives trade in China', *European Scientific Journal* 12 (25): 857–788.

Zubrow, B. (2011) 'Testimony before the House Committee on Financial Services', 16 June, Washington.

Zurn, M., and Joerges, C. (eds) (2005) *Law and Governance in Postnational Europe*, Cambridge: Cambridge University Press.

Index

For the benefit of digital users, indexed terms that span two pages (e.g., 52–53) may, on occasion, appear on only one of those pages.

Printed in the USA
CPSIA information can be obtained
at www.ICGtesting.com
CBHW050803050324
4878CB00032B/4